Judge Your Mother / Nurit Asnash

Judge Your Mother

Question what you think and
turn your life around

Nurit Asnash

Nurit Asnash

Judge Your Mother

Copyright © 2021 by Nurit Asnash

All rights reserved. No part of this book may be reproduced, distributed, or transmitted in any form or by any means, including photocopying, recording, or other electronic or mechanical methods, without prior written permission from the author except in case of brief quotations with a credit given to the author. For more information, visit www.nurit-asnash.com

The Work of Byron Katie and the Judge-Your-Neighbor Worksheet are copyright © 2002 by Byron Katie International, Inc. Referenced and reprinted with permission. For more information about The Work, go to www.thework.com

The author and publisher of this book would like to clarify that the content appearing in this book does not constitute medical, psychological, or spiritual advice or a professional opinion, and it is not a substitute for a consultation with a professional. If you choose to use any of the information in this book for yourself, the author and publisher assume no responsibility for your actions. The author's intent is only to share out of her personal experience regarding a method that supported her in her pursuit of physical, mental, and emotional well-being.

Book cover by Inbal Ohana | Une Studio

Jacket photograph copyright © 2021 by Yahav Gamliel

ISBN: 9798737386962

To Byron Katie

Contents

Introduction: She Is the Cause of My Suffering 9
Introduction to The Work 12
About this Book 17
Avoiding Doing The Work on Mother 19
I Complain About My Mother 22
Facilitation #1: She Deserves Revenge 27
Facilitation #2: My Mother Should Protect Me 41
Facilitation #3: Mom is the Center of My Universe 55
A Turnaround to the Role 76
Facilitation #4: She Thinks I'm Bad 80
No New Thoughts and Common Themes Related to Mother 87
Facilitation #5: My Mother Humiliated Me 94
Facilitation #6: She Controls Me 113
Facilitation #7: She Attacked Me 135
Facilitation #8: Mother Should Say She is Sorry 151
Facilitation #9: She Wants Me to Pay Her 168
The Mother I Want vs. The Mother I Have 186
Giving Advice to Your Mother 192
Facilitation #10: She Focuses on the Negative 195
Facilitation #11: Mom is Mean to Dad 211
Facilitation #12: She Repeats Herself 231
Facilitation #13: My Mother-in-Law is Not the Warm Person I Thought Her to Be 240
Storytellers 254
Facilitation #14: She is Criticizing Me 256
Facilitation #15: She Didn't Say Goodbye to Me 267
Facilitation #16: I Worship My Mother 288
Self-judgments: I-statements 308
Facilitation #17: I Abandoned My Mother (1) 313

Facilitation #18: I Abandoned My Mother (2) 321
I Need My Mother to Love Me 330
Violent, Abusive, and Neglectful Mothers 340
Facilitation #19: I Shouldn't Suffer Because of My Mother 345
Mother Yourself 351
Forgiveness 355
A World Created with a Word 363
Personal Words to Conclude 366
Appendix: About The Work 368
Acknowledgments 375

Introduction: She Is the Cause of My Suffering

It's dawn. I rarely wake up so early. The second my mind's switch is turned to ON, thoughts start pouring in. First, it's a thought about the birds chirping outside: "They sound cheerful." I imagine them hopping on the branches of the tree outside. I catch a thought: "Dawn is the gift to the early risers." Then, I receive my writing assignment for the day—this is how it works, isn't it?! Thoughts and ideas pop in out of nowhere, offering directions. "Where are they coming from?" An early childhood memory from when I was four years old comes back to life and, with it, a thought: "Write about this."

It's the earliest memory I have of my mother being angry with me over an innocent act on my part. In that episode, we were in the kitchen together eating a salad from a shared bowl. When it was finished, there was a tiny piece of cucumber resting in the bottom of the bowl. We both drew our forks to snatch the prize. It was a fun game, the two of us battling with our forks inside the bowl to see who would win the battle over the cucumber. It was playful until, all of the sudden, my mother got mad. Her reaction erupted out of nowhere and surprised me. It was the opposite of the fun we had just a second before. Everything flipped in a split of a moment and then there was confusion and fear.

- - -

For decades, I believed that my mother was the main cause of my suffering. My teenage years were especially awful and I blamed it on her, her way of mothering, and her personality. My unconditional love for her shifted and became conditioned on what she said or did. I compared her to other mothers who seemed to be better, more supportive, gentle, caring, and loving than my mother, and their children happy, worthy, carefree, and safe. I had a fantasy of an ideal mother I wished I had instead of her. Any deviation on her part from the standard of the perfect mother was a cause of disappointment and I put meaning on it—what it personally meant about me and my value in this world.

My suffering in this relationship pushed and motivated me to find ways out of my misery, like running away from home and drinking too much alcohol. But alongside that, I had a deep understanding that getting an education was key to making a better life for myself. I turned to education as it seemed to be a good strategy that had the potential to enable me to step up and become independent as well as climb up the socio-economic ladder. I studied everything I believed could help me heal and become mentally stronger, from the conventional university studies of psychology to all kinds of therapy methods and healing practices around the mind-body connection. They were all enlightening and helpful but, no matter what I tried, deep inside, at the core, I was still suffering.

As much as I tried to self-develop and change myself, my mother-related fantasies did not come true. After becoming a mother myself, I felt stuck between a rock and a hard place: on one side, there was my relationship with my mother and, on the other, with my children. These relationships were especially irritating, demanding, and challenging and I experienced my dreams getting shattered one after the other. I blamed them, it was their fault, they broke my heart. I felt helplessness, loss of control, despair. This wasn't how I imagined my family life. My frustration was growing, my stress levels were rising, the emotional fatigue was exhausting my body and taking its toll. I was occupied with arguing and fighting with reality and it drained the joy of living out of me. Then, I heard about The Work.

- - -

When I finally heard about The Work of Byron Katie, I read her book, *Loving What Is,* and I got curious—this was something different from what I had known. Next, I signed up for a workshop to try it out. There, I was facilitated in questioning one stressful thought about a friend and I experienced the magic of Inquiry (the four questions of The Work). Inquiry made the problem resolve on its own. Like a magician saying "Abracadabra," poof! It was gone. That was a life-changing moment. (I'm still in awe every time I do The Work about how my mind settles down after Inquiry, finding a home with itself. It is a truly magical experience.)

I fell in love with The Work for its effectiveness, clarity, and the brilliance of its simplicity. My practice of The Work supports me as I go back to explore the old salad episode with fresh eyes. As I relive this childhood memory that dawned on me and The Work is living in me, I see images of the little house in my mind's eye. I step into the kitchen… I see Woman, Child, Table, Chairs, Bowl, Hands, Forks, Cucumber. I don't see a good child or a bad mom, no right or wrong, no black and white—I used to evaluate and judge things this way in the past. I see two innocent people acting upon what they are thinking and believing. A mother and a child, both captive in their stories, they experience two separate situations—not one—played out by what goes on in their mind. I have no need to feel sorry for myself or hug my inner child; I'm not a victim of this story anymore. In The Work, I find compassion and understanding for the mother and the child. Forgiveness happens.

November, 2020

Introduction to The Work

"Judge your neighbor, write it down, ask four questions, turn it around."
Byron Katie

The Work is a way of Inquiry born out of Byron Katie's experience. (I use the terms The Work and Inquiry interchangeably.) On the surface, The Work is a process consisting of four questions and a few turnarounds. The questions are:

1. **Is it true?**
2. **Can you absolutely know that it's true?**
3. **How do you react, what happens, when you believe that thought?**
4. **Who would you be without that thought?**

The process works like this: we choose a specific, stressful situation as an anchor to our Inquiry. Then, we turn to the Judge-Your-Neighbor Worksheet (or in short, the Worksheet) that covers six questions that help us identify our stressful thoughts related to this person. As you go back to the situation, become still, and write your thoughts down using short, simple sentences—it is a written meditation.

The questions on the Worksheet are:

1. In this situation, who angers, confuses, hurts, saddens, or disappoints you, and why?
2. In this situation, how do you want him/her to change? What do you want him/her to do?
3. In this situation, what advice would you offer him/her?
4. In order for you to be happy in this situation, what do you need him/her to think, say, feel, or do?
5. What do you think of him/her in this situation? Make a list.
6. What is it about this person and situation that you don't ever want to experience again?

This is what the Worksheet looks like:

Judge-Your-Neighbor Worksheet

Think of a stressful situation with someone—for example, an argument. As you meditate on that specific time and place and begin to feel what that felt like, fill in the blanks below. Use short, simple sentences.

1. **In this situation, who angers, confuses, hurts, saddens, or disappoints you, and why?**

   I am _____ with _____ because _____
           emotion   *name*

   I am angry with Paul because he lied to me.

WANTS 2. **In this situation, how do you want him/her to change? What do you want him/her to do?**

   I want _____ to _____
            name

   I want Paul to see that he is wrong. I want him to stop lying to me.

ADVICE 3. **In this situation, what advice would you offer him/her? "He/she should/shouldn't..."**

   _____ should/shouldn't _____
      name

   Paul shouldn't frighten me with his behavior. He should take a deep breath.

NEEDS 4. **In order for *you* to be happy in this situation, what do you need him/her to think, say, feel, or do?**

   I need _____ to _____
           name

   I need Paul to stop talking over me. I need him to really listen to me.

COMPLAINTS 5. **What do you think of him/her in this situation? Make a list. (It's okay to be petty and judgmental.)**

   _____ is _____
      name

   Paul is a liar, arrogant, loud, dishonest, and unconscious.

6. **What is it about this person and situation that you don't ever want to experience again?**

   I don't ever want _____

   I don't ever want Paul to lie to me again. I don't ever want to be disrespected again.

Now question each of your statements, using the four questions of The Work, below. For the turnaround to statement 6, replace the words *I don't ever want...* with *I am willing to...* and *I look forward to...*

The four questions
Example: Paul lied to me.
1. Is it true? (Yes or no. If no, move to question 3.)
2. Can you absolutely know that it's true? (Yes or no.)
3. How do you react, what happens, when you believe that thought?
4. Who or what would you be without the thought?

Turn the thought around.
I lied to me.
I lied to Paul.
Paul *didn't* lie to me.
Paul *told me the truth.*
As you visualize the situation, contemplate how each turnaround is as true or truer.

THE WORK OF BYRON KATIE© © 2019 Byron Katie International, Inc. All rights reserved. thework.com

After filling out the Worksheet, we have our statements written down and we take them to Inquiry, meaning each statement will be questioned using the four questions. Let's take, for example, a universal thought such as, "My mother doesn't love me," as one of the Worksheet's statements. We choose a specific situation when we had that thought as the anchor for Inquiry. This is not a logical or an intellectual exercise, it is an experience. The Work is meditation and the invitation is to slow down and be still as much as you can to immerse yourself and "sit" in the questions. If you do The Work by yourself, that would be self-facilitation. (You can also sit with a friend or an experienced facilitator who can ask you the questions and "hold the space" of Inquiry.) Meditating on this thought would go like this:

1. "My mother doesn't love me." **Is it true?** (The answer is yes/no. If your answer is no, move to question 3.)
2. "My mother doesn't love me." **Can I absolutely know that it's true?** (The answer is yes/no.)
3. "My mother doesn't love me." **How do I react, what happens, when I believe that thought?**
4. "My mother doesn't love me." **Who would I be without that thought?**

Next, we try the turnarounds that take our thoughts into further Inquiry. In a turnaround, we take the original thought and turn it: 1) to the self, 2) to the other, and 3) to the opposite and we test it to see if it could be as true, or truer, when it is applied this way. The three standard turnarounds are used in statements 1-4 on the Worksheet. Possible turnarounds to the thought "My mother doesn't love me," would be:

1. **Turnaround to the self**: I don't love myself.
2. **Turnaround to the other**: I don't love my mother.
3. **Turnaround to the opposite**: My mother does love me.

(In some cases, you might find more or less than three turnarounds, depending on the sentence.) Find a few authentic examples to each turnaround to check how it could be as true (or truer) as your original statement. Give yourself an opportunity to explore if the turnarounds fit you or not.

Statements 5 and 6 on the Worksheet are turned around in a different way. Statement #5 is turned to the self and the opposite. For example, if you wrote, "She is unkind," it will be turned to, "I am unkind," and, "She is kind." Find authentic examples of how this could be as true.

In statement #6 on the Worksheet, we turn, "I don't ever want to…" to, "I am willing…" and then to, "I am looking forward…" to experience what we have written in the original thought. For example, if the thought is, "I don't ever want to get hurt by her again," we'll turn it around to, "I'm willing to get hurt by her again," and, "I'm looking forward to getting hurt by her again." If you finished an Inquiry on the whole Worksheet and still feel uncomfortable about this turnaround, take any leftover stressful thoughts to a new Worksheet and go deeper in your personal work.

If you are new to The Work, this may sound like a lot, but you'll find that, after a little practice, it's quite simple. The Work is a straightforward and uncomplicated process that is easy to learn and get started with—it is only four questions applied to one thought. You can do it anywhere, anytime. It doesn't require any special setup or equipment, only a pen and a piece of paper, or your phone or laptop. You can do it on your own in self-facilitation with the support of the Worksheet, or with a friend. All he or she has to do is ask you the four questions. You can also sit with a trained facilitator who will hold the Inquiry space for you while you are diving into yourself. (If you are new to The Work, go to the Appendix for additional instructions, information, and available resources.)

You have probably heard this before in other places: "You have the wisdom," and "All the answers are in you," but how do you plow your way to them through the noise and clutter that is inside and outside your mind? On a deeper level, The Work is a practice that enables you to access that wisdom, the answers, the inner truth that exists within you. The Work is a way to self-realization, to self-discovery. The way to hit that spot is to roll up your sleeves and actually do The Work. Reading about The Work or watching other people do it is fascinating and enlightening (even entertaining) but nothing tops doing it yourself!

I love getting right down to business with **Is it true?** I enjoy noticing in Inquiry how a thought affects my life, and how I would live if that thought had not been planted in my mind, left unquestioned—it's a fascinating observation. I'm willing and looking forward to being flipped inside out and upside down in the turnarounds—they open and expand my mind. When my thoughts are met with Inquiry, they no longer run my life—I love that freedom. Mild or wild, Inquiry is personal work and I like experiencing everything that it brings my way. Whacky, crazy, silly, fun, or scary—and always pushing my buttons—Inquiry can be a wild ride, just like life. So, here we go, buckle your seatbelt!

About this Book

This book is a journey of self-discovery into who we are without and beyond our stories about our mothers. It is about finding peace within ourselves when reality is not playing according to our plans and dreams. Inspired by and based on The Work of Byron Katie, this book is full of insights about shifting from suffering, fighting, and arguing with reality to experiencing forgiveness, gratitude, and personal freedom.

When you do The Work on your Mother, you do The Work on everything—you get to question everything—that exists in this world. Your mother (or father) is a central figure and probably the most influential person in your life. Some people love and worship their mother, while others resent and hate her. Some have a wonderful and loving bond with their mom while others suffer in an abusive, violent, neglectful relationship. In this book, you will find a variety of real-life situations that participants shared about their mother as they were doing The Work and meditating on the beliefs that caused tension or suffering in this relationship.

Although the focus here is on Mother, the dialogues, insights and exercises in this book can be applied to your relationships with your Father, Brother, Sister, Spouse, Husband/Wife, Children and so on. Replace "Mother" with another person's name anywhere it seems fitting for you and try it out.

About the participants

The people participating in the dialogues in this book have different levels of experience and interest in The Work. The beginners had some knowledge about The Work and, for this project, they filled out a Worksheet for the very first time and were facilitated for the very first time. The experienced ones are more deeply involved in The Work, practice it regularly, and have attended at least one 9-day School for The Work led by Byron Katie and/or other events with her. Some of them have taken additional courses at the Institute for The Work (ITW) or other training programs that teach The Work.

The participants (we call them *clients*) live in different countries and are spread over four continents and they speak different languages. Male and female, their ages range from thirty to sixty.

The clients' participation in this project was voluntary. They did not pay or get paid to be facilitated.

All names and personal details were deleted or changed to protect the privacy of the participants and their families.

About the facilitations

The dialogues in this book (we call them *facilitations*) are arranged chronologically by the age of the client at the time of the situation they were inquiring about.

Prior to the meeting with the facilitator, the clients were given instructions to choose a specific situation related to their mother that they wanted to work on and to fill out a Worksheet. (Most but not all of them did so.)

As we practice The Work, the facilitations are not about giving advice, consulting, coaching, or offering therapy. Inquiry is about a client and a facilitator sitting in the questions and turnarounds and holding that space.

Most of the facilitations were conducted by the author and some by colleagues. The facilitations lasted from 1.5 to 3 hours and were completed in 1-3 sessions.

The facilitations are edited transcripts of online video conversations. The conversations were recorded, transcribed, and edited by the author.

In the following facilitations, The Work's four questions are marked in bold, while the turnarounds are marked in italics.

Avoiding Doing The Work on Mother

> *"I knew I wasn't dealing with a person; I was dealing with concepts, and once I investigated the concepts about my mother, I had unraveled all my concepts about everyone and everything."*
> Byron Katie

There are many good reasons not to do The Work on Mother and to just avoid it instead. People bring up various explanations, motives, and excuses for not doing an Inquiry on their mother. Here's a partial list of their reasoning:

- IT'S IN THE PAST. It's over. It happened a long time ago. I cannot remember anything from my childhood. I don't remember exactly what happened—what she said, what I said—so I can't do it. My mother already apologized to me so I can no longer be angry with her. It will not change anything anyway.

- IT'S PAINFUL. I don't feel like going back there and getting into that again. It will bring up painful memories and emotions. I will be a mess. It's scary. It's too big, overwhelming. It's too emotionally charged, complicated, explosive. I'm afraid I won't be able to deal with it.

- FEAR, GUILT, AND SHAME. We don't criticize Mom in my family. My siblings only say good things about her. It would be bad of me to criticize Mom. I'd be betraying my mom by saying bad things about her. My mom trained us to protect her... she didn't let us get angry at her... it's not safe for me. She did the best she could.

- FEELING SAFE IN THE PRESENT. She is getting older and weaker. I am an adult now, I set the boundaries. She can't hurt me anymore. She has changed.

- PRIORITIES AND SENSE OF URGENCY OR IMPORTANCE. I have more urgent topics to do The Work on, I have relationships with other people to take care of now. Working on Mom is not a top priority for me right now. It's not that important to me anymore. It's not affecting me anymore. I'm over it.

I remember the first two times I sat in Inquiry on my mother with a facilitator. It felt like World War III was going on inside of me. The physical sensations were terrible. I thought I was going to fall off my chair and faint on the floor. I was restless and couldn't sit still. My mind was running wild. I couldn't meditate. I experienced what I imagined a blood transfusion feels like, old blood being replaced by new blood. In a way, it felt like death. I wasn't looking forward to having that experience again. In fact, I avoided working on my mother for about a year after that. In the meantime, I noticed that my Work-friends and clients rarely showed up to our facilitations with a Worksheet on their mother. They seemed to prefer working on other issues and situations like their husband or wife, partner, children, work, health, friendships, or more current events.

There are many good reasons to do The Work on your mother and not avoid it. If you believe, "I'm over it," I invite you to start by asking yourself: **Is it true?** In my experience, we never get over Mom. She's a major player in our lives, and Mom… Mom always comes for a visit. (Even if you're physically distant from her, if you have cut her out of your life, or even if she's dead, she still visits you in your mind.) You might be accepting of things as they are, believing you've learned how to live with the mother you've got, but acceptance is not freedom; it keeps Mother as the pain in the background.

Mom is a central figure and doing The Work on your mother can open you up to an Inquiry on other people and relationships that you're fearful or hesitant to touch. Mom Inquiries can be a catalyst to other significant Inquiries. "I don't want to do it," or, "I'll do it later," starts a mental combat inside you. It keeps the mind busy and unpeaceful, not at home with itself.

Working on your mom puts you in touch with the young girl/boy that you were. It can bring you back to seeing more clearly what you were unable to see and understand from the perspective of the little child or a teenager that you were. It could bring you forgiveness and peace within yourself, or at least bring you closer to it.

Mom is at the heart of our craving for love, approval, and appreciation and all the anxieties around not receiving that. In Inquiries about Mom, you can get a glimpse of what it would be like to be free from needing and depending on that.

As long as I avoided plunging into these deep waters, my issues with my mother affected my life. As reality would have it, pain and grief were motivators for change. In my case, this issue bugged me too much for too long and I'd had enough. I wanted to be free. Everything else I tried helped—but not enough. And so I dived into what felt like a bottomless pit and did The Work on my mother.

Looking back on my journey, my yellow brick road is paved with Worksheets. On these Worksheets, I have questioned many beliefs I was raised to believe in, other people's truths that I have (sometimes) blindly obeyed and followed. The Inquiries on Mother brought me to question taboos, values, norms, and social conventions. The most valuable lesson I gained on this self-discovery trip was to end my thoughts with a question mark and to trust my inner compass—my own truth.

I Complain About My Mother

Avoidance keeps your stewing about your mother on the back burner. Complaining, on the other hand, brings it forth and might make you sound like a broken record. While avoidance is a strategy that makes you not want to talk about the person or situation that stresses you, complaining keeps you talking about it (repetitively). We are good at complaining and we do it all the time. That's good since complaining opens the door to Inquiry.

Complaining is the first step to identifying your stressful thoughts and beliefs. Instead of keeping them bottled inside, in The Work, we write our complaints on paper. In this sense, The Work is a written meditation. Writing slows the mind and that allows us to go deeper into ourselves.

Mind game

Take a blank sheet of paper and write down: What complaints do you have about your mother? Do you have any judgments or criticism related to your mother about the past, the present, or the future? Do you wish she were different in any way and how so?

If you are new to The Work, try this prompt:

I complain about my mother because she _____

_____

_____

If you need fuel to get started, here's a collection of complaints I have gathered from dozens of people while writing this book. These statements may be a starting point for your personal Work.

Mother's attitude toward me:

She disrespected me
She is using me for her needs
She doesn't listen to me, she speaks in long monologues
She made me feel unwanted
She doesn't support me emotionally/financially
She embarrasses me
She sucks the life out of me
She makes me feel guilty
She doesn't want to see me, she doesn't answer when I call
She thinks I am not good enough
She doesn't love me, she hates me
She is responsible for the way I turned out, for my problems
She is the reason that I'm sad/sick/depressed
She doesn't hug me, she doesn't kiss me
She is bringing me down
She disconnected from me
She is a burden
She needs me
She should know me better than anyone else, she doesn't know me at all
She should comfort me
She should care about what is going on in my life

Her personality, emotional and mental issues:

She is not a loving person, she is cold, distant
She is selfish, she cares only about herself, she is self-centered
She is a bitch, she is a narcissist
She acts like a child
She complains all the time, she complains about everything
She is poison
She is controlling
She is mentally sick
She is a lonely, bitter woman
She made bad decisions in life, she brought this situation on herself
She is bad, she is mean
She is manipulative

Mom, Dad, and me:

She turned me against my father
She disconnected me from my father
She is mean to my father, she said nasty things about my father
She divorced my dad
She used me to get money from my dad
She kept my father away from me
She didn't let me be in touch with my father
She used me as a weapon against my father
She did not care I needed a connection with my father
She loves her boyfriend more than she loves me

Mother's attitude to me and my siblings:

She loves my brother/sister more than me
She wanted my brother/sister more than me
She prefers my sister/brother
My sister/brother is her golden child
She compares me to my brother/sister
She turned my brother/sister against me
She incites trouble between me and my siblings
She should stop obsessing about my brother/sister
She should not prefer my brother/sister over me
She should love her children equally

Parents and children:

They have failed, they are the problem
It's their fault I turned out this way
They are the sun and the moon
They made me cry many nights, they made me hurt myself
I am afraid to talk to them
Children do not have the tools/abilities to cope with reality
Parents should be good to their kids
Children are not responsible for their parents, parents are the ones responsible for the relationships
Society holds family as holy
Society is not aware of the damage that emotional neglect is causing to a child
It's natural to expect my parents to be loving, accepting, supportive

Mom as homemaker:

She doesn't cook for the family
Our house never felt like a home
She kept the house dirty and messy
It is unpleasant to be in her house
She doesn't do anything around the house
She is too busy with her career/hobbies

Mother's body:

She is too fat/too skinny
Her voice is dreadful, too loud, too harsh
She is old
She is ugly
Her touch is unpleasant, the way she touches me is creepy
She is sick

Mother as a grandmother:

She doesn't help me with my kids
She cannot be trusted with the kids
She doesn't support me
She doesn't know how to be a grandmother
She can be emotionally abusive
She is no fun to be with
She bores my children
She lies to herself that she is a good grandmother
She doesn't care about her grandchildren

Comparing her to other mothers:

Everyone I know has good relationships with their mother
My friend's mom compliments her, my mother doesn't compliment me
Other women have a healthy relationship with their mother
Of all the people in the world, I am the only one who doesn't have a normal mother
Other children have a mother who takes care of them
She is not like the other moms
My mother is the worst

Abusive, neglectful mother:

She did not provide a safe home for me
She hit me, she is abusive
She sexually harassed me
She kicked me, she punched me, she pulled my hair, she strangled me
She broke my things
She abused my sister/brother
She complains that I ratted on her to the police
She scares me, she cannot be trusted
She is not good for me, she damaged me
She should not attack me
She is an alcoholic/drug user
She yells at me, she fights with me, she curses me
She forces herself on me
She did not take care of me when I was sick

She is wrong and needs to fix this:

She needs therapy
She says I am imagining things, she says reality is the opposite of what I believe
She says I am wrong about her
She doesn't try to understand me
She dismisses my feelings, my thoughts
She should admit that she screwed up
She should apologize for the past
She should not expect me to parent her
She should admit she is a psychopath
She doesn't have the right to ask me for forgiveness
She doesn't know what real motherhood is

Facilitation #1: She Deserves Revenge

Have you ever had the thought that one day, when you get bigger and stronger, you're going to make your mother pay for what she did to you when you were a kid? Decades after the situation happened, you might still replay the scene in your mind and hold a grudge against your mother for treating you unfairly. Events from the past do arise from the dungeons of our memories and come alive every now and then. This client brought to his Inquiry a childhood memory that happened thirty-seven years previously. It's never too late to go back and investigate what happened.

Early childhood situations can be tricky to inquire because your memory of it or the details might be blurry. Some people see that as a good enough excuse to not touch those hurtful moments. Don't let that discourage you from inquiring into an event you haven't completely forgiven, that still disturbs you (if only just a little) every time you think about it.

Facilitator: Tell me about the situation.

Client: This was a long time ago. I was about nine years old. It was rainy and dark outside. I was at school and I'd just come home and I brought with me a kite that I made with my friend. I had big plans for it. I wanted to put it outside in the wind and watch it fly. That day, I didn't get a good grade in my test. It wasn't so bad, but it wasn't good enough for my mother. I also lost my hat. It was a really cool hat I'd got from a relative in Sweden. (It wasn't easy to get something like that in the 80s, in my then-communist country). And I also made a hole in the hood of my new raincoat. I got home very excited about the kite, and then I told my mother about the grade and that I'd lost my hat and I'd got a hole in the coat, and she got mad. She smashed my kite and she beat me. I was very sad, mostly because of the kite. Here's my Worksheet [reads from his Worksheet]:

#1 I hate my mother because she beat me and destroyed my kite.

#2 I want her to suffer for that. I want revenge. I want her to see how wrong she is.

#3 Mom shouldn't beat me. Mom should be patient, gentle, loving. Mom shouldn't destroy my creation.

#4 I need her to love me, to be gentle with me, to support me, to hold me, to encourage me.

#5 Mom is fucked-up, brutal, unconscious, an awful parent, deserves hate.

#6 I don't ever want to be hurt again. I don't ever want to be in her power again. I don't ever want my creation to be destroyed again.

Facilitator: Which statement would you like to do The Work on?

Client: She destroyed my kite.

Facilitator: She destroyed your kite. What does this mean?

Client: She doesn't respect me.

Facilitator: Should we work on that one?

Client: Okay.

Facilitator: So, you were about nine years old, you came home from school all excited with a kite, and you had some information for your mother about your grade and your lost hat, and a hole in a new raincoat. Your mom beat you and destroyed your kite. Your mother doesn't respect you—**is it true**?

Client: Yes.

Facilitator: **Can you absolutely know it's true** that your mother doesn't respect you?

Client: Not absolutely. No.

Facilitator: As the little boy that you were: **How do you react, what happens, when you believe the thought** that she doesn't respect you?

Client: I'm hurt, I'm really sad. I hate her. I want revenge. I can't wait to grow up so I can beat her. I have a sense this is wrong. There's rebellion in me. I'm tense, my muscles are contracted, I want to run away. I'm very sad about my kite. I saw it in my mind flying and it looked very good. My friend and I made it and I took it home to try it. Now the kite's broken. I hate her. I don't see a way to repair it—it's permanent—the kite and our relationship. There's a feeling of emptiness in my chest, depressive emptiness. I'm so sad for the kite.

Facilitator: How do you treat your mother in that situation?

Client: I hate her, I want her punished, I want revenge.

Facilitator: So, what do you do?

Client: I look at her hatefully. Could be I was saying, "You'll see—when I get stronger, I'll hurt you back." I try to talk her out of it. I panic and keep asking her, "Don't do it, don't do it!" but after she crushed it, I didn't want to talk to her at all. It was done, couldn't be repaired. I don't want to have anything to do with her. I give her a look full of hate.

Facilitator: How do you treat yourself?

Client: I was a victim. I was wronged and damaged. I can't do anything about it. I took it to heart. It was a disaster. I see future images that I'm going to get revenge. I see past images that I've been beaten. It was rather common.

Facilitator: What do you mean by "common"? Common back then, or common in your family?

Client: Both, common in my family and common in the culture. In the early 80s, it was common to beat children here and common for my mother to do it. I wasn't surprised to be beaten, but I was surprised about the kite, to see it being crushed. The past images prove that she's a bad mother.

Facilitator: Back in the situation: **Who would you be without the thought**, "She doesn't respect me?"

Client: I'm in physical pain, I've been beaten. I'm still sad for the kite. Without the thought, it feels a bit easier. I'm not so hurt without the thought. I'm not taking it so much to heart. It wouldn't be so hard for me.

I'd do well to learn from my sister. She was four years younger and she wouldn't have taken it so badly. She'd get beaten and she'd do it again. She'd say, "Okay, I know I'll get beaten, but I want to do it." I wouldn't be so scared. It would be much easier for me to handle. I wouldn't be so hurt from the disrespect, expecting something better, or believing she should be different. Without the thought, it would be easier for me.

Facilitator: Are you ready for the **turnarounds**?

Client: Yes.

Facilitator: "She doesn't respect me."

Client: I don't respect her. Yes. In that moment, I hate her, I want her to be punished, to suffer, I want revenge. I think she's a terrible parent to me. I'm searching in the past for other things she did wrong to me and I don't want to see any example or option that she respects me.

I don't respect me. In that moment, I really hate the situation, I hate my life, so I don't respect my life and I don't respect myself. I'm in her business, taking the beating so much to heart—that's not respecting myself. I was very afraid of being beaten and always took it hard. There were other options, like my sister. She'd say, "Okay, so I get beaten, but I'll do it again tomorrow." Asking her for respect is also kind of not respecting myself. When I don't get it, I make myself feel disrespected.

She respects me. In other situations she takes care of me. I have good meals to eat every day, she cares that I'm clean, that I have everything I need like clothes, etc. She regularly visits my school and wants me to do well in school. That shows respect to me. She wants me to get better grades—she believes I can do better. She takes care of my needs and she wants me to succeed in life. In that situation, she respects me when she's not ignoring me. She did hear me, she heard what I was saying.

Facilitator: What did you write in the next statement?

Client: I want revenge. I want her to suffer for that.

Facilitator: In that situation, you want her to suffer—**is it true**?

Client: Yes.

Facilitator: **Can you absolutely know it's true** that you want her to suffer?

Client: No.

Facilitator: **How do you react, what happens, when you believe that thought**, "I want her to suffer"?

Client: I imagine a future when I'll be strong, and I'll beat her. I get aggressive and I'm frustrated because I can't do it in that moment. I feel weak because I'm physically smaller than she is. When I believe the thought, I'm not myself and there's bitterness in my mouth and I'm frowning at her and I feel helpless, powerless. With the thought, I feel even worse in that powerless situation. I get angry at myself for not being physically stronger than her. My body's tense. It's not a nice feeling to be wishing for revenge and not being able to get it... [laughs]. It makes me weaker. It fuels my hate, makes me righteous, makes her wrong. It makes me feel even worse and more alone.

Facilitator: So, when she beats you and destroys your kite: **Who would you be without the thought**, "I want her to suffer"?

Client: I'd be lighter. I'd have more resources for myself. I could help myself. There'd be one less problem to solve. I wouldn't need to solve the problem of how many years I have to wait for my revenge until I'm stronger than her. I can see the moment has already passed. I take my beating, the kite is crushed, I feel some pain because she beat me, but the worst is already over so I can get some feeling of relief. The worst has passed, I can move on.

[After a pause.] I'm easier, my body's not so contracted. I'm more relaxed. It was over quickly. I wasn't injured. She never beat me hard or injured me. She was always careful to beat me on my legs and butt. Without the thought, I'm more present. I can see the past isn't so bad. I'm better without the thought.

Facilitator: Are you ready for **turnarounds**?

Client: Yes.

Facilitator: "I want her to suffer." What turnaround do you see?

Client: I don't want her to suffer. Finally, once I managed to be stronger, I didn't take my revenge on her [laughs]. In that moment, I didn't want her to suffer. She behaved like that because she was suffering. I don't really want her to suffer. I can't think of any other examples, but I can see how it's true.

I want me to suffer. No, I don't want myself to suffer. I can see how I'm making myself suffer, but I don't want to suffer.

I want her to be happy. If she was happy, she wouldn't have beaten me, at least not so often. That would be good for me. She's my mother, after all. I have a bond with her even in that situation. I want her to be happy, that's true. It feels good when I say, "I want her to feel happy." I feel much better, more open.

Facilitator: What did you write in your third statement?

Client: Mom shouldn't destroy my creation.

Facilitator: You came back from school and she destroyed your kite. "Mom shouldn't destroy my creation"—**is it true**?

Client: Yes.

Facilitator: **Can you absolutely know that it's true** that "Mom shouldn't destroy my creation"?

Client: No.

Facilitator: **How do you react, what happens, when you believe the thought**, "Mom shouldn't destroy my creation"?

Client: I feel sad and hurt. She's to blame. I hate her. I think she's an awful mother. I think of all the people I know, she's the worst mother. Maybe I can find someone in the newspaper who's worse than her. She's definitely the worst I can think of in all the whole neighborhood. I want her dead. If she died and someone else took me in, it would be a great solution. I look at the kite and I feel so sorry and sad... there goes my dream of this kite flying. This is so wrong. She's such a bad mom that I'm ashamed of what a bad mom I have. I'm crying for that kite. There's bitterness. I don't want to consider anything from her perspective. She's completely wrong, completely the bad guy, there's no doubt in my mind at all. And it's done, it can't be repaired. When I believe the thought, "It shouldn't be like that" and it *is* like that, it makes me helpless, hopeless, nothing can be done... it's finished.

Facilitator: **Who would you be without the thought**, "Mom shouldn't destroy my creation"?

Client: The kite's broken, and it can't fly. I could make a better one. I wasn't sure it would fly anyway, I must admit. It was a little fragile. I can find a solution. I can see that I can make a new one by myself. I don't think about my mother at all now. I feel much better. I'm not happy, but I'm not so devastated. I have a solution. I never thought of that. After all, it's not so complicated; two sticks and little paper, and that's the kite... [laughs]. Yeah, that's true. I'm much easier, almost excited about the idea of making a new kite. That feels good. She's not in the picture at all.

Facilitator: "She shouldn't destroy my creation." **Turn this thought around** and find examples how this could be true.

Client: She should destroy my creation. That definitely meant less of a beating for me. She took her anger and frustration out on the kite, so I got spared. That's a good thing, that's true. It gave me a Worksheet to do and a chance go a little deeper in myself.

The kite wasn't completely mine (I made it with a friend). I wasn't even sure it would fly. The paper was too thin for the wind.

Facilitator: In the moment, when she does it, how is it true? Can you find another example?

Client: I don't think she was capable of anything else at that moment. She's full of bad emotions, she gets angry at me and it just pulls out of her.

She should do it to release those emotions. [Pause] I get something out of that, like not to get so attached to things.

Facilitator: "Mom shouldn't destroy my creation." Do you see another **turnaround**?

Client: I shouldn't destroy my creation. I shouldn't destroy my peace by believing that she's so wrong and I can't do anything about that and it's beyond repair, since I can make a new one. I destroy the creative process in me by stopping there and thinking, "It's done and can't be made better."

I destroyed it in my mind repeatedly, that situation, plenty of times. I completely forgot about it and then it popped up ten days ago. When I repeat in my mind how this kite was destroyed, I'm destroying my creation again in my mind.

Facilitator: Do you see another **turnaround**? "Mom shouldn't destroy my creation"?

Client: I shouldn't destroy her creation. I made a hole in my raincoat, which she paid for. She was angry. It was only a few days old, that raincoat. I shouldn't have the fantasy of revenge, destroying her. That didn't do me any good. I don't see anything else.

Facilitator: I see something. Can I share?

Client: Yes.

Facilitator: See if you relate to it. *I shouldn't destroy her creation.* You are her creation. She stays home, she cooks, she waits for you to come back from school, have your meal, and then you come home with all kinds of surprises for her.

Client: Yes, that's true. I can see that. I came home, I got a bad grade, lost my hat, made a hole in the new raincoat… I can see that her afternoon was really destroyed. She's at home, preparing a meal, then I come in and there are surprises. I can see that.

Facilitator: What's in your next statement?

Client: I need her to love me.

Facilitator: When she beats you and destroys your kite, "I need Mom to love me"—**is it true**?

Client: Yes.

Facilitator: **Can you absolutely know it's true**, in that moment "I need Mom to love me"?

Client: No.

Facilitator: **How do you react, what happens, when you believe**, "I need her to love me"?

Client: I feel alone, not loved, vulnerable, helpless. I want another mother. I want this one to go away. I'm unhappy. I don't want to live. I don't want her to live. I feel this is so wrong, completely wrong. I feel sorry for myself. I don't want to be there with her. I don't want to be her son. There's a heaviness in my body. My shoulders and my chest, my arms feel so heavy.

When I see other families, I think, "Oh, they love their children," and I make false images about those families. They don't get beaten, most of them. I get ashamed that mine is the worst mother. I imagine myself with another family where I'd be happier. I'm not happy at all.

Facilitator: **Who would you be without the thought**, "I need Mom to love me," in that moment?

Client: Lighter. More connected with myself. I'd be focused on what's happening and see how it was over very quickly. I wouldn't be happy, but the emotions wouldn't be so big about it. I'd be much better in that situation, and free. More relaxed, more open. I wouldn't be so focused on her. My body's more alive without the thought. I can see she's not the perfect mother. I can have some understanding that she gets angry quickly and she's aggressive, but I won't take it so much to heart. It would be easier for me to handle the situation with the kite and the beating. I feel much lighter without the thought. My body's straighter and there's no heaviness.

I can breathe more deeply. I can even have some compassion for her. She lost her job. There was a court case against her because of that job. She was home all the time. She was unhappy with my father but she didn't leave us, and I can see that her unhappiness had nothing to do with me.

I'd be focused on something else, like my friends. There's a whole world out there like other family members that I love. There's someone special who really loves me. I can find love in other places, that's true. Without the thought, it's really not so bad.

Facilitator: "I need Mom to love me." What **turnarounds** do you see?

Client: I need me to love myself. That's true. One thing is not to wait for her love. Another thing is not to compare myself with other children that I have fantasy images about; that makes me feel bad. I need to focus on myself and not be in her business. I need to consider the situation and my options, to recognize where I can get love, like from my grandmother and my aunt. [After a pause] I need to not feel ashamed to be a part of my family. I was overreacting, overstating how bad it was, especially when comparing myself with other kids and believing that I was in a much worse situation than it actually was.

I need me to love myself because she's not capable of that at that moment, so I'm the only one available to do that.

Facilitator: Do you see another **turnaround**?

Client: I don't need her to love me. When I'm focused on her in that situation, I become very dependent, very attached to her. Without her love, I become much more independent and I really love that about myself.

I don't get love in that moment but I get what I need—I need some lessons, challenges, so in that moment I don't need her to love me. I get other things that I need: I get a challenge.

Quite the opposite is really the truth, *I need her not to love me.* One example is not to be focused on her and to be more independent, more self-sufficient. Another thing is I get some challenges that direct me to investigate myself, go deeper in myself, like psychology and spiritual stuff. These challenges make me feel bad but, when I explore those moments, I can find some direction for me in them.

I don't need her love. It's clear that I needed her not to love me, at least not in that gentle way that I preferred. It gives me the freedom to leave that home and not come back. It feels clear to me that her role was not to love me but to challenge me and that I've benefited from that. I don't see another example.

Facilitator: Can I share one?

Client: Yes.

Facilitator: You don't need her to love you in that situation because she's teaching you her values at that moment—like education is important, you should try harder at school, take care of your belongings and property… your special hat, your new coat.

Client: Yes, I can understand that. It was in the 80s and still a communist regime. It was very expensive to buy new things. I can really understand that she would get upset because of that.

Facilitator: And the third **turnaround**?

Client: I need me to love her. If I want her to be happy, I need to love her. [Pause] I'm not happy with resentment. I need to understand that she got upset because I destroyed a new raincoat, lost a great hat, and got a bad grade. She was already depressed and fucked up. Yeah, I can understand that.

I need to love her for the good things she provided and be grateful. She considered it important to get me fed, that I was clean, had clothes to wear. She directed me to get a good education and get a good job. In her universe, she was giving me important things and I'm grateful for that and love her for that. She really did her best in those things that she considered important. I can see that. I should love her for all that and I should love her for the challenges because that's part of that creation and without that, I'd be interested in shallow things. Those challenges made me feel bad so I needed to dive deeper into myself and I'm grateful for that and that's thanks to her. Without those challenges, I wouldn't have any need to search for psychology, spirituality, and everything else. That's a big thing.

I need for me to love her so that I can be happy and because there are plenty of things that I can be grateful for and I can love her for. Also, I can have some understanding of her situation.

Facilitator: What's in your #5 statement? Read it and **turn it to the self**.

Client: Mom is fucked up, brutal, unconscious, an awful parent, deserves hate.

I was really fucked up. That's true. I was thinking that my family was fucked up, I was fucked up, much worse than my schoolmates, which turned out not to be so true.

I'm brutal. Oh, in my fantasy of revenge, I'm brutal. I think I'd let her live [laughs].

I'm unconscious. Yes, in that moment, I believe that she can make me happy, that she could be different, and that I'm completely good.

I'm an awful son. I don't love her. I don't respect her. I'm not grateful for anything she provides. I think she is completely bad for me. I destroyed a new raincoat, lost my hat, and got a bad grade.

I deserve hate. Oh. Hmm... Why would I deserve it?

Facilitator: Punishment?

Client: I deserve punishment for that coat and hat and the bad grade. I deserve some punishment, that's true.

[Client turns the statements around to the opposite.] Mom is fucked up, *Mom is okay.* She's angry, there are reasons to be angry, and that's okay. She does her chores, prepares meals, and goes to my school to check how I'm doing.

Mom is gentle. I can't relate to that in the situation. Outside the situation, when I was six, she took care of me gently when I was sick and had a high temperature. There was gentleness. In that situation, I wasn't injured when she beat me. She was careful not to injure me. She beat me on my butt or my legs with a wooden kitchen spoon.

Facilitator: And she took some of that anger out on the kite instead of on you.

Client: Yes, that's true. Some of that anger and aggression came out on the kite instead of me. So, the purpose of the kite was to spare me, to save me, not to fly [laughs]. It's good that I took it home [laughs]. I was lucky to have it with me. It was a lifesaver. I can see that the kite's purpose was to be my shield.

Mom is conscious. She's conscious that education is important in the world. She's conscious that we're middle class and, without her job, we don't have a lot of money to spend on a new raincoat.

Mom is a great parent. She's a great parent for giving me some challenges, directing me to get an education and finish school. I always had a meal and something to wear. She washed my clothes etc. I was always clean and always taken care of. I got a good lunch.

Mom deserves love. She gives her best, she deserves love. I can see her situation: she lost her job, and there was a court case against her because of that job. She wasn't satisfied in her marriage, and I can have some understanding for her. I can love her. Everybody deserves love when you get to know them. Everyone deserves love.

Facilitator: And, the sixth statement, "I don't ever want to..."

Client: I don't ever want to be in her power again. *I am willing to be in her power again.* I can see that can happen. It would make me dive deeper into myself.

I'm looking forward to being in her power again. That will be a challenge. I can look forward to learning something from that. I can see some good things in that.

Facilitator: Like what?

Client: Then I have to search for my happiness inside myself. When I'm in her power, I can't do anything outside. That directs me to go into myself and that's authentic happiness and authentic love. I can look forward to that. This feels good. Well done. Thank you.

Facilitator: Thank you.

Facilitation #2: My Mother Should Protect Me

As you go back to a stressful childhood situation, you might find in Inquiry that if it wasn't for what you believed at the time, you could have coped with the situation in a better way. For example, instead of feeling weak and powerless, you could have experienced yourself as a brave child with super-powers. (This is true for adults as well.) As children, we tend to attach to the belief, "I need my mommy," or, "I need my mother to protect me." This Inquiry demonstrates how this thought can make a child feel helpless—unable to stand up for herself in a situation when Mom is not present to save or protect her. We can see that, without the thought that we need Mom to be there for us, we can be there for ourselves and stand up for ourselves.

Facilitator: Tell me about the situation.

Client: I was in fourth grade, about ten years old, and my mother sent me to see a dermatologist by myself. I entered the doctor's office. I didn't know what to expect and I felt small. I put my palm with the wart on his desk and he told me, "We need to burn it." I told him, "I'll come with my mom another day," and he told me, "No, we'll do it now." It scared me. I was afraid of the doctor, an older man in authority. I was afraid that my mom would be angry if I didn't do it right then because he was a specialist and it took a long time to get an appointment with him. I played it cool on the outside but I was in turmoil on the inside. He said it would feel a bit unpleasant—that it would be cold. He applied the nitrogen and I felt overwhelmed by pain. It startled me and caught me unprepared. I was miserable. I left with a sore finger and it continued to hurt for a few days after. I'm feeling pain in my chest just remembering it, God!

Facilitator: Read to me what you wrote on your Worksheet.

Client [reads from her Worksheet]:

#1 I hate my mother because she sent me to the doctor by myself. She wasn't there to protect me, to comfort me, to reassure me.

#2 I want her to accompany me, protect me, reassure me, to not let them treat me without painkillers.

#3 Mom should function as a guarding mother, protecting, defending, soothing, she should accompany me to the doctor's appointment, wrap me in motherhood.

#4 I need my mother to understand that it is her responsibility to take care of who she brought into the world, to care about me when I'm in pain, to protect me, to wrap me up in love, protection, and care.

#5 My mother is weak, a coward, irresponsible, miserable. She brought me into the world out of cowardice and weakness to stand up to my father and say she didn't want to have any more children.

#6 I don't ever want to experience the feeling of isolation and fear that I was confronted with in such situations, the terrible pain and helplessness in front of the doctor, a figure of authority, while I am small.

Facilitator: Thank you. Read to me your first statement.

Client: I hate my mom because she wasn't there to protect me.

Facilitator: "She wasn't there to protect me"—**is it true**?

Client: My mom, even if she was there, I'm not sure she'd have protected me.

Facilitator: I invite you to find the answer, yes or no, only in this situation at the dermatologist's office, not your whole life. "She wasn't there to protect me." Yes or no?

Client: I feel an internal argument with this. If the doctor was gentle maybe the experience would have been different. Also, I could have told him that I'd come again only with my mother. I froze there in the situation. I didn't respond.

Facilitator: Let your answer meet the question.

Client: There is truth in it. It's not like she knew this was how it was going to be and chose not to come with me. It still hurts me terribly that I was there alone.

Facilitator: I invite you to look at it through your eyes then, when you were in fourth grade.

Client: Back then, I didn't think my mom should be there. It didn't cross my mind. I didn't expect it from her. When I thought the thought "I hate her" for not protecting me, examples of those situations came to me, such as when she sent me to the doctor by myself.

Facilitator: So **how do you react, what happens, when you believe the thought** that you want your mom to be there to protect you and she isn't there?

Client: My chest really hurts. These were really horrible experiences.

Facilitator: Let's focus only on this situation with the dermatologist.

Client: I feel small and upset and helpless. Very. Really terrified and helpless. Freezing. Surviving. Miserable.

Facilitator: How do you treat your mother?

Client: I accuse her of being irresponsible, that she doesn't care about me. She doesn't consider the consequences. She gave birth to me, brought me into the world and she doesn't take responsibility for me when I need her. She decides that it doesn't interest her, it's not important to her… not her responsibility to take care of it.

Facilitator: **Who would you be without the thought** that your mom isn't there to protect you?

Client: I can be a brave girl, not so upset. I could have been a heroine—I didn't think about that. What a brave girl I was [laughs]. I went to the doctor alone and he burnt me, and I overcame it. What a stunning girl I am. It could have been an empowering experience and not an experience where my mom's shit. I didn't think about it. Yes, it's a possibility. Yeah, what a relief. I don't forgive her for the other times, but for this specific one, fine.

I'd be independent. Yes. A brave girl with superpowers who can deal with a scary doctor. I could have gone in a completely different direction with it. I didn't think about that. She *is* a shitty mom but I could have been a cool girl.

Facilitator: Let's look at **turnarounds**. "She wasn't there to protect me." "I…"

Client: I wasn't there to protect myself. Definitely. I'm not mad at myself but, yes, I wasn't there to protect myself. I could have told him, "I'm not ready. I'll come back here with my mom or my dad or my sister. I'm not doing this today. I'll come another time." I could have protected myself, but I didn't. That's right.

I could have expressed pain. I didn't have to bury all the pain inside of me. I could have screamed at the doctor that he was a liar, that he'd told me it would only be cold, but it burned. I could have screamed at him; it would have freed me. I was silent there. If I was a girl with confidence, I could have shouted at the doctor that I was in pain. It would have helped me. Yes, I didn't protect myself, either.

Facilitator: "Mom wasn't there to protect me." Is there another **turnaround**?

Client: I should protect her? It's only protecting her in the sense of telling the doctor that my mom couldn't come but I'm not protecting her beyond that. I don't want to protect her.

Facilitator: And another **turnaround**? *She was there to protect you.* Can you take a look at this possibility? Try it...

Client: She wasn't there physically. She wasn't there to protect me. She chose not to be there. She cleaned, cooked, did a thousand housework chores because it was so important to her to clean and cook and do other things. It seemed more important to her than to come with me.

I very much connect to, *I wasn't there to protect myself*, or *I wasn't there to protect her* and tell the doctor she couldn't come. She wasn't even in my thoughts.

Facilitator: What did you write in the second statement?

Client: I want her to protect me.

Facilitator: "I want her to protect me"—**is it true**?

Client: Well, I never experienced protection from her because she never ever did this for me. She doesn't have this feature. It's a heartfelt wish. It's not true, because she never did.

Facilitator: So is your answer yes or no?

Client: No, because she isn't able to. I want some imaginary mother to protect me, not her. She really doesn't know how to do it. And if she does, she does it awkwardly and it would have embarrassed me, and I'd need to defend her *and* myself in that situation. She would shame me. I'd like to experience protection, but not from her. She never did. This isn't a realistic wish at all.

Facilitator: **How do you react, what happens, when you believe the thought** that you want your mother to protect you when you're sitting in front of the doctor?

Client: I want something that doesn't exist, and it causes me suffering. It's like saying I want to win the lottery and suffer, because I didn't. It's idiotic. I want my emotionally crippled mother to get up and dance with me in the town center. It's a thought that causes me to suffer, expecting something futile. It's a stressful thought, really.

Facilitator: **What happens to you**, the girl, **when you believe the thought** that you want your mother to protect you? How do you treat yourself and how do you treat her?

Client: I feel lonely, small, shrinking, becoming smaller and smaller and smaller until I disappear. Miserable. Wanting to die. I see myself shrinking and shrinking and shrinking and getting tiny-tiny-tiny-tiny, and I expect there to be a mother who'll come and pick me up, raise me, and breathe me in, and protect me from becoming so small and lonely.

Facilitator: **Who would you be without the thought** in this situation?

Client: I would be my size, not too small, not too big. Not miserable, not lonely. In fourth grade, I was 1.3 meters tall. A girl who can breathe at the doctor's office. Without the thought, I'd be a normal, fourth-grade girl sitting at the doctor's office on the chair, not shrinking, because I don't have that thought about my mom.

Facilitator: What does this mean?

Client: I'd have told him that I didn't want to do it now and that I'd come back another time. Because when I expect my mom to protect me, then I'm frightened and small, and he's a big doctor who can do whatever he wants. If I don't have the expectation that she'll protect me, then I'm a fourth-grader who says that I don't want to do it alone. I don't know what I'd choose in the end—to be brave, recruit my powers and do it? Or that I don't want to. But I wouldn't find myself forced into the situation. I felt that I didn't have anyone to protect me and I was trapped and, in fact, the doctor controlled the situation and decided what to do.

Facilitator: Let's try the **turnarounds**. "I want my mom to protect me." What turnaround do you see?

Client: I don't want her to protect me. I want to protect myself. Wanting her to protect me won't help me. I want to stop feeling like I need protection in every situation. There are situations that can be overcome safely even without protection. I don't have to be protected and guarded in every situation. Yes, my story of protection is intensified and exaggerated. I feel like it prevents me sometimes from experiencing things. These over-defenses often harm me as well. From the thought that I was unprotected, I created all sorts of stories for myself. She didn't protect me once and I made myself in need of the Queen's Guard. I did myself a disservice. "Protection" sounds like a very nice word but it's not always needed and not in every situation. I also want to be less protected in situations.

Facilitator: Let's look at number 3. What did you write?

Client: Mom should function as a guarding mother.

Facilitator: "Mom should function as a guarding mother"—**is it true**?

Client: Yes. Mom should function as a guarding mother.

Facilitator: **Can you absolutely know it's true**, in the same situation, that your mom should function as a guarding mother?

Client: In this specific situation, not necessarily, because I'm not going to meet a perverted neighbor behind the building. I'm going to see the doctor at his office. This isn't a dangerous situation. I'm going to see the doctor, a person who's supposed to help me. In this specific situation, she doesn't have to protect me. I'm at the doctor's office, there are people at the reception desk who know me and my family. It was the same as going to the local grocery store.

Facilitator: In this situation at the doctor's office, your mom should function as a guarding mother—yes or no?

Client: As a child, I saw the situation as unprotected and defenseless. On the other hand, when you send a child to the doctor, she doesn't necessarily need to be protected. It's not supposed to be a harmful situation. I'm a mother who always goes with my daughters to visit the doctor.

Facilitator: Let's focus on this event. When the doctor is treating you, should your mom function as a guarding mother?

Client: I really wanted to have a guarding mom, but objectively, going to the doctor's office is not a dangerous situation. I was mad at her. I felt lonely and miserable and in pain and I wanted to die. I was really miserable. I felt unprotected and defenseless. Is it the absolute truth that my mom should be there? No. If the doctor had just given me a prescription for ointment and sent me home and it hadn't hurt, I wouldn't have needed her there.

Facilitator: How do you treat her when you believe the thought that she should be there?

Client: I hate her.

Facilitator: **Who would you be without the thought**?

Client: Without the thought, I'd be a girl who's willing to respect her mother. I could have respected her if I didn't hate her so much or was so angry at her.

Facilitator: Who would you be in front of the doctor when you're in pain, without the thought that your "mom should function as a guarding mother"?

Client: I wouldn't have agreed to what the doctor was doing. I'd have screamed at him that he was a liar and that he was hurting me, so maybe he'd have done it more gently. I might have avoided this whole situation.

Facilitator: "Mom should function as a guarding mother." What **turnarounds** do you see here?

Client: I should function as a guarding mother to myself. I would have told the doctor that I wasn't having the procedure that day and I'd have left satisfied with myself—a bit afraid that my mom would be mad at me, but I'd have told him that I wasn't doing it. I wouldn't have let him do it if I was protecting myself.

Facilitator: What other **turnarounds** do you see?

Client: I need to function as a guarding mother to my daughters, which is also a problem. I don't want to constantly be their protector anymore. They need to grow and protect themselves. That's it, enough. I drove myself crazy when I forced myself to do this. This is for another session.

Facilitator: I have to function as a guarding mother to my mother?

Client: Ugh, I want to get rid of that thought. I put a lot of effort into getting rid of it. I'm not supposed to be a guarding mother to my own mother. She had a crazy mom of her own who didn't protect her. It's not my role to protect her. I have this thought, and I don't want this thought.

Facilitation #2: My Mother Should Protect Me | 49

Facilitator: Is there another **turnaround** for "Mom should function as a guarding mother"?

Client: A mother doesn't always have to protect and has to let her child deal with the situation, at the right age, at the right time.

Facilitator: What about when you were at the dermatologist's office? I heard you say that this wasn't supposed to be a dangerous situation.

Client: I want to be a girl who knows how to protect herself. A mother shouldn't feel guilty that she doesn't protect in situations where it wasn't clear in the first place that she needed to protect. I don't want to be a mom who feels guilty that I didn't protect my daughters in situations that were not supposed to be dangerous to begin with. Wow. This is a really important sentence for me! Both sentences. One, that I don't want to be protecting my mom all the time. I'm willing to protect her some of the time, but not all the time. I don't want to. And also—I, as a mother, don't want to feel guilty that I wasn't a protective mom for my daughters in situations that were not supposed to be dangerous, even if in the end it turns out to be a harmful situation. But, if it's not clear ahead of time that it's such a situation where I can say, "Okay, I don't have to be a protective mom there," I waste a lot of energy worrying about it. There are situations where it's okay to not be a guarding mom because it's not supposed to be dangerous or it's not supposed to be my responsibility. Maybe it's my daughter's responsibility to raise herself there. Wow.

Facilitator: Do you see a possibility that your mother shouldn't have functioned as a guarding mother to you because it wasn't supposed to be a dangerous situation?

Client: Yes.

Facilitator: Let's look at the next statement. What are we going to work on?

Client: I need my mom to care about me when I'm in pain.

Facilitator: "I need my mom to care about me when I'm in pain"—**is it true**?

Client: Yes.

Facilitator: **Can you absolutely know that it's true** you need your mom to care about you when you're in pain when you're at the doctor's office and she's at home?

Client: It wouldn't have helped me. It wouldn't have been less painful if she had cared. But I wanted to know that she cared.

Facilitator: **How do you react, what happens, when you believe this thought**?

Client: I'm suffering terribly because the situation is that my mom is in the kitchen with her back to me, cleaning and cleaning and I try to get her attention by telling her I'm in pain and she waves her hand and tells me, "I'm not a doctor. Go to the doctor." She's indifferent. She makes me feel like she doesn't care at all. I remember many situations where she didn't care that I was in pain, when she didn't care that I didn't feel good, when she had her back to me, indifferent, not caring. The pain was even more painful because she didn't care, do you understand? It increased my pain.

Facilitator: How do you treat her when you believe that she doesn't care if you're in pain?

Client: I hate her, I want to make her disappear. I'd be better off as an orphan than with a mom who doesn't care. I'd rather die than be a mother who doesn't care. Wow, wow. I'm full of shit. Wow.

Facilitator: When you're sitting in front of the doctor, **who would you be without the thought** that you need your mom to care about you when you're in pain?

Client: I don't need her. I can handle the situation. I cope better and I'm in less pain. Because I held on to the feeling that I was abandoned, the whole situation intensified. I'd be a girl who could tolerate physical pain. I intensify physical pain because I feel abandoned. If I don't need the thought that I need her to care about my pain, it hurts less. What do you know!

Facilitator: Let's try the **turnarounds**. What do you see?

Client: I need my mother to care about me when I'm not in pain.

Facilitator: [After a pause] What does that mean?

Client: Oh, wow. It means something horrifying. It means that she doesn't care about me when I'm not in pain, so I create pain to evoke her empathy. Oh, wow! That's true... I'd make myself miserable to evoke her empathy and it didn't work if it wasn't a real tragedy. I was very dramatic in order to get her empathy. If she cared when I wasn't in pain, I wouldn't have needed so much physical pain. God! I need to write this down.

Wow, now I understand... God! I have this thing that when I have a lot of drama in my life and it evokes empathy in others, it brings me pleasure. My dad was sick with cancer and I remember feeling for a moment that I had a right to be miserable and get empathy from people because I actually had a big drama in my life. Even though it scared me and caused a big mess, there were also moments when someone would express their caring and empathy toward me, and I'd be pleased with the drama. I never realized that I created dramas out of my heart's desire that it would make my mother care about me. Wow... that's amazing, and it's crazy.

I never understood why even though I was scared in physical situations—let's say a colonoscopy, and things got messed up and I was hospitalized and had a fever, and I was scared to death about a million things... I was also delighted. I had no idea where it came from, why I was pleased while I was also so scared—it's a thing and its opposite. How is it that I feel happy with the drama? Now I understand. For years I've been curious about it and didn't understand where it came from. And my daughter does it, too. She's such a drama queen.

Facilitator: Let's see if there are any other **turnarounds**. "I need my mom to care about me when I'm in pain".

Client: I need me to care less when I'm in pain. I need to reduce the drama, to care less about physical pain. I'm being overdramatic. Every pain is cancer, every disease will kill me. I was over-caring when I was in pain and I need to care less, have less drama, panic less. I doubled and multiplied the pain in order to compensate myself.

Facilitator: Let's take a look at the **turnaround**, "I need to care about my mother when she's in pain."

Client: I need to care about my mother when she is in pain? I'm done with it because she keeps recruiting me. I'm tired of caring about my mother.

[After a pause.] I need to care about my mom when she's in pain? Maybe. I'm disgusted by her, repulsed by her, angry at her. I distance myself from feeling empathy for her—that's right. It wouldn't hurt me to care more for my mother when she's in pain. I try to avoid feeling care toward her. I'm willing to feel a lot of negative sensations in order to not feel empathy for her. I'm willing to be disgusted by her, repulsed by her, hate her, to be indifferent, just not to feel caring. I can't stand this feeling. This is a difficult thought for me.

It's interesting that when I tried to choose a situation and a statement for Inquiry, I thought of, "I'm disgusted with my mother because ...," "I'm repulsed by my mother because ...," "I'm indifferent toward my mother...," and then I realized that it isn't really the feeling, and I tried to identify what I was feeling until I got cornered with "I hate her." But before I got to "I hate her" there were many layers covering it up.

Facilitator: Let's look at statement #5. You wrote: Mom is weak, coward, irresponsible, miserable. Let's do **turnarounds** to "I."

Client: I'm weak, it's my lack of responsibility. I was too weak to resist the doctor. *I'm a coward*, that's true. *I was miserable and irresponsible* toward myself, that's true.

Facilitator: And **turnarounds** to your mother?

Client: Mom is strong. She was strong facing me. She didn't agree to come with me to the doctor. Yes, she protected herself. She was terrible to me, but she was good to herself. Even then, it was clear to me that she couldn't withstand all the situations of motherhood. If she had to run around with me and my siblings to see doctors, it would have been the end for her. She was barely alive anyways. It's clear to me now that she protected herself and that she was strong. She defended herself.

She was brave in being true to herself and saving her energy. Instead of being a by-the-book mom, she was willing to be a good enough mother where she could.

She is not miserable. For years, I was my mom's spokeswoman saying things like, "She's miserable, she had a hard time with my father, a second-generation to the Holocaust, she had a crazy, mentally-ill mother." For years, I protected her. I wasn't angry at her as a child. My mom didn't let us get angry at her. She'd make herself the victim and she'd always be right. She trained us to protect her. I want to find examples not from the position of the girl who protects her mom, but from a position that looks and says she protected herself, she was strong when facing me—she was brave. She's not really miserable, she makes herself miserable.

Facilitator: Mom was irresponsible. What **turnaround** is there?

Client: Mom was responsible. She was responsible for herself instead of being responsible for me. Okay. I'm willing to accept that. I'm not willing to accept that she was responsible for me.

Facilitator: Was she responsible for sending you to the doctor's office?

Client: Okay.

Facilitator: We found one example. Is there another example where she was responsible?

Client: She did other things that were within her responsibility instead of coming with me. She didn't go sit in a cafe, she didn't go on a trip. She was responsible for other things like cooking, cleaning, tidying the house. She was responsible for other things in her parenting.

Facilitator: What did you write in statement #6? "I never want to experience ..."? Read it as a **turnaround**, "I am willing to experience ..."

Client: I am willing to experience the feeling of isolation and fear that I was confronted with in these situations, the terrible pain and helplessness in front of the doctor, a figure of authority, while I am small. He hurt me and I was composed on the outside but in turmoil on the inside. Why would

I want that again? I'm willing to try to experience it again and to see that I'm not dying. But why look forward to it? I'm not looking forward to it, but I'm willing to try to cope. It's hard. [Pause] I'm willing to experience the feeling of isolation. It doesn't scare me. It doesn't scare me to feel the fear again. I can contain it and am willing to experience pain.

I have a hard time with helplessness. I'm not willing to feel helpless and I'm not willing to compose myself on the outside and be in turmoil within. If I'm storming inside, I want to be storming on the outside.

Facilitator: What **turnaround** was most significant to you in this Inquiry?

Client: What resonated with me the most is that I don't always have to be a protective mother to my daughters, and I don't have to feel guilty. I constantly have a feeling that I need to protect them because there may be a situation that turns out to be dangerous in retrospect. I want to be a mother where, part of the time, it's okay not to worry and not protect my girls, and not to trigger myself constantly with thoughts of worry and protection for them as if I need to be a "helicopter parent" looking for the next obstacle where I'm supposed to enlist myself as a guard—because God help me if I didn't identify it ahead of time and been there for them. It resonates with me very strongly.

And, with myself, to be willing to feel isolation, fear, and pain. I still feel it in my body. And also, the question—am I willing to connect with my empathy toward my mother and stop distancing myself from that feeling all the time? I realize how much I've made myself miserable and smaller and just wanted to die from the thought that I needed her. Wow! How much it has castrated me even in that situation… and, on that, I've built hills and mountains out of life situations. Dear God!... Thank you.

Facilitator: Thank you.

Facilitation #3: Mom is the Center of My Universe

Going back to inquire into a recurring painful childhood situation can be an opportunity to see things with a new perspective now that you are an adult. For example, from an adult's point of view, you can see how it was important for your mother not to favor one child over the other and to treat all her children equally—something you were not able to see as a young child. When questioning what you believed at the time, you can find more understanding, not only for your mother but for your sibling and yourself as well.

As a mother herself, the client looks at her interactions with her own children. She finds examples in her role as a parent that brings her to see her mother in a different light, and to get to know her mother better.

Client [crying]: The situation is a repetitive type of situation. I'm in the kitchen and I'm watching my mother and my sister doing some kind of craft or gardening—something they both enjoy. I see how much my mom enjoys being with my sister. She's talking with Amy and she looks happy to be with her. I'm watching them and I'm feeling left out.

Facilitator: How old were you?

Client: I could have been ten, or twelve, thirteen, or fourteen. This happened numerous times throughout my childhood. It's a recurring theme for me. I'll read my Worksheet. [Client is crying as she reads her Worksheet.]

#1 I am saddened by Mom because she likes Amy more than she likes me.

#2 I want Mom to give me the same kind of attention she gives Amy, to be delighted with me and enjoy being with me as much as she does with Amy, and to love me fully.

#3 Mom should see me as special, too. She should love me for who I am. She should love me just as much as she loves Amy. She should show me that she loves me.

#4 I need Mom to be excited and happy during her interactions with me, to approve of me, to notice me, to not be mad and disapproving of me, to give me as much positive attention as she does Amy.

#5 Mom is disregarding me, she identifies more with Amy, she likes Amy better, she is more interested in Amy, she is turning away from me, she prefers Amy, she is disapproving of me, she is disinterested in me, leaving me aside, leaving me out.

#6 I don't ever want to feel that Mom loves Amy or likes her better than she likes me. I don't ever want to experience not being loved enough again.

Facilitator: So, you see them doing some activity together, some kind of craft…

Client: I see my Mom smiling. She looks happy. I can see how much she's enjoying herself, enjoying talking to Amy, being with Amy. I didn't get that!

Facilitator: Let's start with the first statement.

Client: "She likes Amy more than she likes me."

Facilitator: Where are you when you're watching them? Are you standing somewhere when you see this?

Client: It's a very small kitchen, so I'm standing right in the doorway, maybe four feet back, and watching them sitting at the table.

Facilitator: "Mom likes Amy more than she likes me"—**is it true**?

Client: Yeah.

Facilitator: **Can you absolutely know that it's true** that your mom likes Amy more than she likes you?

Client: No.

Facilitator: **How do you react, what happens, when you believe the thought**, "She likes Amy more than she likes me"?

Client: I feel isolated, left out, sad. I feel separate from them. I don't get that kind of attention, even when I express interest in those kinds of things. I feel angry at them for leaving me out. I feel a sense of despair because I tried different ways to get that kind of attention and approval from my mom. It feels like they have a special little club I'm not part of. I feel like I need my mom. I miss her.

My sister seems like she's a little princess. It's like she won the competition before it even started.

[Client asks herself a sub-question.] How do I treat my mom? I watch her interacting with Amy. I might say something to join in and it doesn't work. The interaction is still about them and what they're doing. I feel like giving up. My mind tries to figure out other ways to get her attention. It feels so futile. I'm angry at both of them.

[Client asks herself a sub-question.] How do I treat myself? I treat myself like there's no one there for me. I feel alone, isolated, like they don't care about me. There's a sense of worthlessness. I want to give up. I want to go and hide in my closet and cry. I want to go to my stuffed animal that my mom made me. It's a dog, his name's Brownie. I want to find him and lay my head on Brownie and cry. I feel confused. It's like I'm not supposed to be like me, I'm supposed to be like Amy but I can't be like her and I try to be like her, and it doesn't work.

Facilitator: In that situation, when you're looking at your mother and Amy at the kitchen table, **who would you be without the thought**, "She likes Amy more than she likes me"?

Client: I'd see that my mom looks happy. They're interacting and I notice they enjoy being together. I notice my sister getting my mom's approval and appreciation and it's nice for her. She seems to want that and need it, too.

Without the thought, I'd feel more grounded. I don't need to be a part of what they are doing. I don't know that I need that attention at that moment.

I wouldn't feel so torn up inside. I'd just be observing. I wouldn't feel threatened by the situation. I'd be glad to see my mom looking happy. I'd notice if what they were doing was something I was interested in doing or not, and make that more the basis of whether I got more involved or not. If I wasn't interested, I could just watch them or leave, and if I was interested, I could get closer. I wouldn't feel like I needed anything from my mom or my sister. I'd feel more whole.

Facilitator: Let's move to the **turnarounds**?

Client: Sure.

Facilitator: "She likes Amy more than she likes me."

Client: She likes me more than she likes Amy. She told me that she liked watching what I did because I was adventurous. She enjoyed watching me do things like when I volunteered to go on stage and dance in a school assembly.

She said things were easier for me than they were for Amy. She seemed relieved that she didn't have to worry about me so much. My mom was more concerned about Amy. For example, I loved going on summer camp and, one year, Amy came too and she was upset and afraid, so my mom came and took her home. I was excited about going to camp, to school, to the doctor's office. Mom loved telling stories about how I'd go for it without worrying. I always did very well at school. I wasn't a difficult child. I think she liked that. She taught me how to read when I was three and I think she liked teaching me to read. I remember us together.

She and Amy liked the same things. I wasn't as interested in things like crafts or gardening at the time. She liked me better from afar, that's what it feels like.

Facilitator: Do you see another **turnaround** to "She likes Amy more than she likes me"?

Client: I like Amy more than I like myself. In that moment, I think there's something better about Amy. I think she's the preferred one, so there's something I prefer about Amy over myself. I find myself to be inadequate, insufficient, lacking, and Amy has… whatever she does, whatever she has, is what I need to have to get that kind of attention from my mom. At the same time, I'm angry and irritated with Amy. It's a mix of feelings.

I feel like I should be like her in some ways. I should be somebody who really likes to do those crafts. I'm not really interested in it. I see her as more likable, preferable, or better than me. In that situation, I turned everything against myself. There was some anger against Mom but not much because it was never safe to be angry with my mom. It really wasn't.

Another turnaround would be *Mom doesn't like Amy more than she likes me*. I can't know what Mom likes or doesn't. I can't know what her feelings are. I can't know why she gives more attention to Amy. It doesn't necessarily have to be about liking or not liking. I know there are things she liked about me, that she appreciated about me that I mentioned before.

Facilitator: You said it was a recurring situation. From your little girl's eyes, do you see an example for this turnaround?

Client: It was important for Mom to treat us equally. I know that was important to her. I know, in her way, she tried to. I know she liked that I was "easier." She had four kids, she was busy, and she was working. It was a relief to her that she didn't need to "worry about me."

I see another way it's possibly true that she doesn't like Amy more than she likes me at that moment. I know when my kids are interested in something that really interests me, it's really nice, it's exciting, it's fun. We can dive into it in a different way than if I'm just listening to them talk about something they like—that's great and all—but when they like something I like, like music, there's something different in that for me as a parent.

I know my mom spent a lot of time focused on us—we were her primary focus. She didn't have a lot of friends and she rarely met with a friend. So, to have a daughter who was really into what she liked, I can see how her excitement would be expressed and it wasn't necessarily her excitement about Amy. She was excited because she was doing crafts and gardening, something she loved, and that's where her excitement came from. It wasn't necessarily about liking or not liking Amy but, as a child, that was the only way I could see it. I couldn't see that a mom could be lonely and just love connecting with someone over the things she enjoyed. I couldn't see her as a person, as an adult with her own needs. It doesn't invalidate my needs, it's just making both parts of the picture. It just shows me how big that "I, I, I" is for a child. It's so big.

I'm looking for another turnaround. *I like Mom more than I like myself.* I can see that. I look at her as the one from whom to get the attention I need, the comfort I need, and the approval. I don't see that it's possible at that time to have it come from me. I do find it through my stuffed dog. I'm able to find it there within myself with my stuffed Brownie friend to a fair degree.

For that turnaround, I like Mom more than I like myself. I put my whole sense of whether I'm worthy or not, if what I'm doing is right or wrong—everything—it's all according to her judgment. It's all subject to what she thinks about it. I was looking outward for her approval and disapproval. When I'm looking at her, it's like whatever's going on with Amy and her, that's the way. I don't have a sense of what things I like. Those things have no validity in that moment. I'm more in line with her than I'm in line with myself. I'm in her business, for sure. As soon as I go there, I lose myself.

Facilitator: What did you write in your next statement?

Client: I want Mom to give me the same kind of attention she gives Amy, to be delighted with me and enjoy being with me as much as she does with Amy, and to love me fully.

The one that stands out to me is, "I want Mom to enjoy being with me as much as she enjoys being with Amy." But I'd like to work on the one that hurts the most, it holds more power than the other way. [Crying] "She doesn't enjoy being with me as much as she enjoys being with Amy."

Facilitator: Back in the kitchen, when they're doing crafts and you're watching, "She doesn't enjoy being with you as much as she enjoys being with Amy"—**is it true**?

Client: Yes.

Facilitator: **Can you absolutely know that it's true** that, "She doesn't enjoy being with you as much as she enjoys being with Amy"?

Client: No. I can't know her mind.

Facilitator: **How do you react, what happens, when you believe the thought**, "She doesn't enjoy being with me as much as she enjoys being with Amy"?

Client: I feel alone. I'm deeply sad. My heart hurts, my throat hurts. I feel tightness. I feel very small, withdrawn, and contracted. I see them having fun, enjoying what they're doing and I feel so left out. I'm lost, helpless, stuck on my own, like nobody else is there for me. I'm envious of Amy. Mom's happiness, in a way, is making me sad because I think she isn't happy like that with me, or interested like that with me.

I treat Mom as if her attention is everything—where it's going is the most important thing. I treat Amy as if she's special in some way and I'm not special and I don't know how to be special like that. I see the way they connect with each other and it's very painful to me. It's something I don't get to have that way. I feel completely left out. I feel like I'm holding my breath and I want to leave. I want to get away from the pain. It makes me think of things like Christmas gifts under the tree when I notice Amy's pile looking taller. It makes me think of Mom sharing stuff with Amy about cooking and gardening, and disapproving of me but not disapproving of Amy.

Facilitator: **Who would you be without the thought**, "She doesn't enjoy being with me as much as she enjoys being with Amy"?

Client: I wouldn't need anything to be different. I'd be happy that Mom's happy. It's so nice to see her happy. I see how pretty my sister is and I feel love for her. I'll be able to enjoy the moment. I'd feel calm inside. I'd be free to decide if I want to stay there and watch them or sit down with them or go do something else. It wouldn't affect how I feel about myself. I feel free inside—free from needing anyone's attention or approval.

Facilitator: Ready for the **turnarounds**?

Client: Mom does enjoy being with me as much as she enjoys being with Amy. The thing that comes into my mind is when my kids are with me and I'm interacting with one of them and the other's on the couch, or sitting there doing something else, I love having my kids around me. It could be that I didn't need to be involved with what they were doing for my mom to enjoy having me there. Just my being there was meaningful to her. I didn't need to do anything, or be anything, for her to enjoy me being there.

I wanted so much to be important to her. She loved all of us, each one of us…there wasn't a difference. It's so interesting how the mind wants to pick one thing to focus on but there's so much that plays into someone's behavior. And the more we make it about ourselves, the more we miss the picture.

She does enjoy being with me as much as she enjoys being with Amy. When you enjoy being with somebody, it's a mutual thing. It's not like you can enjoy being with somebody who doesn't want to be with you. My mom was not an expressive person, so her enjoyment was more subtle. She was very calm and kept quiet within herself. So, I'm realizing that, if I enjoyed being with her, which I did, she must have enjoyed being with me and it was a quiet enjoyment, it wasn't lots of laughs and big smiles.

Facilitator: It sounds like just being present with each other in the same space was enough.

Client: Yeah. I think that's it. What's next?

Facilitator: **Turn it around** to the self.

Client: I don't enjoy being with myself as much as I enjoy being with Amy. In that moment, I'm wanting to be there, with Amy, in that place around that table, receiving what she's receiving. I don't enjoy being with myself, standing over there. I want to be anywhere but where I'm standing, feeling like this. In that moment, I'm approving her qualities and I'm not approving the qualities that are in me—a sweet, young girl who loves her mom.

Facilitator: And her sister.

Client: And her sister, that little irritation. Saying that right now makes me feel left out again, so I don't want to go there. I see her as perfect. I don't see myself as perfect in that moment. I definitely want to be in that position that she's in.

I think, in this turnaround, it stands out to me how I'm against Amy in that moment. I love her so much. I'm in a big sister role with her, loving and protecting. We have fun together, we laugh together, and I enjoy being with my sister. In that situation, I miss out on that feeling I have toward her at other times—loving her, being with her. It almost seems like Mom has that role so there's no place for me in the situation. She's the one who guides Amy and is connected with her, watching over her. In a way, as a big sister, there's no place for me with that when Mom's with Amy. I get to see that I'm missing out on how I really feel about Amy—how I love her—when I'm thinking that thought that Mom doesn't enjoy being with me as much as she enjoys being with Amy. There's an immediate negative feeling toward Amy and it's not my overall feeling toward her. What's next?

Facilitator: Let's look at the next statement.

Client: "She should love me for who I am."

Facilitator: "She should love me for who I am—**is it true**?

Client: Yup!

Facilitator: "She should love me for who I am—**can you absolutely know that it's true**?

Client: No.

Facilitator: **How do you react, what happens, when you believe the thought**, "She should love me for who I am"?

Client: There's sadness and despair, hopelessness. There's a feeling that I'm not enough. There's a feeling of pride that she should love me for who I am and sort of wanting to figure out how to get her to love me. I see all her attention is on Amy. I feel like she doesn't care about me. I can see from where I'm feeling as a kid—it feels so strong—the feeling inside is like she doesn't care if I die. Like she doesn't care about me at all!

[Client asking herself a sub-question.] How do I treat Mom? I feel a little bit angry toward her. I feel disconnected. A little bit resentful. I feel angry with her for not loving me for who I am, but I'm not loving myself for who I am in that moment.

[Client asking herself a sub-question.] How do I treat Amy in that moment? I see Amy as being kind of a little princess, snotty, like she's better than me in some ways. She's the prized one. I'm judgmental of her, I resent her, and at the same time it's mixed with loving her. It's confusing and it makes me sad. It makes me feel disconnected from her, too.

Thinking, "She should love me for who I am" makes me feel like I want to leave but if I leave I won't get the attention that I want or the love that I want, so I don't know where to go and what to do. It's painful and I don't know how to fix it.

Facilitator: **Who would you be without the thought,** "She should love me for who I am"?

Client: I start to feel warmth within me. A love for myself comes in when I'm not having that thought. It's a natural sense of appreciation to myself. Love, in a way, wouldn't be personal anymore. Love would be something that's just given. It's not given to this person or that person or the other person. It's just given. Love would feel much more available.

Facilitator: So, **who would you be without the thought,** "She should love me for who I am"?

Client: I'd be completely free to be myself because it wouldn't be about trying to be a certain way so that she would love me. I could be whoever I wanted to be. It's a very happy and free feeling. I'd get to be me, whatever that was, in that moment. I'd be enjoying myself and my own self-expression.

Facilitator: Are you ready for the **turnarounds**?

Client: Yeah. "She should love me for who I am." The obvious: *I should love myself for who I am.*

Facilitator: What would that look like when you're a little girl in that kitchen? What can you do?

Client: I don't know. I'm trying to find something I can do in that moment. It's little things that come into my mind. It's something simple, like looking at my hand. I'd appreciate my hand. My mom always liked the way my hands looked. She had big hands. She said they were big, like a man's, or a farmer's. She'd always look at my hands and say, "You have such beautiful hands." So, I'd be looking at some part of me and start to find places that I love myself and I might begin with looking at my hand.

I might be thinking about something that I'd enjoy doing right now. I love reading. I enjoy playing piano. I could go do something and enjoy it by myself. It's so hard to find the little places to start to love myself for who I am in that moment. To find the first steps, I could start by looking at my hand. I could go look at my hair in the mirror. I always liked my hair. It makes me feel good.

That was a good question you asked. What would I do? How would I do that in that moment? What do I enjoy?

Facilitator: I should love myself for who I am. You mentioned you didn't like so much the specific thing they were doing. Loving myself for who I am would be asking myself, "What do I want?" We're so willing to change ourselves or do things we don't enjoy just to get Mom's love, and that's not loving to us.

Client: Absolutely. Yeah. That's very helpful.

Facilitator: What's another **turnaround** for, "She should love me for who I am."

Client: I should love her for who she is. Well, I'm not loving her that much for who she is in that moment [laughs]. Maybe it's not so easy to do. I don't love that she's giving all her attention to Amy. I'm mad, I'm angry at some level. I wasn't loving her for who she was. I was loving her for what I wanted from her. I wanted love and attention.

I should love her for who she is. That would be appreciating that she's happy. Some of the things I saw in Question 4, "without the thought," were what a pleasure it was to see her enjoying herself like that, to see her feeling connected with my sister. I couldn't see that at the time.

To love her for whatever limitations she has also helped make her the mom that I love. To listen more when she was talking about the things she was interested in. She used to tell us all these stories from *Reader's Digest* magazine and I wasn't interested in those stories. I didn't want to hear that from her. But those were her little stories. That was Mom. Today, I could just listen and I'd enjoy her. She died a few years ago. I could enjoy her. I could enjoy those things.

Facilitator: What's another **turnaround**? How about the opposite?

Client: Mom shouldn't love me for who I am. It didn't occur to me [laughs].

Facilitator: We're trying things out.

Client: The thing that stands out to me is her attention is very much on Amy and the crafting, so in that moment, I'm not so much a part of that picture when I look at what's going on there. The truth is, I don't know that she doesn't love me for who I am.

Facilitator: It's her business and you have no way of knowing.

Client: Yes, I'm in her business when I'm deciding who she loves for who they are. That's funny, the thing that came up for me is that she shouldn't love me for who I am, she should love me for who she thinks me to be [laughs].

Facilitator: It's all she can do.

Client: It's all she can do. Yeah. And that's nice because it takes me out of the equation in a way, and it leaves me free to be myself, oddly.

I'm in her business and she's focused on something else, on someone else, on her own pleasure of sharing something she enjoys. That's what I really see, a lot.

My daughter sometimes says to me that her sister's my favorite, that I love her more, and it's funny because I give her sister less attention, for sure. I'm baffled when she says that. I give her so much attention and, anyway, I can't imagine loving one of my children more than the others. That just doesn't make any sense at all.

Facilitator: You're ten or twelve years old and you see your mother with Amy in the kitchen doing some crafts and your mom looks happy. Be there now and reconnect with the little girl that you were. We're at Statement #4. What did you write?

Client: I need Mom to be excited and happy during her interactions with me, I need her to approve of me, to notice me, to not be mad and disapproving of me, to give me as much positive attention as she does Amy.

The one I'm getting the most energy around is, "I need Mom to approve of me."

Facilitator: "I need Mom to approve of me"—**is it true**?

Client: Yes

Facilitator: **Can you absolutely know it's true** that "I need Mom to approve of me" in that moment?

Client: No.

Facilitator: **How do you react, what happens, when you believe the thought**, "I need Mom to approve of me"?

Client: I feel isolated, separated, and disconnected from her. I feel like she and Amy have their private, little club and I'm on the outside and I'm not invited in. I'm not welcome, I'm not acknowledged. I feel really sad and very alone. I can't enjoy Mom being so happy because I see it as a result of being with Amy and she doesn't feel this way about me. So, it's an overall negative experience for me.

Sometimes, in such a situation, I'd try to go and add something to the conversation and, if I didn't get the attention I was seeking, I'd feel rejected. I might express interest in what they were doing and if I didn't receive the attention, it felt worse and it made trying to get that attention a scary thing.

I can see that I'm putting my sense of self-worth on my perception of what my mom thinks of me. It depends on my interpretation of whatever reaction she shows or expresses. Whether it's about me or not, I don't know, but I take it to be about me.

I feel resentful of Amy and the attention that she gets. I start to feel like I don't deserve the attention. I get harder on myself and I start to feel like I'm not worthy of that attention and that love. There's a feeling of desperation and deep sadness, a sense of futility. I want to close in inside myself, to curl up. I feel tightness in my chest.

I treat Mom like she's an all-powerful being, like she's the center of my universe, which, in a way, she is. I think she's perfect. As a child, I can't see any of her limitations or struggles. I can't see her humanity.

I search in my mind for something to do to get her approval. If she's angry or impatient or dismissive of me, it's just another confirmation that I'm not worth it, I don't have it, whatever it is, the thing that qualifies for getting that approval. I can try as hard as I want to, but I'm not going to get it. It makes me not want to not try at all, just give up.

Facilitator: In that situation, **who would you be without the thought**, "I need Mom to approve of me"?

Client: I definitely feel more grounded in my body. I feel more present with myself. There's a sense of safety that isn't there with the thought. I wouldn't feel that desperation. There's a sense of love around me that's holding me there. I feel accepted.

I feel I have a choice. If watching them interact is causing me pain, I don't need to do that. I'd be taking care of myself, for sure. I'd be respectful of my feelings.

Facilitator: What would that look like at that age of ten or twelve, taking care of yourself and taking care of your feelings?

Client: Maybe I'd leave the kitchen and go do something nice for myself. Go outside, walk around the yard, sit on the grass, watch a squirrel, or something like that, and sit with my feelings for a bit. Maybe I'd write Mom a little letter saying, "Mom, I miss doing things with you. I really would like to do things with you, too. Can we pick something to do together?" A letter would be safer because, if I tell her, she might say something like, "Okay, but I don't have time," and I'd take that as a big rejection.

Facilitator: Sounds like rejection is scary and you feel fearful about it. You try to avoid it. When Mom says, "No," or when she doesn't want to do what you want, you believe she's rejecting you.

Client: Yeah. There are a lot of feelings of rejection and it's so painful. That's why I don't want to try anymore. The rejection is too painful.

Facilitator: You want to see what comes up in the **turnarounds**?

Client: Yeah.

Facilitator: "I need Mom to approve of me."

Client: I need me to approve of her? It brings up to me acknowledging that she's enjoying herself there and it makes me happy to see her happy. I enjoy seeing Mom doing the things she loves to do. I acknowledge that seeing Mom enjoying herself is very good for me. It's actually a need that I couldn't see at that time. I just saw the situation where she wanted to be with Amy, not with me, that kind of stuff, instead of, "Look at Mom! Look how happy she is. Look, look, she's enjoying herself."

Most of the time, my mom worked and worked and worked. When I look back, I see that she was happy when she was sitting at the table doing crafts she loved, and it makes me so happy to see her that way. I missed that when I was having this need to be approved of.

Facilitator: What's another **turnaround**?

Client: I don't need Mom to approve of me. What I get really loud and clear is that my experience was that she didn't. Whether she did or not, I was okay. I felt a lot of painful things and painful thoughts, but I'm noticing that I was okay. If she was focused on other people and what they were doing, it allowed me the freedom to do whatever I wanted.

Another one is *I need me to approve of myself.* That would fix everything. What does that mean to me in that moment? I need to be kind to myself, to be loving toward myself, and see myself as valued, and worthy of love and attention. What I really need is to be in my business, not to be getting into Mom's business and her relationship with Amy... to see if I could ask Mom to do something with me, or maybe offer to help her make dinner or do the dishes, whatever, just to spend time together with her.

Facilitator: Do you see anything else?

Client: I need me to approve of Mom. I think it's something I couldn't do then—accept her as she was, as a human being, and to know that she had stories in her life. She didn't have the resources I have today about recognizing those stories and patterns and addressing them. She tried her very best to treat us equally and love us all and give everything she could to make our lives good lives, and that was because she loved us.

It also will be helpful to me if I can enjoy her being happy. I need to approve of her doing something she wants to do in that moment, and I can write her a note telling her that I want to do things with her and approach her another time. Feeling angry with her is painful to me. I need to approve of her because I don't want to have that pain.

Also, to notice other times when she approves of me. She does approve of me about things like doing well at school or being helpful when other people are struggling and things like that. I can notice the times when she's been approving of me and giving me attention. I can give her credit for those ways and those times. It's not that I wouldn't want more, but I'm not even seeing the approval that she has given me.

Facilitator: What did you write in #5?

Client: Mom is disregarding me, she identifies more with Amy, she likes Amy better, she's more interested in Amy, she's turning away from me, she prefers Amy, she's disapproving of me, she's disinterested in me, leaving me aside, leaving me out. Should I **turn these to "I"?**

Facilitator: Sure.

Client: I am disregarding myself. Yes, I'm way over there seeing them, I'm not present with myself. *I identify more with Amy.* In that moment, *I like Amy better* than me because I definitely think there's something much better about her than there is about me.

I'm more interested in Amy. Yeah, I'm more interested in her than I am in myself. *I'm turning away from myself.* Yup. *I'm preferring Amy.* Yes, I'm seeing Amy as the special one, as the better one in some ways.

I'm disapproving of myself. Yeah, I find myself lacking, inadequate. *I'm disinterested in myself.* All my attention is on them and I'm trying to be a part of them. *I'm leaving myself out.* Yeah.

Facilitator: You want to read it **turned around to the opposite**?

Client: Okay. "Mom's disregarding me." *Mom's noticing me.* She probably notices that I'm in the room, I imagine.

She doesn't identify more with Amy. She identifies more with me. It's like, one of my daughters in many ways is more like me. I identify with her a lot. We have similar personalities in some ways, the same style of clothes, and she receives the least of my attention.

It's possible that Mom's trying to connect. I know sometimes, with my kids, if I'm feeling disconnected from one of them, I think to myself, "Okay, that's the one I need to spend more time with and connect with." Sometimes, there's a concern about someone else more than the other, like when one of them has an illness, or the youngest one might get more attention. So, one kid might not receive as much attention because other people appear to be needing it more. And I feel guilty about that and I try to do more with them. My mom was worried more about Amy, as I would be with one of my kids that I'm more concerned or worried about. That kind of thing. It's that expression, "The squeaky wheel gets the grease," and I don't mean it in an unkind way. It's just good to see it because I resented hearing my mom say to me, "Things always come easy to you." They didn't always come easy to me. I couldn't get her attention!

Seeing it from this perspective—of being the parent—you notice when your child is struggling, and you direct your attention more to that child. And so far, the ones who've been struggling more or needing more attention—either they're going through something, like an illness or social difficulty, or they needed more attention because they're younger. Amy was the youngest and Mom was worried about her in various ways. I can see how moms have limited hours in the day and they always go to the ones they're worried about and try to fix that, and I wasn't the one she was worried about. It puts me in a different position back in that situation in the kitchen, of someone my mom does approve of and can relax more around, not needing to tend to me as much. And she might even be more dismissive of me because she doesn't have to be as careful or as thoughtful around me.

You hear about those roles in families of heroes and scapegoats, or the lost child. I always knew my mom loved me. There was no question of whether she loved me, it was that I believed she loved someone else more, which now I don't believe to be true. But I do believe her behavior toward Amy was often quite different from what it was toward me. I think, when I look into it, I see all these different factors weighing in on the situation. I was the one that many things came easy to. It was easy for me to find things to do, it was easy for me to find friends, to do well in school. So, obviously I wouldn't get as much attention from a mother who has four kids, a job, and a husband who comes home from work and sits with his newspaper and watches TV. She goes to work, she comes home, she cooks dinner, she cleans up, she gets things ready for the next day, she makes sure the kids have what they need. It puts me in that kitchen in a different position. I'm the older sister watching Mom take care of her younger sister in a way that isn't threatening for me. I can see that she does love me. It feels like she doesn't need to take care of me because I'm able to do that for myself. It gives me the position of being the older sister in the kitchen and being supportive of my mom when she gives attention to my sister, rather than being the abandoned child. It places me in a different role that I hadn't seen as a possibility in that situation.

I didn't approve of Mom. I really didn't. I can see times and conversations with her where she would be... Even when she called me in college, sometimes I'd feel like I didn't want to talk to her. I'd be irritated with her, with what she was saying, with how she was being... I don't want to get into blaming myself for not being more present with her back then and missing out on her. It's easy to go there, "Oh, I didn't fully enjoy her when she was alive." That's a good one.

Facilitator: What's the next thought you wrote?

"She likes Amy better." *She likes me better?* I think she liked that I was easy for her. I was an easy child. She liked that. I had friends and school was easy for me, so Mom didn't need to give me the kind of attention she gave Amy.

"She is more interested in Amy." *She is not more interested in Amy.* What's coming up for me is, I think, that she was excited to be doing something she enjoyed doing with Amy and she wasn't interested in one person more than the other. It's not like when I'm with my kids I think, "Oh, I'm more interested in him than I am in her."

"She is turning away from me." *She is not turning away from me.* She's just sitting there, facing Amy. They're facing each other and I look on from a different direction. So she wasn't turning away from me. Wow. Wow! How funny, ha? Wow.

She is not preferring Amy. I think it's the same thing. When you're doing something with someone, you are just doing the thing with them. Preferring is just a thought.

She is not disapproving of me. Gosh, she was not disapproving of me in that moment at all! She was engaging with Amy in that craft.

She is not disinterested in me. She wasn't acting in any way that was showing me any disinterest. She did not dismiss me. It's just that she wasn't interacting with me. It's like when I'm in the kitchen talking with one of my kids—if another one walks in, I may look at them or I may just keep talking. It's not that I'm disinterested in the other child, it's just that I'm doing this thing right now. God, kids really put stuff onto things, holy crap, that's crazy, man! Wow!

"She is leaving me aside." No, *she is not leaving me aside.* She's just doing what she's doing with Amy and I'm there in the kitchen, too.

"She is leaving me out." *She is not leaving me out.* They were already doing the thing in the kitchen when I came in. Hmm. I was more independent, going out on my bike or going on a hike through the woods, or reading. And then I'd come in and see that they were doing crafts, and I'd feel left out and apart from that.

She is not turning away from me. She isn't rejecting me. She isn't saying, "No, we're doing this together, just me and Amy." She never once said to me that I couldn't join in. She'd never do that. Even if I didn't get the approval and interaction that I was seeking from her, she wouldn't leave me out. Phew!

Facilitator: And the last statement?

Client: "I don't ever want to feel that Mom loves Amy more than me or likes her better than me again. I don't ever want to experience not being loved enough again." I'll turn it around.

I am willing to feel that Mom loves Amy more than me or likes her better than me. I'm willing to not be loved enough again. Okay. Bring it on!

I look forward to feeling that Mom loves Amy more than me or likes her better than me again. I can see that there's this painful place that I can go back to and I can be there for myself if I feel that way again. It's an opportunity for me to be there for myself in a way that I wasn't able to then. That feels good.

I look forward to experience not being loved enough again. Yeah... I mean... Achh [laughs]. I feel that by looking back at these situations, I'm getting to know my mom better. I'm getting more insights into her life because I can see it from the perspective of a parent now, instead of just the perspective of a child. I get to appreciate her in a different way. I wasn't able to have that perspective when I was a kid. So, it's nice, I get to know my mom better now and I appreciate that.

I look forward to experiencing not being loved enough again… I can't really get in on that one, but I understand it. It will send it back to me to find the love within myself and to work with people like you, which is always wonderful.

Facilitator: Anything else on your mind about this Inquiry or the Worksheet?

Client: I'm grateful for this opportunity to do The Work on my mom because my mom is one of the three people that I have a lot of resistance to work on. Mom is—you know—it's a big one. Such a central figure. If I'd worked on it by myself, I wouldn't have gone through a whole Worksheet like this, so it really showed me the value of that. I feel a lot of shifting and peacefulness coming in.

A Turnaround to the Role

At times, we are still attached to our story and we are not ready to open up to the possibility that a turnaround can be as true or truer than the original thought into which we are inquiring. This can be challenging, especially when it comes to the complete opposite. If you are new to The Work, here is a brief explanation about the turnarounds.

The three standard turnarounds are: 1) to the self, 2) to the other, and 3) to the opposite.

The turnaround to the self is an opportunity to look at how I am doing to myself the same thing I am judging the other person for, (in the specific moment I am inquiring as well as in other situations).

The turnaround to the other is an opportunity to look at my part in the situation, how I did the same thing to the person I am judging either in my reactions, my behavior, or in my mind, like my thinking and my imagination. I look for examples in and outside the situation.

The turnaround to the opposite is an opportunity to see how it is possible for the complete opposite to also be true, or truer, than the original thought. Here as well, look for examples in and outside the situation.

For example, if the thought is "My mother is not interested in me," it will be turned around this way:

1. **To the self**: I am not interested in myself.
2. **To the other**: I am not interested in my mother.
3. **To the opposite**: My mother is interested in me.

For each turnaround, we look for a few specific, authentic examples that can be as true or truer than the original belief.

However, at times, it could be that we are still attached to a belief and are not willing or able to see how a turnaround may be truthful to us. There could be a few reasons for that, for example:

- We are looking at a childhood situation (sometimes going back decades into the past) and it's challenging to see beyond the perspective of the child or teen that we were.
- The identity we built around the belief is so strong that we are not ready yet to let it go, to allow a shift to happen.
- We have resistance to understanding and forgiving the person we judge on the Worksheet (in this book, our mother).
- We are fearful and defensive about what we might discover once we try on a certain turnaround and so we hold back.

In such cases, positioning ourselves in the role of the person we judge and trying the turnaround this way, could bring insights. For instance, when we become parents ourselves and are facing a stressful situation with our own children, it can bring us to understand differently a stressful event with our mother into which we do an Inquiry. For example, in a previous facilitation, the client judged her mother for not protecting her, and then she had an insight and found an example in the form of a turnaround to the role:

> "I want to be a mother where, part of the time, it's okay not to worry and not protect my girls, and not to trigger myself constantly with thoughts of worry and protection for them as if I need to be a "helicopter parent" looking for the next obstacle where I'm supposed to enlist myself as a guard—because God help me if I didn't identify it ahead of time and be there for them."

When they got stuck in the standard turnarounds (mostly the complete opposite one), the clients found examples in a turnaround to the role—from their perspective as parents themselves. They moved themselves to see the situation as a mother/father interacting with their children in a similar situation to the one into which they were inquiring. From the point of view of their role in the situation, they could see how the turnaround can be true when it comes to themselves as children interacting with their mother. This is another kind of turnaround; I call it the **turnaround to the role**. In this book, the turnaround to the role manifests itself when a client tries on a turnaround and finds examples from his/her role as a parent, and it can be applied to other roles we fulfill in our lives.

Thus, the earlier example, "My mother is not interested in me," will be turned to, "I am not interested in my children" (when I am in the role of a mother or father). If you have no children, try it in your role as an adult—"I am not interested in (someone's) children." Find examples: are you interested in your child at each and every moment? Are you interested every time your son or daughter shows you a scribble or a doodle they made in daycare? Are you listening when he or she goes on and on about something? Do you, at times, think that what you are doing is more important than what they want? Do you pretend to pay attention to them when you are not?

Let's look at another example: "My mother shouldn't yell at me in front of my siblings." We will turn it around this way,

1. **To the self**: I shouldn't yell at myself in front of my siblings.
2. **To the other**: I shouldn't yell at my mother in front of my (or her) siblings.
3. **To the opposite**: My mother should yell at me in front of my siblings.
4. **To the role**: I shouldn't yell at my children in front of their siblings. I shouldn't yell at my children in front of my siblings (or in front of other people).

If you are a parent, have you ever yelled at your child in front of their friends, relatives, neighbors, at school, in a store or parking lot (even if it happened only once)? This is not about making you feel guilty or ashamed, it's about being open and honest when taking a look at yourself and getting to know yourself better. As with the other turnarounds, this is about the truth. Don't take a guilt trip, take a look and try it out, and see how your judgments are true for you in a similar role as a parent or adult.

The turnaround to the role is an opportunity to see how we express the same reaction or behavior we judge in another person when we are in the same position as them. When we can't see it about our mothers in the standard turnarounds, it could be clearer and easier to see it about ourselves when we *shift* (not switch) roles and get to be the parent/adult ourselves. *We put ourselves in the role of the person we judge.* This is not the same as putting ourselves "in their shoes," as we are not pretending to know their experience or trying to guess what goes on in their mind—that would make us leave ourselves and get in their business. Instead, we are looking at *our own experience in the same (or a similar) role as that of the person we judge,* positioning ourselves and observing how the questioned thought applies to us.

The turnaround to the role can be generalized and applied to any role we fulfil in our lives. For example, relating to our workplace, we might have a thought: "My boss doesn't respect me." We take this statement through the four questions first and then we proceed to the turnarounds:

1. **To the self**: I don't respect myself.
2. **To the other**: I don't respect my boss.
3. **To the opposite**: My boss does respect me.
4. **To the role**: I don't respect my employee.

If you have never been in a role of a boss at work, look into your personal life when you were bossing another person. Can you find examples when you were not respecting them?

If you get stuck and cannot find yourself in a turnaround, if you feel not ready or resistant, consider turning the original statement to the role and look for treasures there. As a mother, I give myself the opportunity to explore how I react and act, the same way I judge my mother, and turn it around to see when, where, and how I do the same things to my children as their parent. I find clarity and freedom in that turnaround. It shifts my position from "I know how it should be," "I never do that," or, "I will never do that," with the tension and even arrogance that comes with it, into the softness and quietness that exists in humility and integrity.

Facilitation #4: She Thinks I'm Bad

In this facilitation, the client worked on one thought out of a whole Worksheet. Inquiring into even one thought is valuable and it takes as long as it needs to when you allow yourself to slow down, be still, and meditate on it. Take the time you need. The situation you are investigating might have waited for you for decades—and you finally got to it.

Client: This is about my sister, Lisa. When we were children, she would always come and annoy me. If I was watching television, she'd come and change the channel. She wouldn't ask, she'd just do it to be a bitch, or she'd kick me, or she'd do anything she could to annoy me. If I retaliated, she'd go to Mom and I'd get into trouble, and that was always 100% of the time. I can't remember a single time when I didn't get in trouble.

In this situation, I was watching TV when my sister came and changed the channel and I didn't do anything. Then she kicked me and I didn't do anything and she just kept on doing stuff to annoy me. In this situation, I didn't retaliate at all. Eventually, I went and told my mother what Lisa was doing and I got in trouble.

Facilitator: Read your Worksheet to me.

Client [Reads from his Worksheet]:

#1 I feel rejected by Mom because she doesn't care about me, she thinks that I'm bad. I'm resentful with her because she thinks I'm picking on Lisa.

In this instance, the important thing is that, even though I haven't done anything wrong, she still thinks I've done something wrong.

#2 I want Mom to think I've done the right thing, I want Mom to support me, I want Mom to see that I didn't do anything to Lisa.

#3 Mom should listen to me, Mom should believe me.

#4 I need Mom to care about me, I need Mom to think that I'm doing the right thing.

#5 Mom is uncaring, unjust, unfair, self-absorbed, emotionally abusive.

#6 I never want Mom to think that I'm bad, I don't want Mom to believe I'm picking on Lisa.

Facilitator: So, what do you want to work on?

Client: How about, "She doesn't care about me"?

Facilitator: Okay. Go back to the situation. Where were you and where was your mother?

Client: My mother was in the dining room and Lisa and I were in the TV room. I went to the dining room to tell Mom and she just started yelling at me.

Facilitator: Did you see her do something when you entered the room? What was she doing?

Client: She was reading a book. She started yelling to leave her alone, blah blah blah… I can't remember exactly what she said. But, I remember, the impression is that it's all my fault. She thinks it's all my fault and I should leave Lisa alone.

Facilitator: How old were you?

Client: About twelve.

Facilitator: And Lisa?

Client: About eight.

Facilitator: So, you walk into the dining room, and your mother's there reading a book. You tell her your complaints about Lisa. She starts yelling at you, "Leave me alone," yes?

Client: Yup.

Facilitator: So, your mother doesn't care about you—**is it true**?

Client: [After a pause] No.

Facilitator: **How do you react, what happens, when you believe the thought** that your mother doesn't care about you?

Client: I feel hopeless, like I can't do anything right. No matter what I do, I'm always in trouble with this woman, my mother. Even when I'm doing the right thing, I'm doing the wrong thing. I feel rejected and I feel hopeless. I just don't understand. I just want her to listen to me, to see what's really going on. She just doesn't care. It's like she hates me.

I don't know what to do. I tried everything I can. I tried dealing with Lisa myself, I tried not doing anything to Lisa and letting Mom deal with it and I get in trouble and I don't know what to do. She doesn't want to listen to me. I have resentment toward her just for that because she won't listen. If she'd just listen and see, then she'd understand and I'd feel it was justified, that the right thing had happened, that there's justice. I feel that, no matter what I do, she'll always hate me. That's it.

I think I should be acknowledged because of the effort I've made. I should have that acknowledgment that I've done the right thing and I'm not getting it. I think she should see that I'm good and it turns out that I'm just bad. No matter what I do, I'm bad.

I have so much resentment for Lisa. I hate Lisa because she knows what's going on and she takes advantage of it. She knows exactly how it's going to turn out and I know exactly how it's going to turn out, and I resent my mother for allowing it to happen. I resent the fact that Lisa can come and do whatever she likes to me and then it's like a double-whammy that I end up in trouble when Lisa does whatever she wants to me and I get in trouble with Mom. I hate them both.

I want Mom to see I've done the right thing. I just don't understand why I get this special treatment from her. I give up. I give up trying to tell her. I give up trying to do the right thing. It becomes a pointless thing to me. It's like a futility that I have. I just want that woman to love me like she loves my brother and sister. I see the difference, so clearly obvious. I feel like I need to do better, to do more, and I'm lost. I don't know what more I can do.

I'm frustrated and I don't understand why she doesn't care to listen, why she always makes that same judgment. She calls me names and I don't even know what they mean and I don't know why she's calling me those names. I remember she called me a chauvinistic pig. I want to start defending myself when she starts yelling at me but, at that moment, it's hopeless. It's a waste of time saying anything. I might as well talk to a post, it doesn't make any difference. This woman's going to hate me no matter what.

Facilitator: **Who would you be without the thought** in this situation, "She doesn't care about me"?

Client: I'd see a woman who is frustrated and angry and she wants peace and quiet. She wants to read a book and doesn't want to be disturbed [laughs]. She wants to get back to her own business as quickly as possible [laughs]. She's somebody who isn't interested in what I have to say and it's not a bad thing, she's just not interested.

I'd be peaceful and I'd see it's not personal. I'd be calm and see that she has her own issues, and she's not capable of dealing with a life of a child, and not interested really in dealing with children, and it's not personal, it's just her wanting to get some kind of happiness, some kind of peace, some kind of enjoyment, and she doesn't want to be disturbed. That's it, yeah… [laughs].

Facilitator: "She doesn't care about me." What **turnarounds** do you see?

Client: I don't care about myself. Yeah, in that situation I'm thinking I'm bad no matter what, even when I try to do the right thing. I'm not seeing that I haven't retaliated to Lisa and that's a good thing. I'm seeing it as a bad thing. I'm not acknowledging my own efforts to make peace and get along with Lisa to resolve the issue in a different way.

I don't care about myself when I stop trying to explain what's going on. I don't care about my thoughts and my opinions of the situation, I don't care about my version of the event. I give all power to my mother.

Facilitator: "She doesn't care about me."

Client: I don't care about her [laughs]. I don't care that she's reading her book and she wants peace and quiet. I don't care that she doesn't want to be disturbed and this is her enjoyment, her happiness, because she enjoys reading a book. I don't care about her being upset and angry and feeling frustrated or irritated or whatever she's feeling. I don't care about her opinion that whatever's going on is insignificant, not important to her.

Facilitator: "She doesn't care about me." What's another **turnaround**?

Client: She does care about me. She didn't beat me [laughs]. I don't know. She does care about me. I don't know. Can you see anything?

Facilitator: She does care about you, but in that moment, you're annoying her. It has nothing to do with caring or not caring about you.

Client: Yeah, that turnaround just doesn't work.

Facilitator: She's a woman, a mother with two little kids in the house, fighting. She wants to read her book. Leave her alone.

Client: [laughs] Yeah. Okay.

Facilitator: It's one more quarrel between these two children…

Client: [laughs] Okay.

Facilitator: So, can you find an example that she does care about you in that moment?

Client: In that moment? No. Well, she talked to me. She yelled at me, so she didn't completely ignore me. This turnaround is really not going to show anything because there's nothing there that I can see in that situation where she cares about me. I mean, I can go through my life, and—well—she fed me and clothed me and sent me to school and there are other situations where I can see that she did care about me but, in this situation, I can't see one.

Facilitator: Was there a **turnaround** or an example that was significant for you in this Inquiry?

Client: Yeah, I suppose *I don't care about her* when she just wants peace and quiet. She wants to be able to read her book. She doesn't know how to communicate properly and I'm not seeing it. I'm not caring about her inability to communicate her needs. I don't care about her frustration or impatience with the situation.

And the other one was the turnaround to the self—*I don't care about myself.* I'm not caring about how I've done the right thing, and how I try to resolve the issue, at least in my mind. I'm not caring about myself or my opinions, or explaining myself and what's going on to my mother, so I'm not sticking up for myself.

Facilitator: Do you have anything else to add to this Work today? What did you see when you answered "No" to Question 1?

Client: I don't know what she cares or doesn't care about. I can't get into her mind. That was the main thing, that was the "No." And in Question 3 was how I felt, what was going through my head and how I thought it was hopeless, I can't do anything right in that situation and that showed how I got to the turnaround to myself. And the turnaround to the other, this made me look at my mother and the situation. It showed me that all she wanted was peace and quiet [laughs] and it had nothing to do with me.

Facilitator: Can you relate to that as a parent? [**Turnaround to the role**]

Client: Oh, yes, [laughs]. 100%. It's something I felt very guilty about with my daughters because I'd come home from work, I'd be worn out, and my daughter would want to play and talk, and all I wanted to do was collapse on the couch. A lot of the times I'd send her off with, "Go play with your sister. Go do something. Go play a game." Just go [laughs]. Yeah.

I'm going to do a Worksheet on Lisa, too, because I hate that, even to this day, I feel so much resentment toward her for that. And you know something? It's the only thing that I resent her for because other than that, I don't really have any problem with Lisa. It's interesting.

> **More Work to do!**
>
> As you sit in Inquiry, take notes of additional judgments that come up. Many treasures can be found in questioning even just one thought. More sticky, stressful thoughts that are connected to the belief you are inquiring into will float to the surface and reveal a story and an identity that formed around it. For example, in this Inquiry:
>
> She thinks it's my fault.
>
> She hates me.
>
> She thinks I'm doing the wrong thing.
>
> My mom allows my sister to do whatever she wants to me.
>
> My sister takes advantage of this.
>
> My mom gives me special (negative) treatment.
>
> Mom favors my sister/brother over me.
>
> She doesn't love me as much as she loves my sister/brother.
>
> She thinks I'm bad.
>
> She's not interested/capable of dealing with a life of a child.
>
> She doesn't want to be disturbed.
>
> She doesn't know how to communicate (her needs) properly.

No New Thoughts and Common Themes Related to Mother

Together, we suffer alone

As Katie says, there are no new thoughts; all thoughts are recycled and some thoughts are universal. For example, "My mother doesn't love me," "She doesn't listen to me," "She doesn't care about me," "She doesn't respect me," "I want her to be happy," and "She ruined my life." Although they are universal, it doesn't mean that they are ultimate, absolute, unshakable truths. While millions of people on Earth think these thoughts and believe in them, each person will find their own answer to the question **Is it true?** There is no right or wrong answer; yes and no are equal. An Inquiry is an opportunity to start questioning what you were taught to believe and what you might have blindly believed and followed. Avoiding the truth, ignoring it, looking for it outside yourself, and obeying other people's truths without doubt leaves you unsettled—it just doesn't feel quite right. It is never too late to reexamine, reconsider, and reassess those beliefs and stories you have been attached to for so long.

For several weeks, I did The Work with a friend about our mothers. We were finally ready and willing to dive into the deep waters that we had avoided for so long. At some point, it hit me—we have the same mother! Although we come from different backgrounds, live in different countries, and are from different cultures, we were thinking the same thoughts, experienced similar situations, and we had the same complaints and judgments concerning our mothers. And so I began to collect stressful thoughts from other people about their mother. For example, have you ever had the thought, "I had a difficult childhood"? The thing is, when we find ourselves caught in a stressful situation, we might feel isolated and lonely, even unique or exceptional in our misery and misfortune. We make up a story composed of beliefs like, "I have the worst mother," "Other children have better homes," and, "My family is the most dysfunctional." Have you ever had such thoughts running through your mind?

So far, I haven't heard any new, original thought. Each time I facilitated someone or have been facilitated, I discovered parts of myself and my life in other people's Inquiries. Their Worksheets were my Worksheets; we believe the same thoughts about our mothers (and if not about mothers, we find them relevant and applicable to other people). You might have already found some of your own stressful thoughts sprinkled lightly or heavily in the facilitations or in the "I complain about my mother" list.

I have bundled some of these thoughts into common themes and you can explore which ones are relevant to you, which beliefs are still alive and painful, causing you distress, wanting your attention, and waiting for Inquiry.

The right order of things

We believe we know how things should be when they work properly in reality. We have opinions about what is right and what is wrong, what is normal, and what is abnormal. We know. Anything that deviates from these beliefs can be labeled as a disorder, mental illness, abnormality, mistake, or chaos. We hold on to core beliefs such as, "Mothers should love their children (at first sight)," "Mother's instinct is a natural thing," "Mothers should nourish their children (physically and emotionally)," "Mothers should provide a safe environment for their children," "Mothers should nurture and cultivate their children's self-esteem and self-worth," "Mothers should be gentle with their children," and, "Mothers should put their children's needs first."

In reality, things don't always turn out that way. Who would you be without your thoughts of what's right and what's wrong about the order of things on planet Earth?

Entitlement

Children believe they have rights—birthrights that they expect their parents to fulfill. Whether it's true or not, reality has a way of showing us. Some children take it a step further and innocently believe they have all the rights while their parents have no rights beyond providing for them.

(Some children still believe it when they become adults.) With beliefs such as, "She brought me into this world," and "It wasn't my choice to be born," a whole world of expectations is born as well. "She gave me life, [and therefore] she is obligated to me, she owes it to me to take good care of me."

We have expectations: "I want...," "I need...," and "She should...." For example: "She should cook for me, feed me, do my laundry, give me attention when I need it, not interfere with my life when it suits me, show me affection, support me emotionally, and buy me things. It's my birthright to live with her and be taken care of until I am able to stand on my own two feet."

How would you live your life if you dropped the belief that your mother owes you anything? What would your relationship with her look like?

Role switch: Who is taking care of whom?

We want—we need—Mom to be Super-Mom: strong, healthy, sane, someone who is available to us when we need her. It can be challenging to see our mother as fragile, vulnerable, weak, sick, tired, addicted, mentally ill, struggling, confused, or helpless, especially when we are young. (Some people never grow out of it.) It is our heart's desire that our mother is someone we can lean on, rely on, and someone who will always be there for us as support in this world. We believe that "Mothers need to take care of their children," and, "Children don't need to take care of their mother," at least not while the children are young and before the mother gets old.

Other variations to these beliefs are: "She is supposed to take care of me, not the other way around," "She expects me to take care of her. She should take care of me," and, "I shouldn't be the one taking care of her." "She is acting like a child, I was the parent," "I was the responsible adult," and "I was a parental child." "She was/is not a source of support."

Reality shows that, for various reasons, mothers (and fathers) don't always take good care of their children, and in some families, children take care of their mother, even at a young age.

Who would you be without the story that your mother should support you or be someone you can lean on?

The love triangle: Mother, Father, and Me

The Mother-Father-Child triangle includes dynamics such as competing with Father for Mother's love and attention, competing with Mother for Father's love, accusing Mom of taking Dad's side against you, or vice-versa. Separation or divorce of the parents brings another kind of tension to the triangle. It can be a dynamic triangle when teaming up with one parent against the other changes over time. Preferring one parent over the other, forming a team of two against the third person, or giving someone the title of "bad guy" or "good guy" are some of the ways we play roles in this love story.

What aren't you able to see when you believe the thought that your mother sided with your father against you (or the other way around)? Who would you be without the story that your mother has treated your father unfairly?

Competition and rivalry with siblings

Competing with a sibling over Mom's love and attention can be a cause of distress for a child. Believing that Mom loves your brother or sister more than she loves you, that she has a favorite one and it's not you, or that she is choosing sides between you and your brother or sister is painful. It can continue into your adult life. You might have plenty of evidence that your brother or sister (or you) is the prized one, the prince or princess, the golden child or the black sheep, and so on. Giving people roles and labels creates a world of stories and identities.

It doesn't have to be a human sibling for you to feel neglected or less loved by your mother. It can be anyone and anything she devotes her time and attention to—a friend, a pet, a plant, even her special curtains that she attends to that can make you jealous and feel less important to her.

There are as many mothers in the family as there are children. Each child has a different Mother-experience with the same woman. How would you live your life without the thought that your mother favored your brother or sister over you?

Competition and rivalry between Mother and me

Power struggles and/or competition with your mother is another recurring theme in this relationship. It could be around position and status in the family, feeling powerless or wanting to feel powerful when facing her, comparing yourself to her, and feeling inferior or superior. It can be over talent, skills, a sense of importance and strength, physical appearance, etc. with thoughts like, "I am smart, she is stupid," "She is jealous of me," "I am more talented," "She thinks she is prettier than me," "I'm a better cook," and, "I am a better mother than her," and so on.

Who would you be without making comparisons between yourself and your mother?

Not taking "No" for an answer and fear of rejection

It is inevitable that, at times, what we want or need will conflict with what Mom wants or needs. When we ask and Mom says, "No," "Not now," or, "I don't have time for this," we might take it personally and perceive it as a rejection of us. When she is not complying with our requests and not giving us what we want, we might see it as proof that she does not love or care about us. A story is created around her "No"—how and why she says "No"—and what it means about me and her. There are unquestioned, naïve, and childish underlying beliefs like, "I come first," and, "Mothers put their children's needs first."

Who would you be without your story that what you want or need is more important than what she wants or needs?

Needing Mom's love, approval, and appreciation

The things we do for love… to receive love from our mother, we try to be good sons and daughters. Because we want Mom's attention and show of affection, we can find ourselves doing things we don't necessarily like or enjoy. To spend some one-on-one time with her or to win her over our siblings, we can become pleasers. It gets us involved in her business, guessing how and what she would like us to do or be, trying to find the thing we need to do to extract that magical love from her as proof that we are worthy.

We believe our happiness and well-being depends on her approving of and loving us. We believe that when she is happy, it is because of something related to us, something that we said or did. This mindset can leave us feeling that we are not good or that we are never good enough for her. This could be a cause of frustration and resentment toward her when we believe she failed to make us happy or we have failed to make her happy.

Can you absolutely know that it's true that you need your mother's approval or show of affection to feel good about yourself?

The fantasy of the ideal mother

The ongoing longing for the perfect mother to show up—that nurturing, good, gentle, kind, and unconditionally loving mother—keeps us in a position of arguing with reality. It can be challenging to accept our mother as human, a person—the wholeness of her—and to allow her the right to be happy and free in and beyond her role as our mother.

While we continue to expect the ideal mother to pop out of her hiding place inside the body of the woman who is in front of us—our birth mother—we lose clarity in the present moment. We mentally make comparisons between two images of a mother—the one we want and the one we have. Waiting, hoping for our mother to change (for the better, of course), to surprise us with new reactions and behaviors other than the ones she shows is met with disappointment.

Even by her deathbed, we might still be hoping she will give us what we want, or that she will change. It's her last chance to show us how special we are to her or to admit that we are her favorite child.

Who would you be without your story of the mother that you want vs. the mother that you have?

I want my Mommy

We can be twenty, thirty, forty, fifty, even sixty-years-old and, in one swift moment, we can mentally go back to being like little children wanting our mommy. Even as adults, we sometimes want to be snuggled like toddlers. Mom is the go-to person we want to be able to reach out to and show her our kindergarten drawing or to boast of our success at work, as well as cry about our failures and difficulties.

From birth till death, we want our mother to be there for us, to be gentle and sensitive with us, to put our needs first, kiss our bruise, and make the pain go away. As we get lost in a dream, forgetting for a moment that we are grown-up men and women, we become children again wanting to be cuddled by our (ideal) mother, even if just for a moment, to put our heads on her shoulder, rest, and find solace in her arms.

Facilitation #5: My Mother Humiliated Me

Facilitator: Tell me what the situation is.

Client: This is a situation that recurred many times. I am the oldest daughter and went through a lot of humiliation in front of my brothers and sisters. My mother would ostracize me, telling them, "Don't go near her. She's bad. I don't allow anyone to talk to her," and telling me, "Leave the house. Take yourself and go." I didn't know if I could return home, when I could come back, or whether she would let me back in the house or not. This was accompanied by verbal and physical violence. I expected my mother to show respect, empathy, to be inclusive. My dad loved me very much when I was little; I was his favorite. In retrospect, I realize he did not really love me. He loved that I was smart because it served all sorts of purposes for him. He definitely preferred me and loved me more than my siblings and held me in high regard and gave me a lot of attention. When I grew up, he took my mother's side and they would both take their anger out on me. I felt betrayed, helpless, and abandoned. The issue of getting kicked out of the house and humiliated in front of my siblings when she'd say about me, "She's bad, don't go near her," was repeated many times.

Facilitator: What age were you?

Client: I think I was thirteen or fourteen years old.

Facilitator: Where were you in this specific situation that you want to work on?

Client: At home. It was summer break. My mother had to go to work. The situation was difficult. There was physical violence toward me. My little brothers watched as she dragged me out of the house and I begged for my soul, "No, no, no!" I experienced humiliation when I saw all my little brothers watching in horror. I begged her. It was August and very hot outside. I didn't have any water, I didn't have food, and I didn't have anywhere to stay. She didn't show any mercy for me. She yelled at me, "Get out of here!" She dragged me out of the house very violently—I'm not going into detail right now—even though I begged and screamed. She ordered my brothers, "No one opens the door to her. No one. I warn you. If I find out someone opened the door for her there will be consequences." She locked them in the house, took the key, and went to work. I was left outside alone. For hours I wandered in the August heat through the streets, with no food. I felt like I was about to pass out. I went into an alley... I was a very trendy and popular girl. To this day, there's a dissonance between how I look on the outside, how I'm perceived by others and my successes, and what I manage to create, or rather fail to create, in intimate relationships. I felt like I was about to pass out, but I kept my dignity. I didn't want to be pitied. I wasn't the type of person willing to be perceived as miserable or weak. I was walking down an alley and suddenly my grandmother found me and asked me, "What are you doing here?" I told her and she was very angry with my mother. She took me to her house and gave me a drink. And then I experienced humiliation a second time when my mother came there and yelled and said how bad and horrible and dreadful and terrible I was.

Facilitator: When was the peak moment in the situation you described—when she dragged you outside?

Client: Yes, that moment when everyone's watching and not allowed to talk to me. When I'm screaming helplessly and begging for my soul in front of everyone. Such humiliation. That's the worst moment, when she drags me outside in front of everyone and the fear that I don't know what will happen on the streets. I don't know if I can go back home, how I'll survive the day, or where. I want to stay at home. I want her to treat me like she treats my other siblings. She never behaved like that to my siblings, only to me, so I felt there was something wrong with me and I was really bad. It's a fact that she acted fairly toward my siblings. By the way, they're all married and everything's good with them, but not for me, as I keep recreating these disconnections in my relationships. This is how I feel in my relationship every day. I don't know if my husband will leave. I don't know if I'll leave. I don't know if my daughter will have a father. I don't know if I can even keep a relationship at all. Maybe not.

Facilitator: Let's go back to the peak moment. Let's focus on this specific situation like an anchor and go back to it throughout the Inquiry. Read to me what you wrote in the Worksheet.

Client [Reading her Worksheet]:

#1 I am angry and hate my mother because she humiliated me, she beat me in front of everyone, she took her rage out on me, called me names. I was helpless and humiliated.

#2 I want my mother to treat me with the same respect she shows my brothers and sisters, to love me like everyone else, to support me, show affection, and give me safety and comfort.

#3 She should love me, give me warmth and love, be caring and emotionally close before she lashes out at me, remember that I'm her daughter, count to ten, and only then talk pleasantly after she calms down and is available to talk. She shouldn't have yelled and cursed and resorted to physical, mental, or verbal violence.

#4 I need her to speak to me respectfully, inclusively, to explain herself and not to scream or curse or beat me or attack me with any physical or verbal violence.

#5 Mother is a monster, mindless, crazy.

I hated her. I'm uncomfortable saying it, but I really hoped she would die. In the end, it happened. I want her to stop existing in my life, I wish I'd never been born.

#6 I never want to experience again my mother humiliating me violently in front of my brothers and sisters and kicking me out of the house.

Facilitator: Let's start with the first statement. Choose one thought.

Client: She never loved me.

Facilitator: Is that what you wrote on the Worksheet?

Client: No.

Facilitator: Choose one statement that you wrote on your Worksheet.

Client: She humiliated me. The abandonment comes back all the time in my life but I didn't address it in what I wrote.

Facilitator: "My mother humiliated me." Let's focus on that one, in that specific situation, not throughout your entire history together. Only that day and that moment. I invite you to take a breath… we'll do it slowly. Look inside yourself for the answers, for your truth.

Let's go back to that day. You said it was the summer break, and you were thirteen or fourteen years old. Your mother wants to leave the house and go to work. She drags you out and says violent words to you. She's physically violent. You see your siblings watching. Your mother locks the door. They're inside, you're outside. This is the moment. "My mother humiliated me"—**is it true**?

Client: Yes.

Facilitator: "My mother humiliated me"—**can you absolutely know that it's true**?

Client: Of course. Yes.

Facilitator: Look through your eyes then, at age thirteen or fourteen. **How do you react, what happens, when you believe that thought,** "My mother humiliated me"?

Client: I'm terribly confused. I believe that I'm wrong. Every time it happened, I fought with myself that the situation would end differently, that she wouldn't make me believe again that I'm so bad, or that I'm different from my siblings and they wouldn't be allowed to approach me.

Facilitator: What happens to you in this specific situation?

Client: Complete helplessness. Total chaos inside.

Facilitator: How do you treat her in that moment?

Client: I feel a big crisis. Huge disappointment. I really hate her. I disconnect from myself.

Facilitator: Is there anything else?

Client: I'm shut off. I put on a poker face. Pretend I'm strong, going out into the street to survive. Inside, I hate everyone. Disconnected from myself, hating myself, disappointed in her, disappointed in myself. Fact is—it doesn't happen to the others, it only happens to me. I'm angry at her… I'm furious at her. Inside, I'm angry at myself for recreating the situation again, again I'm bad, again no one's allowed to talk to me. I think every time this happens, it makes me emotionally disconnect from myself because, if I give any room for emotion, I'll go insane. If I feel sorry for myself or let others feel sorry for me, I'd commit suicide. I can't stand being pitied. I'd rather have everyone hate me for being a bitch and strong than for someone taking pity on me. So, I disconnect myself from any emotion.

Facilitator: Let's look at this situation again. Nothing has changed. **Who would you be without the thought,** "My mother humiliated me"?

Client: I think confident, safe. I was restless and insecure about my place at home and where I'd go. I was looking for stability, security.

Facilitator: In the situation when you're at home and your mother wants to go to work, she drags you out and you see your siblings watching. Do you see it?

Client: Yes.

Facilitator: **Who would you be without the thought** that your mother is humiliating you?

Client: Safe. Worthy. Happy.

Facilitator: Let's try the **turnarounds**. For each turnaround, try to find examples inside and outside of the situation. "My mother humiliated me." What turnaround do you see?

Client: I can't do it.

Facilitator: Let's try again. We're just trying to look and see. This is an opportunity to go back and see what was going on in the situation while it happened because you couldn't see it at the time when you believed the thought and reacted to it. Now that you can go back and look again, are there things you can see now? This is an invitation to look. "Mother humiliated me.' What **turnaround** do you see?

Client: I humiliated her?

Facilitator: That's a turnaround. Can you look and see the things you said, the things you did?

Client: Yes, I can see it. I'll tell you something that might be relevant. I'm not trying to promote myself or brag, but I was a very, very smart girl. Above average. Very! When my mother was young, she faced a lot of cognitive difficulties. She didn't talk when she was a child.

Facilitator: How does this relate to the situation?

Client: I'm telling you how this was humiliating for her. I humiliated her without meaning to. She had a teacher who called her a deaf and a mute. She yelled at her in front of all the kids in the class. About me, everyone would say at school and kindergarten, "What a smart girl," "She needs to move up to the next grade. She's gifted." My dad said many times that I was smart. On the other hand, about her, he'd say that she was gullible, naive, and didn't understand what was being said to her. So, even without intending to, or being rude, she often experienced humiliation when compared to me because, even as a little girl, I was a smart girl and, compared to me, she experienced a lot of difficulties. I know this because she said it all the time.

I think she had a hard time with me because I was quick to grasp and understand in-depth subtleties and my dad would give voice to that. Many times, my dad would say about me, "Wow, she's a genius. How smart," and he'd make fun of her. So, without actively doing anything, I'd make her feel humiliated next to me due to the circumstances. When I grew up, I did use it. She really wasn't at a high cognitive level and I often knew how to hurt her easily when I was angry with her.

From a young age, without me even doing anything, she hated me, probably because of this as well. Slowly, I developed a resentment toward her, and I knew where my strengths were, where I could demote her and hurt her. I wasn't physically as strong as she was. I couldn't defend myself against her, and I couldn't maintain my status in front of my siblings but I was smarter than her and that's where I could hurt her because it was a terribly painful spot for her. I think I used that power I had over her a lot as a kind of defense that I created for myself to feel strong when facing her.

She throws me out of the house, she frightens me, she's stronger—but she's not as smart as I am and I can hurt her in areas she can't deal with. I think this turnaround is true in this sense.

Facilitator: And in this specific situation, do you see an example of this turnaround? "I humiliated her"…

Client: I think what preceded all this mayhem was a sentence I threw at her. Most of the time, her outbursts were probably the result of words I threw at her in order to feel the power and strength I had over her, and then it would start. This was also proof that I'd succeeded in my goal of humiliating her and hurting her, when she defended herself and the situation I described came about. So, I think what preceded it was something humiliating that I said to her and then she'd burst. I made her feel stupid and she couldn't bear the thought that she was stupid so she reacted that way.

Facilitator: Do you see another **turnaround** to "My mother humiliated me"?

Client: No.

Facilitator: May I suggest one?

Client: Yes. I'd appreciate it. Help me.

Facilitator: "*I humiliated myself.*"

Client: I humiliated myself? How did I humiliate myself? That I begged to stay and didn't just get up and leave?

Facilitator: I don't know. Check with yourself.

Client: Yes, in this situation *I humiliated myself*. That's not to say she didn't do it. She did humiliate me.

Facilitator: Slow down.

Client: What does "I humiliated myself" mean? I think it's survival. I could tell her, "I don't care about you. Shame on you for behaving this way as a mother. Bye!" and leave. But I begged for my place, yes, desperately. If I had looked at it from the side, it would have been very hard to watch, I'm sure. You know, it also repeats itself in my relationships the same way. When your partner's abusing you, you could get up and leave and believe in yourself… instead, I stay and humiliate myself. I cry. I beg. I settle for crumbs. Even as an adult, even after I got divorced when I was already twenty-plus and I was working—I had a career, I was a manager in one of the biggest companies in the country—I would have died to get away from home. But I didn't dare to get up and rent even a little housing unit for my peace of mind and not go through these humiliations with my partner. Yes, I humiliated myself. To this day, I probably recreate the same thing.

But as a child, what could I say? "Bye," and leave? That's a bit absurd. Yes, I humiliated myself but I don't know if a child at this age is able to get up and leave. I don't know, maybe yes. Maybe there are kids who'd say "Bye" and go to their grandparents' house, tell them what she did and that they can't live in that house anymore. It's possible that, yes, with the maturity I had, it suited me very well. So yes, I humiliated myself in that situation when I begged to stay at home.

Facilitator: Look at yourself. What do you do, what do you say in the moment that's humiliating for you?

Client: I beg, "Please, no. I'll be a good girl." I tell her, "I won't do it anymore. I promise to change. Please, please!" I get physical beatings and I fight. I stay there and I receive more and more beatings and I fight to not leave instead of ending the situation as quickly as possible and not getting beaten and shamed in front of everyone. I could have complained or done all sorts of things within the law or the family—I had a lot of supportive extended family around. Instead of doing these things that would raise my self-worth, I chose a position of humiliation and war. To this day, even in my relationships today, I try to change myself to attract a partner who can contain me and suits me. I constantly try to change myself because I'm not worthy of love. I'm flawed.

Facilitator: Is there another **turnaround** for, "My mother humiliated me"?

Client: I don't know. Maybe you can help me and then I'll know how to think. I need to open my mind in this area.

Facilitator: There's the turnaround, "*My mother did not humiliate me.*"

Client: No, no, she definitely humiliated me, a lot. She beat me and told my siblings not to approach me. Is this humiliation? Yes.

Facilitator: What's the opposite of humiliation?

Client: She was proud.

Facilitator: Do you want to try and look into that?

Client: She was never proud of me. Never. Not even in the depths of her heart.

Facilitator: What did you write in the next statement?

Client: I want her to treat me with the same respect she shows my brothers and sisters, to love me like everyone else, to support me, show affection, and give me safety and comfort.

Facilitator: Choose one that we'll work on.

Client: I want her to give me love.

Facilitator: Let's go back to the situation. It's summer break, your mother wants to go to work. Your siblings are home, she drags you outside, she shows verbal and physical violence toward you. Are you there?

Client: Yes.

Facilitator: "I want my mother to give me love," in this situation—**is it true**?

Client: Yes.

Facilitator: "I want my mother to give me love"—**can you absolutely know that it's true**?

Client: Yes.

Facilitator: **How do you react, what happens** to you **when you believe that thought**, "I want my mother to give me love"?

Client: I feel frustration, hatred. Everything repeats itself. Abandonment. Disappointment. I'm convinced it's never going to happen and she will never love me. On the other hand, I never give up, so I do these manipulations because I want a different ending to the story.

Facilitator: How do you treat her when you believe the thought that you want her to give you love?

Client: I distance myself emotionally. Feel disappointed... very angry. It's always the same emotions. There's fear, anger, abandonment, hatred, disconnection.

Facilitator: In the same situation, **who would you be without the thought**?

Client: More relaxed. More rational. More confident.

Facilitator: Let's try **turnarounds**. "I want my mother to give me love."

Client: Ugh, it's so hard. I'm so in it, in those beliefs. I'm really trying. It seems a bit fake to me. I'm trying.

Facilitator: I invite you to close your eyes, take a deep breath, and we'll just try, just check what else is possible. Holding on to the story causes us suffering...

Client: I want to love myself.

Facilitator: *I want to give myself love.*

Client: But I don't want to give myself love. I want her to love me like everyone else. I don't want to give myself love. I want her to love me like the others. Why am I different? Why am I so humiliated? I want her to give me love like everyone else. That's more accurate. I don't want to be an exception.

This is the most painful, most castrating thought. I want to be loved like everyone else. I don't want to see everyone in the situation looking on in horror and feel that I'm different or unusual. I can't be loved. Everyone else, yes, but not me. I don't want to.

Facilitator: Can you see how, in the situation, you can give love to yourself?

Client: No. I'm disappointed in myself again. I'm even more disconnected from myself. In the end, it's not her. I'm the bad guy, it's me who caused the situation to happen, it's me who's being kicked out of the house. I just want to be loved the same as my brothers and sisters.

Facilitator: Do you see another turnaround? There are a few.

Client: I'm stuck. I don't know how to do this. I can't see any.

Facilitator: Let the turnarounds arise from inside of you. Take your time and sit with it. "I want my mother to give me love," like she did with everyone else.

Client: I can't. This is the thing I want the most.

Facilitator: Close your eyes, go back to the situation, and look at it as if you're watching a movie. Look at the characters—you, your mother, your siblings—as if you're watching a movie. There are a few **turnarounds**:

I don't want my mother to give me love like everyone else.

I want to give myself love like everyone else.

I want to give my mother love like everyone else.

I want my mother to give me love unlike everyone else.

Is there one you feel you can relate to? How can it be true? Your truth?

Client: No. None of these make me feel like I'm truly relating to them. I do want her to love me like everyone else. I want to love her like everyone else? I never loved her. This is exactly where I get stuck with the turnarounds. It's been my life's goal that never came true until she died, so it will never happen. She never loved me. I don't know if I did love her. I was just so broken because of her. I want to love her like everyone else? I can't relate to this.

Facilitator: I want to give myself love like everyone else? As you love other people, you want to love yourself?

Client: I don't think I know how to love other people. For real. It's so sad, but I'm disconnected. I don't know if I know how to love other people. I only know how to love my daughter. It's very easy for me to disconnect from people. There's no one I love at all costs, absolutely not. Except for my daughter.

Facilitator: Can I offer an example?

Client: Okay.

Facilitator: In a situation like this, where your mother's violent toward you, and in the moment you don't experience her as loving, and this is your subjective interpretation—you don't know if she loves you or not, because it's her business...

Client: I know because she tells me she doesn't love me. She also tells me she hates me.

Facilitator: ... and therefore I see that, in this situation, I only have myself and I have to give myself love in that moment because, in my experience, there's no one else. In this situation, I only have myself to comfort me, to calm me down, to tell me things like, "You're smart, you're able, you're capable, you're okay," because that's what I need in that moment and no one around me is able to give it to me.

Client: True.

Facilitator: You're the only person in the situation who can give this to you.

Client: It's always like that.

Facilitator: I also see an example for, *I want me to give my mother love,* in that moment because I see how she is—she might look crazy and insane and irrational to me. She's miserable and I've no idea what she's going through. When I look at her, I see a woman in need of love. I may not be able to give it to her, but I can see a woman who needs someone to give her love…

Client: True. She really was miserable. She really needed love. Certainly. But I absorbed all her rage.

Facilitator: … and I can also see in this situation—you say you're the eldest daughter—that you're not like everyone else because you're older. You said you were smarter than everyone else, so you're not like everyone.

Client: I've never been like everyone else. Even today, I'm not like everyone else. But how does that help me? Because I'm not like everyone else, I can't receive love other than giving love to myself?

Facilitator: Let's leave this question open and see what you find out in the Inquiry. What did you write in the next statement?

Client: Mother needs to be emotionally close to me. Mother in general, even the term "mother" …

Facilitator: Your mother, in this specific situation.

Client: Mother should count to ten before she lashes out.

Facilitator: Let's go back to the situation again, imagine yourself there, like in a movie. The advice you have to give her is, "Mother should count to ten before she lashes out"—**is it true**? Not "Mother"—your mother—in this situation.

Client: She doesn't do that.

Facilitator: The answer is yes or no.

Client: Yes.

Facilitator: **Can you absolutely know it's true** that this is what she should do in that moment?

Client: This is a tricky question. She doesn't do it. She's not a person who thinks. She should, that's obvious. That's my judgment. In my world, yes, you should count to ten before you lash out.

Facilitator: And your mother?

Client: I want her to. By my standards of behavior, this is what should be done—one hundred percent.

Facilitator: And return to the situation. Yes or no?

Client: No. She would never do it.

Facilitator: **How do you react, what happens, when you believe the thought** that she should count to ten before she lashes out at you?

Client: Frustration, complete misunderstanding, distance. A feeling that we will never, never, never connect. We're so different. Loathing her… superiority over her.

Facilitator: What else?

Client: Distance. These are two completely different worlds. It would never happen. I also don't want to be a part of it. Anger, disappointment. Desperation.

Facilitator: In the same situation, **who would you be without this thought**?

Client: It's hard for me to be without this thought. I don't know who I would be without it. If I'm not so critical and judgmental of her, I may have more compassion for her, then I'll be calmer. Less upset and angry.

Facilitator: Are you ready for **turnarounds**?

Client: Yes. *She shouldn't count to ten.*

Facilitator: Do you see examples in this situation?

Client: Examples? No. She lashes out.

Facilitator: **Turnaround to yourself**.

Client: I should count to ten before I lash out? It's a turnaround that's really easy for me to do. Yes, in my mind, I'd lash out at her endlessly. Maybe I should have stopped, counted to ten, and understood and seen the difficulties she was facing, to understand that she's not emotionally available.

Facilitator: What are you doing in that situation?

Client: In my heart, I curse her, hate her, disconnect from her. I think she's psychotic, mad, abnormal, that I have an insane mother. I have a lot of confusion, insane chaos, even if it doesn't show on the outside. I'm afraid it's pretentious to say that I should count to ten before I react because, in that moment, I receive such humiliation that it's a bit hard to count to ten. I can look at this turnaround and see it. I don't know if it's possible to execute it. But if I judge someone, then I should see how hard it is for me to implement it and then understand that I can't expect someone else who's also as flooded with emotions as I am to implement it.

Facilitator: What else comes to you?

Client: I can't see anything else. Can you help me?

Facilitator: My mother shouldn't count to ten. You said it because it's difficult for her. You realize for yourself how hard it is, once you start boiling, to stop and count to ten before you lash out.

Client: When I boil, I try to count to ten. I have a daughter. I hope that I'll manage to count to ten and not do such horrible things. I try very hard.

Facilitator: It brings us back to ourselves again. *I should count to ten before I lash out at myself.*

Client: Wow. That's really true. Before I started becoming self-aware and going through processes, I had a lot of disconnections and self-hatred, self-disappointment. I'd beat myself up all day, from the morning when I woke up until I went to bed. This is something that's less true for me today. But, let's say, until last year, it happened all the time. It's part of the emotional disconnection from myself.

Facilitator: Let's look at the next statement.

Client: I need her to speak to me respectfully, inclusively, to explain herself and not to scream or curse or beat me or attack me in any physical or verbal violence. In short, I need words and not violence.

Facilitator: I need my mother to...

Client: Explain herself, to not discharge her anger. To talk, to explain what hurts her. I need communication. There's no communication. She never explained herself. Always screaming, beatings and cursing. There were never words or a conversation.

Facilitator: In the situation, what do you need?

Client: Communication. If I jumped her fuse, instead of her using violence and nothing good coming out of it, I need her to sit with me and talk to me—find out what happened, like I do with my daughter. If she does something unusual, I stop everything, we have a conversation, we talk about what hurts her, what hurts me, and what's going on. We don't escalate the situation. We behave responsibly. I didn't have communication. I need my mother to know how to communicate with me.

Facilitator: So, we'll get back to the situation. "I need my mother to know how to communicate with me"—**is it true**?

Client: Yes. I did all this to get her to communicate with me for once.

Facilitator: "I need my mother to know how to communicate with me"—**can you absolutely know that it's true**?

Client: No.

Facilitator: **How do you react, what happens** to you at that moment **when you believe that thought**?

Client: I explode with rage and disappointment. Maybe more than communication, I need her to see me. To see me without all the provocations I throw at her.

Facilitator: How do you treat her when you believe ...?

Client: I hate her. I'm disappointed in her. I can't see her as a mother. I see her as an obstacle, a worthless thing. I try to get some kind of understanding from her, to see me as a person, listen to me, look at me. I'm so angry and disappointed and don't know how else to try to get her to listen to me, see me, talk to me once about feelings, a mother-daughter conversation without rage and explosions like a volcano. A really big disappointment.

Facilitator: **Who would you be without the thought**?

Client: Free.

Facilitator: She does what she does, only you don't have the thought ...

Client: I think I'd have left. I'd go and take care of myself. Independent. Free. I'd act with complete independence and spare myself the humiliations and disappointments of trying to get from her something that's impossible.

Facilitator: "I need my mother to know how to communicate with me." **Turn it around**.

Client: I need to know how to communicate with myself.

Facilitator: What does this mean?

Client: I continuously blamed myself and took my anger out on myself because I couldn't get what I wanted from outside. And I also got ricochets that I am different, and everyone gets it from her, only I don't because I'm wrong, I'm bad, and I wish I didn't exist. If I'd known how to communicate with myself, it would have released me to be independent and free.

There's also the turnaround, *I need me to know how to communicate with my mother.* That's definitely true. In the same situation, it means I wouldn't have said the sentence that provoked her into this Dance of the

Demons in the first place. But as a child, my whole being awakened things in her that made it very difficult for her. No matter what I said, it would swell inside her head to higher volumes and greater dimensions. Today, I understand why it was only directed at me and not my siblings. I won't pretend to be innocent. I know that, many times, I'd cause an explosion on purpose because I wanted revenge on her for the pain and suffering she caused me. Yes, I needed to know how to communicate with her. I needed to be smart and give up revenge because, in the end, she always won. I think I drew happiness and satisfaction from those moments when I felt how explosive and weak she got because of what I said. So, I needed to know how to communicate with her, yes.

Facilitator: Another **turnaround** would be, *I don't need my mother to know how to communicate with me.*

Client: I don't need it. Need? No. Want? Yes. Of course, I want her to know how to communicate with me. Otherwise, there's complete indifference, like walking next to each other at home like air. I want to, yes. Do I need it? I won't survive without it? No.

Facilitator: "I need my mother to know how to communicate with me." Is there anything else you see in the turnarounds?

Client: I'd be happy if she could. Apparently, she couldn't.

Facilitator: Can I share an example?

Client: Yes.

Facilitator: I need to know how to communicate with my mother and myself. Like you said, you provoked her, and she lashed out. You had no control over her reaction. Her reaction was her business. So go back to yourself and look. What are your motives in that moment? What are you trying to achieve? What kind of attention are you trying to get from her? What are you trying to prove to yourself or to her? What are you trying to show your siblings?

Go back to yourself. You need to communicate with yourself clearly so that you're clear in your thoughts and take responsibility for what you do and say. Be connected to reality, with what's happening in that moment. Your mother can't count to ten and she can't love you in that moment and she's also unable to sit down with you for a conversation and calmly explain to you what she's experiencing at the moment because you said something that turned her on and she exploded.

Client: Yes. So, we did The Work. How does it manifest itself as a change in life? I'm with a partner who behaves like my mother. He doesn't know how to communicate, he lashes out, he has problematic beliefs about relationships, and he doesn't know how to talk about it. He doesn't know how to control his emotions when something explodes inside of him. I feel like I'm wasting my time. We haven't had anything between us for two years. I have a daughter who I want to show a model of a good relationship and a happy and loving home. I have a huge fear of getting up and leaving. The question is, how does The Work help a person experience change in their life? I feel stuck. I realized that I can't get what I need from outside. First it's my mother, then it's my husband—it doesn't matter who. If I'm not able to or can't get what I want from the outside, I have to do it for myself. The question is, how can The Work help me escape this position so I won't humiliate myself again? So I won't stay in places where I only get crumbs, violence, and humiliation, and I don't get what I want? How will I be able to make the right decisions and do the right things, to be whole with myself and not regret it after? How does it help me make a change from within—to be there for myself, be true to myself, love myself? I don't want to be stuck anymore.

Facilitator: My experience is that you do it one situation at a time, one Worksheet at a time, until you feel like your Work is done. It takes stillness and slowing down, and meditating on your thoughts, being open to what shows up, loving the truth, and letting the answers meet the questions.

Facilitation #6: She Controls Me

Facilitator: Please tell me, what is the situation?

Client: I'm sitting with friends in their living room. I'm looking out the window and I see the lights of my mother's car approaching.

Facilitator: How old were you?

Client: I was fifteen. It was a birthday party and there were other friends there. Should I read my Worksheet?

Facilitator: Yes.

Client [Reads from her Worksheet]:

#1 I am ashamed of my mother because she picks me up too early from a party.

#2 I want my mother to let me be young with my friends.

#3 My mother should be aware and sensitive to my needs.

#4 I need my mother to let me be and make my own experiences.

#5 My mother is controlling, overruling me, insensitive, dominating, making a fool of me, doesn't meet my needs.

#6 I don't ever want to be controlled again.

Facilitator: So the moment is before she enters the house?

Client: Yes. I just see her coming and I wish she hadn't come to pick me up.

Facilitator: Read your first statement to me again.

Client: I am ashamed of my mother because she picks me up too early from a party. I'm ashamed even by the mere fact that I'm being picked up.

Facilitator: Close your eyes and be there now, in your friend's house. There's a party, and you're fifteen. You see your mother's car coming. "She picks me up too early"—**is it true**?

Client: Yes! Definitely!

Facilitator: She picks me up too early. **Can you absolutely know it's true**?

Client: In that situation, it feels like it. Yes.

Facilitator: **How do you react, what happens, when you believe that thought** that she picks you up too early?

Client: I feel noxious. I'd like to throw up. I feel humiliated, I feel like she's overruling me. She's grabbing me and holding me. I feel that she's suffocating me in her need to take care of me and look after me. I'm sad. There's anger, but mostly sadness. [Pause] I'm ashamed of her and I'm ashamed of myself in front of my friends because everyone else is staying and I have to go home.

Facilitator: When you see the car coming, how do you treat your mother in your mind?

Client: I want to punish her by not speaking to her, by not being forthcoming, by not being a good daughter. I want to make her feel how unhappy I am, so I'm disrespectful and give her the silent treatment. I don't talk back to her, it's not possible, so I give her silence and the feeling of me not approving her.

Facilitator: Anything else comes up with that thought, "She picks me up too early"?

Client: No.

Facilitator: **Who would you be in that situation, without the thought**, "She picks me up too early"?

Client: Often, I don't like to stay at parties that long. So it's nice of her to pick me up seeing as it's nighttime and I don't have to think about how to get home. Without the thought, I'd appreciate her concern about me. I'd talk with her when I get in the car and I'd tell her about the evening. I'd share with her what happened and be more connected with her, definitely. I'd be happy. I'd be thankful.

Facilitator: You're ready for the **turnarounds**?

Client: Yes.

Facilitator: She picks me up too early.

Client: She picks me up on time. Often, at that age, I got really tired when it got that late. Thinking back, I might have been asleep on the sofa at some point before she came. Perhaps it was the right time.

Facilitator: Look at your experience. Is it true that she picked you up at the right time?

Client: Related to this particular situation, it's hard to say. Regarding other situations… this is really hard.

Facilitator: What time was it?

Client: It was around midnight.

Facilitator: This party happened forty years ago. Go back to that time, you're fifteen and it's around midnight. "She picks me up on time." Is this turnaround true for you?

Client: Right now, I don't see anything else.

Facilitator: Do you see another **turnaround**?

Client: She doesn't pick me up too early. Even though I was with friends, I sometimes felt insecure, not knowing what to say or what to do. When I look back, it's so funny, I get this feeling that she didn't pick me up too early, because in a way, I didn't know what to do or what to say, so it was nice to be taken out of the scene. But I had to react against her because I was young so I was supposed to be with my friends but, actually, I felt like she was saving me from not knowing how to be with my friends.

Facilitator: She supported you in that situation.

Client: She came to pick me up so I could go to bed.

Facilitator: And leave the party not because of you but because of her.

Client: Yeah. It's like being saved by the bell because I was insecure even with friends. [Pause] It's really hard to find examples for this one. Often in the evenings, when it got late, I got so tired and perhaps she knew that I needed to rest and to be in my own company—that might be the case.

Facilitator: What does it mean to you, when you're fifteen and your mother comes to pick you up from a party at a time that is, in your opinion, too early?

Client: It shows how insecure and not-an-adult I am that I have to have my mother pick me up.

Facilitator: Does it mean she humiliated you, she didn't trust you? What does it mean to you?

Client: She's scared that something might happen to me so she wants to control me. She wants me to be in this spot where she knows where I am, and she really did. She imagined us living together for years and years after I'd grown up. I was escaping. I tried to get out of the house, find a man I could move in with—and that's what happened. She was really controlling. She was nice to me but she wanted to know where I was. She made me feel the world is dangerous and it was much better to stay together in our little community, just me and her and our animals. She was afraid to be alone. I felt smothered and I couldn't breathe.

She didn't pick me up too early? No, it was her rule. She said how and when and how much. That's how it was. One time, I wanted to go to a disco and she said, "No," because then she'd be home alone. It was her rules and I was just to follow.

Facilitator: Let's go back to the party and the turnarounds.

Client: She didn't pick me up too early, she picked me right on time because it was her rule.

Facilitator: Do you see another **turnaround**?

Client: I picked her up too early. I don't see anything. Do you see anything?

Facilitator: I think we should try, "She controls me." It sounds like the issue for you here. "She picks me up too early," and that means "She controls me." Sounds good?

Client: Yes.

Facilitator: You're sitting in the living room with your friends, you're fifteen, you see the lights of her car approaching. "She controls me"—**is it true**?

Client: Yes.

Facilitator: **Can you absolutely know that it's true**—"She controls me"?

Client: I want to say yes but…

Facilitator: **Can you absolutely know it's true**, "She controls me"? Sit with it.

Client: Actually, yes. Yes.

Facilitator: **How do you react, what happens, when you believe that thought,** "She controls me"?

Client: I get angry. Right now, I feel so angry. I think it's so unfair. She's ruining my life. I feel tense in my body and I feel like crying with anger. I call her names in my head. I'm ashamed as well because I think about what my friends think about me and my mother, but especially what they think about me. I'm angry and fearful and sad. I feel trapped without any possibility of doing anything.

Facilitator: How does it feel in your body?

Client: I feel anger in my stomach and tenseness in my shoulders and at the same time I feel small because I'm ashamed and sad that it has to be like this, that I have this mother. There are two sides fighting in me. When I'm with my friends, I have this attitude: I don't show any anger but I reject her in front of them. And when I'm with my mother in the car, I don't talk to her, I reject her, and when I'm alone, I'm sad and frustrated, and ashamed as well.

Facilitator: Do you see any images of past and future with the thought, "She controls me"?

Client: Yes. She controlled me a lot. She'd say, "You can do this but you can't do that." It's a feeling of never being able to do what I want. She's always there to say what I can and can't do.

Facilitator: Sitting in the living room, at a party, here comes your mother's car—**who would you be without the thought,** "She controls me"?

Client: I would be Buddha. I'd think she was a caring mother. I'd think she was doing what she could to make my life easy and good. I'd feel loved, actually. I'd feel that she cared so much about me that she wouldn't like me going out into the dark night, and I was really scared of the dark, so she was very comforting and compassionate about me. Without the thought, I'd feel the most loved child. She really cared about me. She did. I have to digest that now.

[After a pause] I know she loved me even though, sometimes, it didn't feel like it. She took care of me and she wanted to meet my needs on many levels. She did. She wanted to do the best she could for me, so, of course, she wanted to pick me up after dark. She was tired as well, I guess. So it had to be early.

Facilitator: Midnight.

Client: Yeah. I'd been there for many hours. We had fun and dinner. We danced. No boys—only girls—and it was fun. She loved me and I can see that. She loved to protect me the best way she could, so nothing bad would happen to me.

Facilitator: Ready for the **turnarounds**?

Client: Yes. Give me the sentence.

Facilitator: She controls me.

Client: She doesn't control me. Well, I had my free will. I could have said, "I don't want to go home. Don't come and pick me up. I won't go with you. I want to decide for myself." I could have said that and I didn't. I let her be in charge. [Pause} Well, later on, I did what I wanted, kind of. Some of it wasn't so smart. So she didn't control me. I did some things behind her back.

Facilitator: Is there another **turnaround**?

Client: I control her. In this situation, I controlled her with my anger and not wanting to let her into my life. There was a lot of stuff I didn't tell her about because I was giving her a hard time.

At some point—it's really crazy—I thought I could do some hypnosis on her [laughs], like some mind thing, "I want you to let me...." In my head, I was doing mind control. It didn't work [laughs]. It must have been in those years. I wanted to stay overnight with my boyfriend and I knew she wouldn't let me. It didn't work, but I'd have liked to control her in that way.

Facilitator: Can you see an example in the situation of how you controlled her?

Client: I was afraid to go home in the dark. Even though I didn't want her to pick me up, she had to pick me up because I couldn't go home in the dark. It's kind of controlling both ways. And, well, I might have taken a long time to go out to the car when she came. That's a way of controlling.

Facilitator: Do you see another **turnaround**, "She controls me"?

Client: She gives me freedom. I want to try that one because, actually, I think she did. I was afraid of so many things when I was young and, in a way, it could feel as if she put it on herself to restrict me so I wouldn't have to face so many fears. She'd take care of me, she'd pick me up, she'd make sure I didn't get into situations that would be hard for me and make me afraid. So, in a way, by controlling me—it sounds odd, but it feels true—she gave me the freedom to not be in charge. She helped me not be so afraid. She was protecting me from a lot of tough things in the world. I don't like it today, but in the moment it seemed okay.

Facilitator: Sounds like she gave you freedom within boundaries that she set for you.

Client: Yes. Freedom within boundaries—that's actually a good one. She kept me a child for a long time and actually, I enjoyed being a child for a long time. In a way, when I think about it, it's nice [laughs]—in a weird way, but it was.

Facilitator: That's a thought you can question as well—"She kept me a child." [Pause] What about the **turnaround to the self**: *I control myself?* Can you see something in it?

Client: [Pause] I had to control myself with my mother because I was afraid of throwing a tantrum in front of her because that wouldn't… well, I couldn't do that. I saw my sister do it and she got away with it, but in my world, I couldn't do that so I had to control myself when I felt something different from my mother.

[Pause] I control myself very much. I need to write that—I have to control myself. That's one of my issues still today. Sometimes I feel I have to control myself to be in this world, to do the tasks I need to do, and not just to say "screw it all."

Facilitator: I see something. Can I share?

Client: Yes.

Facilitator: I control myself by restricting myself and restricting my freedom because I have fears about what's going to happen, like consequences, or something bad that will happen in the future.

Client: Yeah, it feels very true. I'm controlling myself by restricting my freedom.

Facilitator: Let's look at the next statement. In this situation, how do you want her to change? What do you want her to do?

Client: The first thing I see is I want her to stay away. And then actually, I want her to ask me what do I want. She kind of just says, "I'll pick you up, this and that." I want her to ask me, "What do you want?"

Facilitator: Is the moment when you see her car approaching, or when she enters your friend's house, or is it before the party?

Client: I want her to ask me ahead of the party, "Do you want to stay? Do you want me to pick you up?" I wish I had the choice. I don't feel like I have a choice in anything.

Facilitator: So, you want her to give you a choice?

Client: Yes. Yes! Actually, that's it. I want her to give me a choice.

Facilitator: And this is when you see her car approaching?

Client: Yeah, I wish she'd given me a choice. She could have said, "Call when you want me to pick you up," or something.

Facilitator: Okay. So, go back to that moment as if you're there right now. "I want my mother to give me a choice"—**is it true**?

Client: I have to say no.

Facilitator: You don't have to do anything.

Client: I really don't know. I feel it in my stomach, it's running around. I feel I don't really know. I can't say a definite yes. That makes me say no.

Facilitator: **How do you react, what happens, when you believe the thought,** "I want my mother to give me a choice"?

Client: I feel anger and I feel something in my throat. She makes me so angry and I can't talk to her. She's really pissing me off. I don't want to talk to her. She never listens to me. She never lets me try anything. I feel helpless, unable to do anything. I'm just somebody she can do with whatever she wants to and I can't say anything.

Facilitator: How do you treat her when you believe the thought, "I want my mother to give me a choice"?

Client: [Laughs] I give her the silent treatment. I get sour and I must be a pain to be with. I feel sorry for myself. I feel depressed and I know it makes her feel bad but I don't care. I get stubborn so I can keep up this position of not wanting to be with her or talk to her, and I can be like that, silent, for days. And then I'd feel helpless. I'd be the victim. I feel that she really didn't want to do anything good for me at all, she was just trying to have her own way all the time.

Facilitator: Anything else comes up with this thought, in that moment?

Client: I shut down. I create a distance, retracting, and going into my own space. I'm being a victim who has a right to be sad, to be heavy. I want to crawl into myself, to be in my own world, and let my thoughts go round and round about this. She just always had it her way and sometimes I felt like I didn't have any life.

Facilitator: Let's go back to when you're sitting in the living room and you see the car coming. In that moment, **who would you be without the thought,** "I want my mother to give me a choice"?

Client: This is a hard one. I'm having a hard time doing this one.

Facilitator: Start like the Morning Walk exercise[1]: take a mental walk. Notice, what do you see? Give things a name, without any thought.

Client: I see a caring mother who wants to take care of her child. She makes me feel safe. She would never abandon me and she shows it by

---

[1] The Morning Walk is a silent exercise. We walk in silence and look at everything we see as though it has no name. We see it as though we have never seen it before and don't know what it is. As we walk, we begin to notice what our eyes rest upon and mindfully begin to name it as if we were God naming things for the very first time using only one-word (Katie calls it "first-generation") names, for example: flower, sky, shoe, bird.

picking me up and taking me home in the middle of the night. I see it as I'm being loved. I feel loved. I always saw it for something else.

[Pause] I can be who I am and I know she'll be there for me. She'll pick me up even though she could say "You're old enough to find your own way home." She wants to take care of me. This makes me feel warm inside to think that she really cared about me and I'm grateful for that.

Facilitator: **Who would you be without the thought**, "I want my mother to give me a choice"?

Client: I'd be excited about it. Yeah! She's there to pick me up and she cares so much that she goes out on a cold night, in a cold car, and I don't have to walk home and that's pretty big. Right now, I feel excitement in my body. It's nice! It's so weird but now I feel pretty happy. I have the best mother who really, really cares about me. She's so sweet. She is.

[After a pause] Knowing me at that age, I was ready to go to bed. So, seeing her without the thought, "I want my mother to give me a choice," I feel like she's rescuing me to take me home so I can rest because I need rest. I'd appreciate that she knew me so well, that she knew it would be good for me to be picked up and not have to walk home. I've already been at the party for six hours. In a way, I'm grateful that she shows me that she honors me so much and she knows how I'm feeling and how I'm wired in my head and she comes to get me. I feel grateful and I feel loved and, right now, I feel happy. I feel myself smiling, I feel seen—she sees me. That feels so good. Thank you so much. That was a good insight for me. [Pause] Yes, this part of being recognized is so special. It contains more than knowing she loves me. She knew me.

Facilitator: Are you ready for the **turnarounds**?

Client: Yes, let's do it.

Facilitator: "I want my mother to give me a choice."

Client: I don't want my mother to give me a choice. The reality is that she doesn't [laughs], so, how about that? She often didn't. That's how it was. I wasn't mature enough.

According to what I just realized, she knew me much better than I did. She knew how I was wired in my head and what I needed. So, apparently, she was much more aware than I was.

Facilitator: Can you find an example of how this turnaround could be true even at that moment when you see her car coming?

Client: Even at that moment, I think I was tired and I was filled up with impressions from a great night. In that moment, I didn't want my mother to give me a choice. If she gave me a choice in that moment, I'd have to take responsibility for myself and my choices and I might have chosen to stay and it might have not been pleasant for me. I don't want her to give me a choice, I want her to take me home. Yes.

Facilitator: Silly teenagers.

Client: I was a baby at that time. I was naïve and I was really a baby.

Facilitator: Another **turnaround** to this thought: "I want my mother to give me a choice"?

Client: I want me to give my mother a choice. This is a hard one. Must be good. I could ask her, "You want to come in and say 'Hi'?" because everybody loved my mother, everybody thought she was great. I was just, like, "Oh my god, they don't know anything," [laughs] and she was sitting in the car, waiting for me to come out.

Earlier I mentioned I gave her the silent treatment and that left her with no choice at all. She's just hanging there. If I was more open, there'd be more choices for her as well. Instead of me sulking and not wanting to talk and… well, I was expected to answer but I'd give her the shortest answer ever. So, I could give her the choice that we could talk, or we didn't have to talk, instead of pushing her away.

I want to give my mother a choice. Oh my god, if I look at it from a longer perspective, I didn't give my mother many choices. I was keeping her at a distance [makes an "at arm's length" gesture]. In a way, I didn't want to involve myself and my feelings with her.

I see that, as an adult, she often called me and would say, "Oh, nobody called me this weekend. I'm alone." She even used that at that time, "You can't leave me alone." She might not have said it many times, maybe only a couple of times, but it stuck to me like glue and it made me want to push her away and not give her any choice of intimacy or connection.

I remember a specific one when I wanted to go to a disco with friends and she said, "Then you're leaving me alone." I want to give my mother a choice… I feel it turned around and blew in our faces. When I became an adult with family and children, I turned it around and put it back on her. I didn't give her a choice. I want to give her a choice. I feel that now. Yes.

Facilitator: What choice would that be?

Client: The choice of connection, a choice of being part of my life. Even though she always said, "I'd love to come and see you because you welcome me," it was still so nice when she left. I can't say she wasn't there for me, but it took so much energy. It feels like right now, if I'd given her the choice to be there, just letting her be, it would have been easier. I don't know, but it feels like it right now.

Facilitator: Do you have another **turnaround**?

Client: I want to give myself a choice. Oh my goodness, in this situation, I didn't. I just accepted that she set the rules and said, "I'm picking you up. You're going home." If I had gone out and said, "I don't want to come with you. I want to stay," she'd say, "No, you're getting in the car," and I'd reply, "I won't. I think I'll sleep over." I didn't give myself a choice. I played along with what everybody else said. Oh, my goodness, that's so true. Even now. I need to be clear about what I want and don't want.

Also, I want to give myself the choice of being authentic—honest with myself—and if I was feeling sleepy, I don't want to blame my mother. I made her the one who was breaking this party up for me. I could say, "Oh, I thought I'd party all night but I really feel like I want to go home." Being honest and saying I want to go home—yes, that's a big one. Being honest with myself. This is it. Great. Is there another turnaround?

Facilitator: Do you have something?

Client: I want my mother to give me an ultimatum? No, that's too big. A boundary?

Facilitator: I want my mother to decide for me?

Client: Yeah, to decide. That was the bottom line. Overall, I didn't want to take the responsibility. I wanted her to decide for me. It was so much easier. And I could blame her, then—it's my mother's fault. In this situation, I could blame her and say, "My mother won't let me."

Facilitator: Let's look at statement #3.

Client: Yes. My mother should be sensitive to my needs.

Facilitator: My mother should be…

Client: [laughs] How could she be sensitive to my needs when I'm not being honest with myself? She doesn't know. She *is* sensitive to my needs.

Facilitator: Let's go with the questions. "My mother should be sensitive to my needs"—**is it true**?

Client: No.

Facilitator: **How do you react, what happens, when you believe the thought,** "My mother should be sensitive to my needs"?

Client: I start blaming and become a sourpuss. I want her to read me like an open book, so I don't have to explain myself to her or take responsibility. Oh, my god, I'm just horrible. I treat her with silence and a sour face and act spoiled and unforgiving. Oh my god, I can see this face of a teenager [laughs]. I'm giving her a hard time, not by shouting or yelling, but by being sour and depressed and not talking to her and pulling away from her. Yes.

Facilitator: You said, "I want her to read me like an open book"—**is it true**?

Client: No, of course it's not true. No. I don't want her to read me like an open book [laughs].

Facilitator: **Who would you be without the thought,** "My mother should be sensitive to my needs"?

Client: I'd be fair to her. I'd treat her with respect and I'd be honest about what I think and feel. I wouldn't be fearful. I was fearful of my mother. I'd talk to her about what happened in my life instead of being afraid of her. It would be so much easier for both of us. It would be so much easier for me. I'd be open and I might realize some new things about her that I didn't know because I didn't want anything to do with her. It's really interesting. I never thought of her as being sensitive to my needs but I think she was more sensitive than I ever thought.

Facilitator: Are you ready for the **turnarounds**?

Client: Yes.

Facilitator: "My mother should be sensitive to my needs"

Client: She shouldn't be sensitive to my needs. It's not her job, it's my job, and even though I was a teenager and I was naïve and stuff, I needed to get my experience from something! It's like she shouldn't be sensitive to my needs in order for me to grow up. She was really taking a lot of care of me. It was done with a good heart, I'm sure, but she shouldn't be sensitive to my needs.

In that situation, she shouldn't be sensitive to my needs because I wasn't sensitive to them myself. So why should she be sensitive? She's just doing her own stuff and because I wasn't doing anything, she took over.

Facilitator: "She should be sensitive to my needs". Is there another **turnaround**?

Client: *I should be sensitive to my needs.* I didn't look out for my own needs. I looked for, as teenagers often do, what the group's expectations and needs were, and the tone of the party. It's normal, but it was my responsibility to be sensitive to my own needs and I should have told my mother and my friends what my needs were and acted accordingly.

Facilitator: I have an example.

Client: Yes.

Facilitator: Some needs may conflict and create confusion. You have a need to be part of the group, to be with your friends, to be a teenager and party all night and all the stories you have around that. And there's your need to rest and go to sleep after you've been at the party for six hours. So, in relation to, "I should be sensitive to my needs," it could be hard to choose which needs.

Client: Yes, and as a teenager, it's really hard to be sensitive to your needs. In retrospect, I can see that at the time, it was a tough job.

Facilitator: You had a need to stay and you had a need to leave.

Client: Yes.

Facilitator: And your mother was aware of your needs.

Client: Yeah, true. I wanted to go home and sleep and still, I kind of lost my sensitivity about how I was feeling, how I was. I put all my sensitivity into the outside, not the inside. I'm sure I was tired and I was probably sitting there, not saying much, and instead of putting my attention and sensitivity into myself and my needs, I looked outside at the others and thought that I needed to stay at the party.

It relates very much to where I am today. I sometimes lose my sensitivity and get so confused when I do that. It wears me out. I should be more sensitive to my needs, what goes on in my head, my heart, and my body in total.

Facilitator: There's another **turnaround**: *I should be sensitive to my mother's needs.*

Client: At the time, I felt I should be sensitive to my mother's needs all the time. That was a feeling I had and the reality was that I wasn't. I was thinking she wanted to pick me up at that time because she wanted to go to bed to sleep, so she didn't want to pick me up later.

In hindsight, I see that I should have been sensitive to my mother's needs also because she was an old lady. She was close to sixty when I was a teenager. I'm glad I don't have young teenagers these days [laughs]. And she was alone. She didn't have a husband. At the time, I felt I had to be sensitive to her needs and still it wasn't out of respect that I was doing it. I'd sulk when she wanted me to do something. Do you know what my mother used to say?

Facilitator: No.

Client: She'd say, "Oh, my daughter—she's such a nice girl. She's so easy." She said that to everybody. I didn't make a big fuss, fighting her in public or anything, I was just being a sourpuss and that might have been easier than the other stuff.

I should have been sensitive to her needs. I was, a lot, but not the need to be close and connected. I didn't do that, but the need to have an easy daughter—I think she needed that. She didn't need any more disturbance than necessary. I was willingly an almost-nice girl and easy to handle, not the kind who's into parties and boys and stuff like that.

Facilitator: Let's look at the next statement.

Client: Yes. In order for me to be happy, I need my mother to let me make my own experiences.

Facilitator: In that situation, "I need my mother to let me make my own experiences"—**is it true**?

Client: No.

Facilitator: **How do you react, what happens, when you believe the thought,** "I need my mother to let me make my own experiences"?

Client: I treat her badly, as I said before. I make a fuss inside of myself and with my mother. I push her away and disconnect from her.

Facilitator: How do you treat yourself?

Client: It makes a mess inside of me because I'm angry inside and I just sulk. I keep it inside and it grows inside of me like a monster, getting bigger and bigger, and I don't know what to do with it. My stomach is so disturbed and thoughts are running inside my head. I can't get a word out, it's like my lips are glued shut. I make it so hard on myself. It's bringing me down. It's like turbulence, a storm, it roars, taking me down… it's laying the ground for depression. I see that. I keep it inside of me and I suffer so much and I want her to suffer as well, and I make her suffer. I do.

And I'm—I just see it—I'm so powerful in my punishment, I'm so powerful in my suffering. I put it on her and I put it on myself and it's really trash. I feel so horrible inside.

Facilitator: Sitting on that couch at your friend's party, **who would you be without the thought,** "I need my mother to let me make my own experiences"?

Client: Just being in that moment. Seeing her pulling the car in the driveway. Sitting with my friends and thinking, "Oh, my mother's here. Do I want to stay? Do I want to go?" I'd check with myself and find what I really need or want and decide from there, then notify my mother and my friends. I'd be much more whole and authentic, and I'd take the decision on myself instead of blaming others. I'd be calm and connected, especially with myself, but also connected with the other people, connected to the situation, and connected with my mother. I'd say, "It's so wonderful you came to pick me up. Who could have a better mother than you?" But I was only fifteen. Just feeling this, having a choice and making my own experiences by saying "No, yes and I'll think about it," is divine. I have a choice. I can make my own experiences. I'd be connected and collected.

I'd be a much nicer person. Not depressed, but happy, content, in tune with the flow of what's happening inside and outside of me.

[After a pause] I'm so happy we're doing this. I didn't think there was so much in it. I'm grateful. Thank you.

Facilitator: Thank you. Let's **turn it around**. "I need my mother to let me make my own experiences."

Client: I don't need my mother to let me make my own experiences. It's not her obligation, it's not her duty—it's mine. In this situation, I need to make my own experiences. She can't do it for me. I have to make them and address her in a polite and good fashion and say, "I want this or that." I need to enable myself to make my own decisions.

Facilitator: "I need my mother to let me make my own experiences."

Client: I need my thinking to let me make my own experiences. I was thinking that she was the one making all the decisions. My thinking was hampering me. I didn't have the awareness that I needed to put up my own boundaries about making my own experiences and that it was my choice. I didn't feel I had a choice. In this situation, I need my thinking to know that I can allow myself to make my own experiences. At that time, I didn't imagine that I could do that.

Facilitator: Look at yourself at that age. What were you able to do at the age of fifteen? What can you do to let yourself or your thinking make your own experiences? Be there now, at the party, with your friends, watching the car coming.

Client: I could let myself be a normal teenager. I didn't rebel against my mother at all. That's why she thought I was such a nice child. I didn't do what a teenager is supposed to do. I just went to the car. I didn't do what I was expected to do as a teenager. It's the age when you push your parents aside and say, "I'm going to fight my own way," and I needed to do that in that situation. I needed to push my mother aside and say, "I need to make my own experiences," and I didn't. I should have.

Facilitator: These are wonderful thoughts to take to Inquiry: "I didn't rebel," "I didn't do what a teenager is supposed to do," and, "I didn't do what I was expected to do as a teenager."

Client: I've thought about it a lot during my life that I wasn't a real teenager when I was a teenager. I didn't rebel, and when I rebelled, it was by smashing myself inside. It could be really nice to do some One-Belief-at-a-Time Worksheets on that.

Facilitator: Let's look at statement #5.

Client: My mother is controlling, overruling me, insensitive, dominating, making a fool of me, doesn't meet my needs.

Facilitator: I am… **Turn it around.**

Client: I am controlling. I am. In that moment, I give her the silent treatment and all that. *I'm overruling her.* Ohhh. In that moment, I don't know.

Facilitator: In your thoughts, in your mind?

Client: Yes, in my thoughts, exactly. I'm giving her a treatment in my mind. If I'd said that out aloud, she would have… Yeah, I'm overruling her. *I'm insensitive.* Of course. I don't care that she's elderly. That's not my concern. I want her to pick me up later. I don't care that she needs to go to bed. *I'm dominating.* Yes. I dominate her with my mood. I set the mood in the house sometimes. That's dominance.

I'm making a fool of her. Of course I did. She was the scapegoat. She was the one to blame. It had nothing to do with me. I felt that she was so old compared to the other parents and I thought it could have been so nice to have a younger parent. She wasn't.

I do not meet her needs. I'm sure she wanted to talk. She wanted to share with me about her things and hear about what I'd experienced, and I didn't meet her needs. She was just a driver, the one who made sure I had food and was safe in the house. Yeah, I didn't meet her needs.

Facilitator: **Turn it to the opposite.** "She is not…"

Client: She is not controlling. That's still a hard one for me. I know I'm controlling, but I feel she was controlling as well. I'm becoming more and more aware that it comes from love and wanting to make things good for the child.

Facilitator: In that specific situation, just that night?

Client: My mother's not controlling. She's just picking me up. It was a nice, kind thing to do. It might not have been controlling. It might have been a kind gesture.

Facilitator: It might or it was?

Client: It's still a "might" for me. There's a lot more in this controlling stuff. I need to go deeper into that. It's not done here.

Facilitator: More Worksheets.

Client: More Worksheets.

Facilitator: Let's look at the next one.

Client: My mother is not overruling me. She isn't at that time. She's picking me up and I didn't say that I didn't want to be picked up. I got in the car. It's only in my mind that she's overruling me. That's true.

My mother is not insensitive. Quite the opposite, I think she is sensitive. I just didn't see it. I had no clue.

She is not dominating. If she hadn't taken any steps toward doing something, nothing would have happened because I was doing nothing. It was so in my mind that she was dominating and I didn't interact with her at the time. I don't think she was dominating, she just felt something needed to be done. If she didn't do it, it wouldn't be done.

My mother is not making a fool of me. Actually, she isn't because I'm perfectly capable of doing that myself by pointing the blame at her. When I look at it, saying or thinking, "Oh, it's my mother and she's picking me up," just shows how little I understood and how irresponsible and lacking in authenticity I am. So, I'm doing it. That's on my account.

My mother is meeting my needs. Yes. I must say, in most cases, when I look back, she met my needs. I didn't know it, but she did.

Facilitator: Let's look at #6. I don't ever want to...

Client: I don't ever want to be controlled again. *I am willing to be controlled again*. Oh god, it really feels like... Arrrrrrr. It's a good one.

I look forward to being controlled again when I'm not aligned with myself, when I'm out of tune with myself, when I fall into the pit of being unaware and not sensitive to what I want and need. So of course, I'm looking forward to being controlled again, yes. I feel this very deeply because then I'll need to look at where I'm out of tune with myself.

Facilitator: Or someone will show up and show you.

Client: Yes! I know! [Laughs] Oh my goodness, this was so good. This is good.

Facilitator: This is fun.

Client: Yes. This controlling thing, I need to do something about it.

Facilitator: More Worksheets, more situations.

Client: Yes. Thank you.

Facilitation #7: She Attacked Me

Client: I'm the sixth of seven children so my mom was quite overwhelmed with all the children. By the time I came along, she was quite depressed. My father is an alcoholic but he's a nice guy so I was daddy's girl, aligned with him. She was the bitch, she was miserable, sort of crabby, worked hard, took care of us but she was not particularly loving or affectionate, and my father was.

This incident was when I was seventeen and it was a life-changing incident for me with my father—I've done a lot of Work on that incident. I started questioning my dad. I was negative toward him. I wasn't adoring anymore. In this incident, he was standing in the driveway sweeping and I came out and he verbally attacked me in all sorts of ways. I was devastated by that. That had never happened to me before.

After that, I went up to my room, hysterical, and my mom came into my room and she just jumped all over me as well. So that's the situation. She was screaming at me, "The truth hurts, Kathy, doesn't it? The truth hurts." She kept saying it and I was totally confused. She was glad to see this had happened to me. She said I was selfish and I deserved to be talked to that way by him.

Facilitator: What did he say to you?

Client: He said I was selfish, that I was a spoiled brat, that I needed to get a job. He called me a whore. I wasn't sexually active at that point. He had lost it.

I come from a blue-collar family and I was focused on my own success, my education. I wanted to go away to college. It was not seen as supportive in my family, to go away. They felt... he felt particularly rejected. The expectation was that, if I had to go to school, I should only be a nurse or a teacher and I should stay home. He felt rejected, like I was leaving them and rejecting them. Too big for my breeches and all that. It was the "whore" thing that mostly got me with him and I didn't understand why. I do now but then, at the time, I didn't. After that I just iced him, I iced her, I just cut them off. I never trusted them again, either one of them, emotionally. It changed my life. Later, my dad apologized. My mom never did.

Facilitator: What did you write in your Worksheet?

Client: [Reads from her Worksheet]

#1 I'm upset and confused with Mom because she didn't understand what had just happened to me and attacked me herself.

#2 I want Mom to listen and comfort me, to help me deal with what happened.

#3 Mom should reserve judgment. She should be a bridge to my dad. She shouldn't attack me with something else on top of what had just happened.

#4 I need Mom to love me, comfort me, help me to understand what has happened.

#5 Mom is oblivious, selfish, clueless, cruel, enjoying my distress, competitive with me, angry, and miserable.

#6 I don't ever want to be vulnerable and needy with someone so unreliable.

Facilitator: Can you choose one of the thoughts you wrote in your first statement?

Client: She didn't understand what had just happened to me.

Facilitator: Going back to the situation, "She didn't understand what had just happened to you"—**is it true**?

Client: I hope this is the reason she did what she did, so I'm going to say yes.

Facilitator: In your seventeen-year-old eyes, she didn't understand what had just happened to you. **Can you absolutely know that it's true**?

Client: [After a pause] No.

Facilitator: **How do react, what happens, when you believe the thought**, "She didn't understand what had just happened to me"?

Client: I'm floundering. I don't know what to do. I'm confused about what happened. The whole ground beneath me is gone. These people are aliens. I'm helpless. I keep replaying what he said. How can she say, "The truth hurts"? Does she know what he said? How can that be true? I'm confused, like they took the world away, there's no safety in the world now, this is nuts and I don't know how to navigate it. I don't know how to find comfort in this world that has become crazy.

She'd never done that before either. Who were these people? He'd never done anything like that before. She'd always attack, but when someone else attacked, she would always defend. So there was nobody. It was another wave knocking me over. I didn't know what to do. At some point, I told her to go away, leave me, get away. I was hysterical.

Facilitator: How do you treat her when you believe she didn't understand?

Client: I was very disrespectful. I told her, "You're nuts." I still needed her and I was angry. I told her to get away from me. There was an element of disgust with her like, "What kind of mother are you? How can you be so stupid? You have no judgment. You have no understanding." I was attacking her, disgusted by her and I expressed that, I'm sure. I dismissed her.

I had waves of shame, thinking I'd done something really bad. I was thinking, "What's the truth?" I was questioning myself about that, too. What am I missing here? What happened that was so terrible? I was defensive and, under that, there was shame and guilt. Withdrawal.

The physical sensation—I was shaking. My whole body was shaking. I felt like I lost any sense of connection to myself. I was floundering, I needed someone, I felt desperate and alone in it, like I'd got nothing.

Facilitator: **Who would you be without the thought**, "She didn't understand what had just happened to me"?

Client: I could separate her from the other incident with my dad. I could ask her, "What do you mean—the truth hurts?" I could have been curious about what she meant. If I hadn't been so in the story of devastation from what had just happened, I could have clarified things a little. I could have separated him from her and dealt with her in the moment. I could have been able to see her instead of this hostile entity that walked into my room in that moment. I could have asked her to help me. I'd be more peaceful and open. I could have talked. I could have asked her to clarify it.

Facilitator: Ready for the **turnarounds**?

Client: Yeah.

Facilitator: "She didn't understand what had just happened to me." **Turn it around**.

Client: I didn't understand what had just happened to me. I made it mean something way more than either of them intended. That's true. Mom kept saying, "The truth hurts, doesn't it, Kathy?" and I kept thinking, "What truth?" I didn't understand what had happened to me but I acted as if I did. They probably didn't mean it that way. We weren't talking about the same things. I took it my way and held it, so I didn't understand that I made a story, a meaning, but she was talking about something else.

Facilitator: "She didn't understand what had just happened to me."

Client: She did understand what had just happened to me. She did, from her own framework. She did understand what had happened to me in the sense that I got a talking to that I very much needed, in her mind, from him. Finally, he said what a spoiled brat I was and that I was pretty entitled and all that, so she did understand that piece—that he was confronting me about my behavior, my critical-ness, my lack of appreciation, and so on. I can see that.

Facilitator: Do you have a specific example of how you were a spoiled brat? You said you could see that.

Client: She knew he'd yelled at me. She didn't know what he said. She understood that he confronted me about my lack of appreciation for what they did for me and me asking for more and all that. She didn't understand how I took it. She was operating from what she understood.

I didn't understand what had happened to her. Yeah. In the situation, I didn't know what he'd said to her. I didn't know what he told her about what happened. So I didn't understand what had happened to her. I didn't understand what it was like for her to be with him. I didn't understand what had happened to her because of me—how I treated her all those years. I didn't understand her history and her childhood issues. I didn't understand what sort of thought system she was operating out of. I'd already dismissed her years earlier.

I didn't understand what had happened to her and how it was for her to be the heavy one, the bitch, the not appreciated one of the two of them. She got all the work, he got the adoration. That seems like the big turnaround in that one. I didn't understand what had happened to her.

Facilitator: What did you write in your second statement?

Client: "I want Mom to comfort me."

Facilitator: When you're in your room, shaking, then she comes in, and she keeps saying, "The truth hurts." You want your mom to comfort you—**is it true**?

Client: Yes. Yes.

Facilitator: **Can you absolutely know that it's true** that you want your mom to comfort you?

Client: [After a pause] I'm getting a no.

Facilitator: **How do you react, what happens, when you believe the thought**, "I want Mom to comfort me"?

Client: I feel desperate and needy and scared. I want someone, but not necessarily her. That's where the "No" came from—I already didn't trust her. It's like I want her to be someone else. I need a mom to comfort me, and so I think it's hopeless because she can't do it and she won't do it. I feel helpless and hopeless.

In terms of images, now I'm thinking of how she was rough in her touch. I remember her trying to clean my face and she'd be rough about it. I don't like her touching me. I don't want her to. I can't get it from her. It wouldn't be good.

It's like this loop of there's nobody, I'm alone, I've got to deal with this myself. I'm judgmental and angry with her and disgusted by her flaws and lack of love and softness. Mostly, it brings up this hopeless and helpless feeling. I feel like curling up. I want her to go. I've just got to comfort myself. I want to hide. I want her to get away from me.

It's like the desire to be comforted by her, the longing for that, is immediately met with believing it can't happen. I don't stay in that feeling for more than a minute or second. Immediately it's like, "Get over it. It's not gonna happen. She doesn't do that." Under that, I can feel the longing in this moment, "Could you please do that right now? Could you please be that somebody who can help me right now? I'm so desperate," and there's no hope that it can happen.

Facilitator: **Who would you be without the thought**, "I want Mom to comfort me"?

Client: Wow, boy, I feel like laughing. I'm shocked right at this moment but there's a sort of joy. I'm okay. I know she can't do this, I know her. I can see her… she's doing the best she can and I'm okay with that. I'm not taking it personally. I'm appreciative of her, of how she does it, how she takes care of business. Without the thought that I need her to comfort me, I don't need her. I'm okay. I know that she'll be there in the way she's able to be there. I could get the comfort the way she can do it.

Without that thought, I'll have my own resources. I'll be able to think. I could ask what she's talking about—"What do you mean?"—and not add this whole layer of meaning about what she's doing to me now. I'd be present and I'd see her straight. I wouldn't be confused. I could see what's going on with her—this is what she does—and not take it personally, just be as fine as I could be in that sort of a moment.

Facilitator: Are you ready for **turnarounds**?

Client: Yes.

Facilitator: "I want Mom to comfort me."

Client: I want me to comfort me. I want me to be more gentle with myself. I want me to remember to look around the room to see all that's there, all the comforts, to not make this incident so big. I want to know in myself that I'm alright, that she was doing what she does and it doesn't have to do with me necessarily. I have my resources, my thinking, my nurturing, my knowing what I know.

Another one would be, *I want me to comfort her.* Pffff... [laughing]. [After a pause] There's a lot of shame in that one. I want me to... Boy... I want me to say, "Gosh, I left you alone, haven't I? Gosh, you've been really alone. Gosh, this has been really, really hard for you, I bet."

I want me to comfort her. I want to not be so mean to her. Gosh. I wish I could have helped her more. Even then, I knew she didn't understand and I wish I'd comforted her.

I don't want her to comfort me. Because she just couldn't. She didn't know how to. So how could she? It wasn't what I needed right then and she couldn't do it, so I didn't want it. And it's okay. I'm grateful for what she could do.

Facilitator: Look at yourself in that moment, from your business, "I don't want Mom to comfort me."

Client: I wouldn't have received it. I wasn't open to it. I would have attacked her back and made it worse. I was barely holding it together and I could have lost my total sense of self then. I couldn't have handled her comforting me. I needed the anger. I needed the victimhood and I couldn't have dealt with it, I think.

The whole world wasn't falling apart and I could focus some of my distress on her. I could get in touch with my anger and that helped in that moment.

Facilitator: What did you write in your next statement?

Client: "She shouldn't attack me on top of what had just happened."

Facilitator: In your room, your mom comes in, repeating a couple of times, "The truth hurts." "Mom shouldn't attack me"—**is it true**?

Client: Yes.

Facilitator: "Mom shouldn't attack me"—**can you absolutely know that it's true**?

Client: Yes.

Facilitator: **How do you react, what happens, when you believe the thought**, "Mom shouldn't attack me"?

Client: I feel really scared like I can't take it. She shouldn't be doing this to me right now. I feel I'm going to fall apart. This isn't fair. This isn't right. I start defending and, at least in my mind, I'm attacking her, judging her—"You stupid bitch." I feel it in my throat. I can't cope… this will do me in. I see myself trying to hold on to something, trying to grab onto something to be okay but I want to puke. Fear. This is too much, this shouldn't be happening, this is more than I should have to bear and I can't imagine how I can live through the next minute. There's nothing to hold onto. I'm falling apart. I can't imagine how I can be, how I can live, how I can go on.

Facilitator: How do you treat her?

Client: I'm in shock that she's saying all this. I treat her with contempt and hate, rejection, and I think I said, "Shut up and leave me alone. Go away!" So—rejecting and judgmental, and attacking.

Facilitator: **Who would you be without the thought**, in that moment, "Mom shouldn't attack me"?

Client: I feel myself settle. I can feel my feet on the ground. I'm not falling apart, I'm coming together. Settled more in myself. Just looking, listening. I'm contained. I don't feel frantic. I'm present with what's happening. I can feel the curiosity.

Facilitator: "Mom shouldn't attack me." **Turn it around**.

Client: The most juice seems to be in *I shouldn't attack her*. I was vicious to her. I left no opening for her. I immediately dismissed her. I didn't let her in. I wouldn't even consider her, in that moment. I'm not sure if I didn't tell her to get out first before she even said anything. I attacked her first. I was usually like that with her. I just took from her and was disgusted by her.

I shouldn't attack myself. I was seventeen years old, I didn't understand what was going on, and I shouldn't attack myself. I was doing the best I knew in the situation I was in. It was all a big dynamic. I was a struggling human, just like them, and I could cut myself a lot of slack here. I couldn't have understood, and I didn't need to attack myself for this.

Facilitator: Do you have examples of how you attacked yourself and you shouldn't have?

Client: In the practical sense, I totally cut myself off from them. I refused to be close to them anymore, if I ever was close to my dad. With her, I attacked myself by not allowing forgiveness. I attacked myself after the fact. I was really busy with school, so when the semester was done, I got a job and I worked constantly. I was harsh. I broke up with my boyfriend—I wouldn't be "that." I called myself, "that." I made sex a dirty thing. I wouldn't let myself be comforted.

Years afterward, I tightened up so I won't be in a position where I can be attacked like this again. I'm not going to be needy. I'm not going to ask for things. I'm not going to ask for help. I'm going to do it myself. For years, I was unhappy. I went away to school and there was no way I wouldn't be successful there. I was harsh, I attacked myself this way. I wouldn't take it easy.

In the moment, I attacked myself with all the shame and I believed it all. I believed what he said. I believed I was terrible for not helping around the house more and focusing on school and myself, wanting success that was about myself and not contributing to the household. I believed that I'd done a terrible thing.

Facilitator: And the **turnaround** to the opposite? "Mom shouldn't attack me."

Client: Mom should have attacked me. She had a point. She should have attacked me because some of it was true. I didn't contribute. I didn't help around the house, so that's true. It's how she saw it and that's what she was talking about. She should have because that stance I had in the world helped me a lot. It made me very successful in some arenas [laughing]. It really put me on a path—how she was, in general, certainly put me onto, "I'm going to understand things. I'm not going to be like that." It really pushed me out of the house. It gave me the strength to leave my family of origin. It's absolutely true. It gave me the impetus. I plowed through.

Facilitator: We're at statement #4. What did you write?

Client: "I need Mom to love me."

Facilitator: "I need Mom to love me"—**is it true**?

Client: Yes.

Facilitator: In that situation, **can you absolutely know that it's true** that, "I need Mom to love me"?

Client: Yes.

Facilitator: **How do you react, what happens, when you believe the thought,** "I need Mom to love me"?

Client: I feel desperate. I'm shaking. I can't settle. I feel like I'm going to come out of my skin. The world feels like it's falling underneath me and I'm looking for something to hold onto. I'm playing over what my dad said to me in the fight or whatever it was, and what she says. I keep putting it together and I can't get it to make sense. I'm feeling like there's no ground, I'm not safe.

I'm incredulous with her. I can't believe what's happening and what she's saying. I saw the opposite—I think she hates me, she wants me to suffer, she wants me to feel horrible. I'm judging and swirling in confusion and feeling hysterical and I have to get away from her, there's something wrong with her. I rejected her and was disgusted with her and wouldn't look at her anymore.

Facilitator: "I need Mom to love me." How does it feel in your body in that moment?

Client: I can feel it in my throat, it's sick, it goes all the way down to my chest and heart. The feeling in my arms is numb. I could throw up.

Facilitator: When she enters your room, do you see images of the past or the future?

Client: In the future, thinking how am I going to live in this house? How can I walk down the stairs? How am I ever going to be able to see these people ever again? They're going to make fun of me for this. They're going to tease me and bring it up in embarrassing situations. How am I going to live? That's how it will be if you get in trouble. They'll announce it to the family and in other situations. I'll keep hearing it, and it'll keep happening. There's not going to be a way for me to escape it.

Facilitator: **Who would you be in that situation without the thought**, "I want Mom to love me"?

Client: Present to it. I'm still upset with my dad, but I'm not putting both of them together. I'm not so frantic, receptive to what's happening right now. It's not a happy thing, but I can take it. I can sit there and see what's happening. I'm not defensive. I'm open to whatever's happening right now. Open to seeing it.

Facilitator: Ready for **turnarounds**?

Client: Yes.

Facilitator: "I need Mom to love me."

Client: I need me to love myself. I needed me to be gentle with myself, and connected to myself with all that confusion. I'd be non-defensive. He can say that, and she can say that, and I don't need to be defensive. I need to be with myself no matter what somebody else is doing. I really needed that in that moment. This was very dramatic—I was seventeen. I needed to give myself time, figure life out and not have such expectations that I should be ten steps ahead. I can make mistakes. I could be seventeen years old, making mistakes or doing things wrong that others can criticize.

Facilitator: "I need Mom to love me."

Client: I don't need Mom to love me. I was okay in that moment. I was crying and hysterical, but I was okay. I was okay after it. I survived that whole thing. I learned from it. It's not true that I need her to love me. I was alright. I went to other people and I got myself through.

I need me to love her. That's where all the juice is. I cut myself off from her at a very young age. I needed to love her, with all her imperfections and confusion and struggles, to be softer with her, and gentle with her. Just love her.

I needed me to love her, not be judgmental. I could have had this with her if I weren't the one rejecting her. I needed to love her the way that she was, in the way that she loved, that I've learned over the years. She took care of business, she did the work, she took care of me. She wasn't the soft and cuddly type, but she'd do the job that I very much needed.

She didn't get why I was the way I was with her, or why I wanted what I wanted, and she'd bitch and complain, but she'd do the job. She made my outfit to be in the band. She'd say, "This is a waste of time. It costs money. You shouldn't do this," but then she made the dress for me late at night. She made this dress that I needed. She gave me the money that I needed. She'd be bitching and complaining, but she would do it. She took care of things, like the time I went away to college. I didn't know what that woman must have been doing all this time in terms of cooking and cleaning and folding all my clothes in stacks. I just threw my dirty laundry in a pile and my clothes were returned to me in a stack. It didn't occur to me how that happened [laughs].

Against the world, she'd be on my side. I knew that. She was loyal. I could be wrong, and she would still be on my side relative to the rest of the world.

I could have recognized that. I just thought she was bitchy. So, I need for me to love her.

Facilitator: What did you write in your next statement?

Client: Mom is oblivious, selfish, clueless, cruel, enjoying my distress, competitive with me, angry, and miserable.

[Client moves to the turnarounds] *Mom is not oblivious.* She wasn't. She knew there was a big thing. She could see my upset. She came in to talk about it. *I was oblivious.* I was confused, I didn't know what her motivations were, what she was trying to do, I assumed it was… she was soft in her saying it. She might have been trying to help me—there's a new one! I haven't realized that I'm responsible for this and I can fix it then. Could be. *I* was oblivious.

Selfish. *She is not selfish.* I can't even find where she's selfish. She was remarkably giving in that situation. She came up there. She didn't ignore it. She tried to do what she knew to do. *I was selfish.* Yes. I didn't care about anybody but myself, clearly. How is this affecting me? How can I get what I want? How do I…? Me, me, me—what's going to happen to me? I had no regard for her life or what it was like for her.

Clueless. *She was not clueless.* About a lot of it, she wasn't. She'd beat me over the head with the idea that my dad was who he was. She could see that I had a distorted perception of him, and she would beat me over the head with it. I needed to see that he could turn on me because he turned on her a lot of times and she wasn't clueless in that respect. Oh, shit. *I was clueless.* I didn't get her at all, really. I didn't understand what she was talking about or what she meant. I was totally confused and I couldn't see any good in that. It just seemed that she was trying to hurt me, and she wasn't.

Cruel. *She was not cruel. She was kind.* She came into the room. *I was cruel*, I rejected her but she still stayed. She didn't leave. Afterward, they never brought it up like I was afraid they would. She never brought it up again. She softened out. I was cruel to her and myself, extremely cruel, just hard ass.

Facilitator: How? What did you do?

Client: I was harsh. I closed right off and I put on this huge armor with her and myself. I gritted my teeth and withdrew from everybody. The walls went up, the doors clanged shut. I left myself alone, cut off. It was harsh and cruel. In a very significant way, I never let them back in, I never let her back in. It was just a wall.

She is not enjoying my distress. Right now, that's hard to believe that she enjoyed my distress. She didn't enjoy her children's distress and in that moment she was trying to shake me awake and I don't think she was enjoying it a bit. I was mean to her and she didn't enjoy that. *I was enjoying my distress.* Yeah. I was enjoying the drama of it. Yeah, I was dramatic, playing the victim. Poor me. I can see, looking at it now, it's a big drama like in soap operas. Falling on the bed, crying, and all that. There was some enjoyment in all that drama.

Competitive with me. *She was not competitive with me.* She had already won the game years before and I didn't know it.

Facilitator: What do you mean by that?

Client: The triangulation dynamic that was going with my dad. Before that situation, I thought that I was ahead of her and she already knew that wasn't the case. I'd lost that game. He was way more aligned with her and I had a distorted perception of my own power and importance. She wasn't trying to compete. She was just saying this is how it is, look at what you're dealing with here, in her unsophisticated way: "This is the truth. It does hurt." It did hurt—that's true—that he could do these things. I saw him do that to her and my sisters. He'd go off and say horrible things. She knew. She was there with me saying, "This is how he is." It freed me up in that way. It wasn't to compete with me. It was just, "The truth hurts," and it did. So, her intention was different, not to compete with me.

I compete with her. There's always a winner and a loser. I have to get ahead, be on top. I couldn't just be with her or him. I couldn't figure out how to be with both of them, so I was always competing with her, trying to be better than her, and be more important to my dad. Jeez.

Angry. *She wasn't angry.* It's like there was an opening and she was trying to get through. *I was angry*, that's for sure. I wanted to hurt her.

Miserable. I think she was miserable. *I was miserable.* Miserable in that dynamic. Miserable alone. Yeah. Do you see anything else?

Facilitator: There was something about telling the truth and in, "I need me to love me." I was thinking about your teenage years and the tools and abilities you had back then to help you deal with stressful situations. Part of it is to be honest with yourself, like asking yourself, what have you done to contribute to the situation? So, in "I need me to love me," let me be honest with myself—what have I done? And you touched on that in the turnarounds. So, when your mother came and told you, "The truth hurts," meditate on that—what *is* the truth? If you're honest with yourself, what is the truth that hurts so much? Because it makes you miserable and angry and you shut her off and all those things.

Client: Yeah, there's a lot in that whole "truth" thing. That word was... that was what the defense was about. To look at the truth and be non-defensive. It's so exhausting to keep the armor up. To love myself would mean not doing that. It would mean being present to it and taking it in, looking at the parts that are true to me and the parts that aren't, without the defense of, "She's doing this terrible thing to me. She's supposed to be my mother and protect me from all of this." She wants to say, "Look at the truth. That's what protects you. That's the path. Just look at it." That's the living turnaround, right? That's how you love yourself, right? That's how "I love myself" means to look at the truth, whatever that is.

Facilitator: Your truth.

Client: Yeah. I wasn't a whore, but I was self-absorbed and all that and not appreciative of all that they did and were doing for me—both of them, but my mother particularly, and my dad. Yeah. There's that. Yeah, that feels way better. Thanks for putting it together.

Facilitator: What don't you ever want to experience again?

Client: I don't ever want to be vulnerable and needy of someone so unreliable. [Client turns it around] So, *I am willing to be vulnerable and needy of someone so unreliable. I look forward to being vulnerable and needy of someone so unreliable.* Yes, I can. Yup. I can say it and mean it.

Facilitator: Any leftovers left when you say that? Anything comes up?

Client: No. The word "unreliable"—it's like I want it even if they're unreliable. I want to be living the truth and not be scared, period. I want that. I'm willing. I look forward to it. I want it all. Give it to me straight, whatever it is, and I'll be alright. I want the truth and I'm willing.

Facilitator: Thank you.

Client: Thank you.

Facilitator: Good stuff.

Client: I want to go hug her right now. They're both remarkable in lots of ways. They're not educated but they've done so much better compared to whatever they had growing up. Wow, they've really done their very, very best, both of them. I'm looking forward to seeing them tomorrow [laughing]. I'm glad I still have time with them.

Facilitation #8: Mother Should Say She is Sorry

Client: My mother is a complicated character in my life and in itself. She suffers from schizophrenia. She hasn't had an outbreak for a few years now but, throughout my childhood, she had many psychotic outbreaks. It's difficult to differentiate between the symptoms of her disease and her personality, so I don't separate her from her disease. I had a hard time choosing a situation to work on because there are so many. My mother is the most untreated aspect of my life. I take care of myself and constantly improve myself, and this issue remains untaken care of because it's the biggest challenge in my life, it's the thing that triggers me the most. It's the most painful thing, the toughest thing to deal with in my life. The most difficult times and moments in my life are related to her psychotic outbreaks.

I've known about her illness since I was twelve years old. I went to visit her while she was hospitalized in mental hospitals and saw difficult things from a young age. I witnessed her suicide attempts. My parents instilled shame and suppression in me. They asked me to not tell anyone that she was ill, so I couldn't share my hardships with anyone, not with professionals and not with friends. From the age of twelve until I was twenty, I went through difficult experiences at home. I wasn't treated, and it damaged me. I feel angry and like a victim for growing up like this.

My parents were never a source of mental support to me. They were a source of financial and physical support, but not mental. The roles switched and I became their parent at some point. I have a lot of anger that, regardless of her illness, my mother's not a motherly type. She's a victim and has a pessimistic nature. She is unmotherly. For example, there was a situation when my brother was lying on the couch, covered in a blanket. She was cold so she asked him for the blanket and took it. It's the most unmotherly thing to do. It's the opposite of motherly, in my opinion. She puts herself first, expecting us to look after her and take care of her. She once told me she has this dream that I... I'm the successful child in the family... my siblings didn't go to university. I'm the only one. So, she told me it's her dream that I will study medicine, become a psychiatrist and find a cure for her illness. It's such a heavy burden to place on an eighteen-year-old girl's shoulders. It frustrates me. She's my mother—she's supposed to help me, she's supposed to solve my problems, she's supposed to support me, not the other way around. She never expressed sorrow or remorse for anything that I went through because of her illness. It's not her fault, but I want her to show some grief about it, to see me. She doesn't see me. She only sees herself as the victim of this thing and as a victim in general.

There are many situations and I can't decide which one to work on. There's the situation with my brother and the blanket and there's another situation that was the most difficult in my life, and there's a more recent, casual situation that happened a few days ago which I wrote my Worksheet on because it brought up memories of her as a victim and a pessimist.

Facilitator: Get still and check within yourself, which situation is asking to be worked on today?

Client: [After a pause] The situation that was... I don't know if it was about her, since she was in a deep psychotic outbreak, and on the other hand, what I experienced there was very, very painful.

Facilitator: Take a few seconds. Close your eyes. Take a deep breath. Let the situation meet you. See what, out of all the things you brought up, rises and asks to be worked on.

Client: The most painful one. Shall I tell you the situation?

Facilitator: Yes.

Client: I remember a specific situation. It's one of the most difficult moments in my life. I was about nineteen years old. My mother had been experiencing a psychotic outbreak for several weeks and had reached the stage where she needed to be hospitalized. When we arrived at the mental hospital, they examined her and recommended that she stay. My dad and I were about to leave and then something went off in her mind and she started to run away. We started running after her, trying to stop her, because we had no idea what she was going to do. We thought she might be dangerous to herself. In a specific moment I was holding her, hugging her from behind so she wouldn't run away, but she fought me and tried to escape. I was calling the nurses, asking them to help, but they said that they couldn't intervene as they were legally forbidden to do anything, so they just stood there and watched. [Client holding back her tears.]

I remember holding her from behind so she wouldn't run, and she was physically fighting me, really fighting me. [Crying] I asked the nurses to help me but they said they were sorry but they couldn't. I was looking up at the sky; it was blue and slightly cloudy—I remember this picture—and I thought to myself: "I want this to stop. I can't take it anymore. Will someone end this nightmare?" I was scared. There was fear about what's going to happen next.

Facilitator: Let's fill out a 'Judge-Your-Neighbor' Worksheet together. Anchored in that moment, can you identify what emotion you feel toward your mother when you hold her and try to stop her as she tries to run away?

Client: Fear. I feel great fear about what's going to happen.

Facilitator: [Reads Statement #1] "I am fearful about my mother because she…."

Client: Because she is unpredictable. She is dangerous to herself.

Facilitator: [Reads Statement #2] In that situation, how do you want her to change? What would you want her to do?

Client: I want her to see what it does to us as a family, what it does to me. I want her to calm down and stop physically fighting me. I want her to return to sanity, to have self-control.

It's difficult to say what I want from her because she's having a psychotic outbreak. I want this psychotic episode to end. I've always perceived this psychotic episode as if the devil got into her, so I want the devil inside her to leave.

Facilitator: [Reads Statement #3] In that situation, what advice would you offer her?

Client: Mother should stop the madness, stop for a second so that we can explain to her what's happening. Mom should stop the struggle, stop fighting us, she should come back to us. She should see me... see that I'm falling apart.

Facilitator: [Reads Statement #4] In order for you to be happy in that situation, what do you need her to think, say, feel, or do?

Client: To be happy in that specific situation?

Facilitator: Yes.

Client: I really need her to come back to herself. I need her to speak logically, to cry. Usually, when she comes back from the illness, she cries because she understands what's happened. I need her to say that she's sorry. [Holding back the tears]. Yes.

Facilitator: [Reads Statement #5] What do you think of her in that situation? Mom is...

Client: [Tear rolling down her cheek.] I think she's sick. I don't blame her; she's done nothing wrong. That's what I think about her illness, her other personality, her paranoid personality, which I think is the basis of all evil in the world. She's not there.

Facilitator: What do you think of your mother in that situation? What do you really think about her in that moment? Look at it through your nineteen-year-old eyes.

Client: In this situation, I separate her from the disease. I tell myself this is not my mother I'm fighting in that moment, I'm fighting her disease. I think it's the other personality inside her that I'm fighting. I think this personality is the foundation of all evil. It's like the devil—it's the worst thing there could be. I don't think my mother's the devil, I think the personality inside her is the devil, and my mother's not present. I can't say what I think about her. She just isn't there.

Facilitator: [Reads Statement #6] What is it about this person and situation that you don't ever want to experience again?

Client: Helplessness. Total helplessness, great fear, a sense that I can no longer do this, an enormous emotional overload. A desperate need for help. I literally begged for help. Neediness… I can't do it by myself.

Facilitator: Now that we've filled out the Judge-Your-Neighbor Worksheet, let's start the Inquiry. I invite you to go back and look at the situation through your eyes when you were nineteen. You drove with your father to hospitalize your mother, who willingly agreed to it. Then, suddenly something in her mind flipped and she started running away. You ran after her, and you hugged her from behind and tried to stop her. You looked up at the blue sky. Be there now. What thought would you like to work on from what we wrote in statement #1?

Client: "Mom is dangerous to herself."

Facilitator: "Mom is dangerous to herself"—**is it true**?

Client: Yes.

Facilitator: "Mom is dangerous to herself—**can you absolutely know that it's true**?

Client: [After a pause] No. I don't know what she'll do if I let her go. She might not do anything.

Facilitator: **How do you react, what happens, when you believe that thought** that your mother is dangerous to herself?

Client: I'm in fear. I'm fully harnessed to the situation. All my strength, all my resources, all my thoughts are directed to stopping her. I have a lot of power and, at the same time, I feel helplessness and fear. There's a sense of ability alongside a sense of inability. On the one hand, I can take control of a woman that goes crazy like this, a grown woman, and manage to hold onto her. But on the other hand, I'm afraid and I feel like I can't take it anymore. A feeling of running out of battery.

Facilitator: How do you treat her when you believe the thought that, "She is dangerous to herself"?

Client: I treat her like an object, like an animal I have to control. I don't see her as a person. I'm not even trying to talk to her. I see myself fighting another entity, and it's not my mother. I see her as her illness, something bad that wants to break out, and I have to gain control over it. It's a physical, forceful war. There's an emotional disconnect from her, as well as fear. I focus a lot of energy on the physical effort it takes to hold and take control of her.

Facilitator: How do you treat yourself in this situation?

Client: This is also a dual position. On the one hand, I'm strong and resourceful. I control it. All the people standing around are watching; no one does anything but me. On the other hand, I'm weak and helpless because I feel like I can't keep doing it anymore—like I'm about to collapse. It's a very dual position I see myself in that moment, both strong and weak.

Facilitator: Does anything else come to your mind about this?

Client: I feel focused and completely detached from my ego. I don't care what people think of me, I don't care what it looks like, a nineteen-year-old wrestling with her mother. I feel purposeful. Now, I start to see that I'm very strong in this situation.

Facilitator: In this situation, **who would you be without the thought** that your mother's dangerous to herself?

Client: If I thought she wasn't dangerous, I'd leave her, I'd be less alert, more relaxed. If I didn't believe that she was dangerous to herself, I'd leave her and wait to see what she'd do. I'd feel less helpless, less fearful. It's possible that I'd be less alert because my focus stemmed from the thought that if I left her, she'd kill herself.

I'd be watching from the side and feeling less in survival mode. Without the thought, I'd be less in a state of war. I'd be curious to see what would happen. I'd be more attentive to the surroundings. I might feel embarrassed. Even though it's a mental hospital, it's still embarrassing when it happens to you. I'd probably feel more shame.

Facilitator: Let's try the **turnarounds**. "Mom is dangerous to herself."

Client: I am dangerous to myself?

Facilitator: That's a turnaround.

Client: In the situation, it's hard for me to put myself at the center because everything was done to stop her. Everything was negligible compared to that. I can't see how I'm dangerous to myself.

In other situations, I understand that all the destructive effects that her illness had on me were created by me, by my own thoughts. In this way, I'm dangerous to myself. I never had suicidal thoughts or anything like that, but, in a way, I cause myself emotional, spiritual, or mental destruction. I have a lot of thoughts of self-pity.

Facilitator: Could you give a specific example?

Client: I tell myself that I had a difficult childhood. I tell myself that I saw things that a child isn't meant to see. I tell myself that I'm a parental child who has parented her parents and that my parents weren't a source of support for me. I'm ruining myself, sabotaging myself.

Facilitator: And another **turnaround**?

Client: I am dangerous to her. The question is, who is 'she'? I'm dangerous to her illness because I try to expel and destroy her illness. It may be that I'm dangerous to her when I aggravate the problem when I hold her. I'm igniting her thought that we're trying to hurt her. It could be that, if I let her go, she'll run and see that no one's chasing her, and then she'll stop. So maybe I aggravated the situation by fighting her. I don't know.

Facilitator: Do you have another example?

Client: I'm dangerous to her because I have strong judgments about her and, for sure, it reflects through my behavior. So, I'm dangerous to her self-image. My mom always says she feels that we don't love her. I don't know if it's dangerous, but it's a feeling I give her—that I don't love her.

Facilitator: And the third **turnaround**, "She is dangerous to herself."

Client: She is not dangerous to herself. The proof is that, despite everything that's happened, all the outbreaks, she's still with us [laughs]. All her suicide attempts were visible. She had plenty of opportunities to hurt herself and yet she didn't. This is proof that she's not dangerous to herself.

Facilitator: And in that same situation when you're with her at the entrance to the hospital building?

Client: She tries to save herself. The rationale for her running away is that she thinks we want to hurt her—that, in the hospital, they want to drug her. She's scared. So, if she's scared, she wants to help herself, so she runs away. It contradicts the fact that she wants to kill herself or do something to herself. She tries to save herself in the situation she imagines is happening.

Facilitator: Let's move on to the second statement.

Client: "I want her to see what it does to me." This is one of the most recurring thoughts I have about all her outbreaks.

Facilitator: When you hold your mother as she tries to escape and you want it to stop, you want her to see what it does to you—**is it true**?

Client: Yes.

Facilitator: **Can you absolutely know that it's true** that you want her to see what it does to you?

Client: Yes, I want her to see what it does to me.

Facilitator: **How do you react, what happens, when you believe that thought:** "I want her to see what it does to me"?

Client: I'm disappointed because it doesn't happen. I feel lonely because my mother is supposed to be the one who supports me, and she doesn't even see me. I'm angry that she's focused on herself and doesn't see me, as well as a feeling of neediness and weakness. I'm self-centered. I want her to see me when she's experiencing a psychotic attack [laughs]. I am a victim. I am the unfortunate one.

Facilitator: How do you treat her?

Client: I'm angry. Disappointed. I think she's not the motherly type. I feel a lack of love, disconnection, and that I'm not connected to her. Disgust. I'm shutting off. I repress the need for her to see me.

Facilitator: In that moment, **who would you be without the thought,** "I want her to see what it does to me"?

Client: I'd be more focused. I'd concentrate on her. I'd be more task-oriented, feel less victimized, feel mentally stronger, less needy. I could be more present for her.

Facilitator: Are you ready for **turnarounds**?

Client: I want me to see what it does to me. Yes, in that situation, I don't pay attention to what it does to me. I create a painful memory for myself and I'm not aware of it, and it's still traumatic for me to this day. In that moment, I don't see what it does to me, and I don't think that fifteen years later, I'll still cry when I think about it.

Facilitator: And in other situations?

Client: I deal with the issue of how my history with my mother affects me. I want to see what it does to me. I want to discover which obstacles present in my life today originated from this so that I can find compassion for myself and solve some of these issues.

Facilitator: Is there another **turnaround**?

Client: I want to see what it does to her. I see what it does to her. All my focus is on that. This sentence causes a strong resistance in me. I have resistance to focusing on her again. What does it do to her? That's her problem. She's my mom, she should deal with it, talk to a psychologist, a psychiatrist. I'm not supposed to solve her problems. I don't want to see what it does to her. I'm not interested. I want to focus on myself.

Facilitator: "I want her to see what it does to me." Do you see another **turnaround**?

Client: I don't want her to see what it does to me. If she understood the meaning of what it does to me, it would cause her grief and emotional instability, and that would trigger a schizophrenic outbreak, so it might be better if she doesn't see what it does to me. It would make her sad. What will I get out of it? Nothing. She'll feel sorrow for things she can't control, and this may trigger her illness. I want her to focus on recovering, so I don't want her to think about what it does to me. I want her to think about herself.

Facilitator: In the third statement, you said, "Mom should stop the madness, the struggle, to stop fighting and come back to us, to see that I'm falling apart." Can you choose one of these?

Client: "Mom should come back to us."

Facilitator: What does it mean "to come back to us"?

Client: In psychotic outbreaks, she's not present. It's as if there's another personality taking over. She even looks different. She has a look in her eyes and you see that she isn't there. It's not her—it's like another soul inside her body, like some demon has taken over her. So, to come back to us means that the outbreak will be over. For me, it's interpreted as two different personalities.

Facilitator: So, your mom should come back to you—**is it true**?

Client: No, she doesn't need to do anything.

Facilitator: **How do you react, what happens** to you **when you believe that thought**, "Mom should come back to us"?

Client: It's like trying to push a wall. It's like doing something impossible. It's discouraging. I'm helpless because there's nothing I can do about it. I'm fighting something I have no chance against. I'm angry because, no matter what I do, it won't stop.

Facilitator: How do you treat her when you think, "She should come back to us"?

Client: I'm angry with her even though I understand that she's not in control. My anger isn't directed at her because it's like being angry with a person who's unconscious. I'm angry at the situation because I understand that she isn't present.

Facilitator: Do you see images from the past or have any thoughts about the future when you believe "She should come back to us"?

Client: I have some optimism because I know she'll come back in the end. She always does. I'm concerned about the future because I expect it to happen again and again and again and again. There is a relief because I know it's temporary, but there's also the difficulty of not knowing when this nightmare will end; it always catches me off guard. In the past, I had concerns about what would happen in the future, when I was away at university. Would I quit my studies for a month? What about when I have children? I'm worried about the future because I can't stop my life all the time to be with her.

Facilitator: How do you treat yourself?

Client: There's a dual perception. On the one hand, a feeling of heroism that I'm in control of the situation. On the other hand, there's also weakness because I'm fighting something that I have no chance against. I can't make her come back to us and there's a feeling that I can't take it anymore.

Facilitator: **Who would you be without the thought**, "Mom should come back to us"?

Client: I'd fight it less, mentally. There would still be the physical fighting. I'd still hold her because I'm afraid she'll hurt herself. There's no way of knowing what she'd do, but I won't have the feeling of a mental war.

Facilitator: Are you ready for **turnarounds**? "Mom should come back to us."

Client: I should come back to myself. During that time, I paused my entire life. I was at home for a long time. I wasn't in touch with my friends… I was cut off from people. I disappeared. It was a secret; no one knew why I cut myself off. I should have gone back to being authentic with others around me, with my friends, with those who could support me. I wasn't authentic by not telling anyone I was going through these things. In that sense, I should have come back.

I should have returned to my routine. During that time, I was sleep-deprived. I wanted to return to myself. I should have gone to sleep at night and been awake during the day. I should have gone back to eating, being calmer, being in touch with people. I should have gone back to functioning like a normal person.

Facilitator: "Mom should come back to us." Is there another **turnaround**?

Client: Mom shouldn't come back to us. How am I supposed to know what should be? I've no idea. I don't understand His plans. Mom shouldn't… I have a very strong resistance to saying that. Obviously, she should—what else, she should keep on being crazy? I resist that sentence.

Facilitator: For you to be happy in this situation, what do you need your mom to do or feel?

Client: I need Mom to say she's sorry.

Facilitator: "I need Mom to say she's sorry"—**is it true**?

Client: [After a pause] No.

Facilitator: **What happens** to you in that moment, **how do you react, when you believe that thought** that you need your mother to say she's sorry?

Client: It weakens me. It makes me feel dependent on her, on what she'll say. When she's in the middle of a psychotic outbreak, it's not the time to be sorry [laughs]. I don't need her to be sorry in that moment. I need her to come back to herself. We're in the middle of a war. I'm disappointed that she's not sorry, and it throws me back to that she's never sorry. It also throws me forward and I know that she will never be sorry for this; she won't say it.

Facilitator: So, **who would you be without the thought**, "I need Mom to say she is sorry"?

Client: I'd be less needy, more independent, stronger. I'd feel less victimized. It would make me more proactive. I wouldn't need anyone else to do anything to make me feel better. It would be irrelevant whether she's sorry or not. I need to take care of myself and make myself feel better regardless of whether she's sorry or not.

I'd be more focused on her and the others than on myself, less egotistical. I'd be a more supportive figure in my family. When I become less absorbed in being a victim, I'd be able to see them as well and help them more. I'd be happier, or not as sad. Happier is a little too extreme in this situation [laughs]. Without that thought, I would be mentally stronger.

Facilitator: "I need Mom to say she is sorry." What is a **turnaround**?

Client: I need to say to Mom that I am sorry. Yes, because I hold her body and treat it in a way that's even a bit violent while she's not present in it. I'm sorry that she has the disease and that she's going through these experiences. Looking more broadly, I'm truly sorry, and I've never told her that, now that I think about it.

Facilitator: "I need Mom to say she is sorry." What other **turnaround** do you see?

Client: I don't need Mom to say she is sorry. I need the physical fighting to stop and for this madness to end. This is not the time to apologize, while we're in the middle of a serious battle. She can ask for forgiveness later, not in this moment. I don't need her to be sorry in that moment.

This is a sentence that has stuck with me for many years. Now, as I break it down, I can see clearly that I don't need anyone to feel sorry so I can feel good; it wouldn't have helped. I don't need Mom to tell me that she's sorry because I want to learn to forgive people, even if they're not sorry. This gives me a challenge that requires spiritual transcendence. I need her to focus on herself and to heal. If her attention goes into feeling remorse, she might not be able to recover as quickly.

Facilitator: What do you think of your mom in this situation? You said that she's sick, not present, not there, that you're fighting not your mother but fighting her illness, a different personality. Which of these do you want to work on?

Client: My mom is sick.

Facilitator: So, let us go back to the situation. Your "Mom is sick"—**is it true**?

Client: Yes.

Facilitator: Your "Mom is sick"—**can you absolutely know that it's true**?

Client: No.

Facilitator: **How do you react, what happens, when you believe that thought** that your mother is sick?

Client: It fills me with compassion. It makes me think that it's a disease, that she's not responsible for what she's doing. On the other hand, when I look at it as an incurable disease, it makes me feel helpless. Such misfortune. It's so depressing that she's sick. It also creates a fear in me that her disease could be hereditary and I could get sick as well. One of the biggest fears I had was that, during pregnancy, I too would become like her, as pregnancy can increase the risk of a psychotic disorder if it's in your genetic background. Even without a genetic relation, there's a fear… it's a disease and it could happen to me as well.

Facilitator: **Who would you be without the thought** that your mom is sick?

Client: I'd feel more anger because, if she's not sick, then why is she doing this to us? [laughs]. There would be no compassion. I'd be more curious to understand what she was thinking and where it came from. I'd be more accepting. I'd be curious to get to know her and this condition.

I had moments of curiosity when I wanted to ask her, "How did you conclude that the government was chasing you?" She gives explanations that are illogical and, at some point, my curiosity disappeared because I told myself it's a disease, that the brain doesn't transmit the messages properly and something's wrong, and that's it. If I didn't think it was a disease, I'd investigate it—I'd dive into her madness with curiosity and try to understand how she came to this delusional conclusion. Without that thought, I'd be more curious.

Facilitator: **Turnarounds**?

Client: My mother is not sick. In the situation itself, she's not physically ill; she can fight me physically. Physically, she's in great condition, unfortunately [laughs]. We want her to be a little weaker so we can take control of her. In the bigger picture, there are many chunks of time where she isn't sick or experiencing an outbreak. There's crying when she returns, and that shows sorrow. Her other personality never cries, so the fact that she cries is a sign of health. Beyond that, generally, she functions, cooks, speaks to the point, more or less, acts like a normal person, gets up, eats, goes to sleep, and takes actions that show that she isn't sick. My mom is not sick, depending on how you define sickness.

Facilitator: And a **turnaround to the self**.

Client: I'm sick? I'm sick in the sense that when this situation occurs, I go crazy with her. She doesn't sleep at night—I don't sleep at night. She doesn't eat—I don't eat. She fights with me—I fight her back as well. In that situation, we both fight each other physically, and I'm kind of like her. I act kind of like I'm sick.

I don't know if it can be defined as sick, but I have recurring mental states of immense and irrational fear. It's an uncontrollable state of mind, just as her illness is an uncontrollable state of mind. In that sense, I have an illness. I have fears, anxieties.

Facilitator: Are these fears like movies running in your imagination?

Client: Yes, my fears are like movies that are disconnected from reality. In that sense, I *am* sick, only it's not defined as a disease—my fears—but, in my definition, it is. It's very much like her disease because I believe my imagination. I believe and react to something that's unrealistic, like when I imagine there'll be a shooting or a terrorist attack at my children's daycare and I respond to it with hysterical fear.

Facilitator: Like the government chasing after your mom?

Client: Yes [laughs], it's not a lot different from that. She makes up a story that an article was written about her in the newspaper and that she's scared about it. And I tell myself there'll be a terrorist attack in the daycare or someone will come and shoot everyone and then I worry about it. It's the same pattern of making something up. Theoretically, it's possible that the newspaper article may be about her. There's also a possibility that someone will go into the daycare and carry out a shooting. So, it's making up something that's very unlikely to happen and then reacting emotionally to it with fear. It's the same pattern of her illness that recurs in me and is very present in my day-to-day. There's hardly a day that goes by that I don't have morbid thoughts of something bad happening to my children.

Facilitator: What is it about this person and situation that you don't ever want to experience again?

Client: I never want to experience helplessness, fear, a feeling that I can't take it anymore, an emotional overload, needing help, feeling desperate for help. [Client turning the thought around] *I am willing to experience helplessness again, fear, a feeling that I can't take it anymore.*

Facilitator: And "I am looking forward to…"

Client: It's tough [laughs], *I am looking forward to experiencing helplessness, fear, a feeling I can't take it anymore again.*

Facilitator: I never want to experience an emotional overload, needing help, feeling desperate for help. I'm willing to...

Client: I'm willing to experience an emotional overload, needing help, feeling desperate for help. I look forward to experiencing an emotional overload, needing help, feeling desperate for help. When I think about these turnarounds it makes me think that this state of helplessness and the feeling that I can't take it anymore, an emotional overload, are exactly what make me grow. These are exactly the moments that I grow from.

Facilitator: Is there anything else?

Client: This was interesting. There were a few 'Aha moments' throughout the Inquiry, like I don't need her to be sorry. It's something that I wanted, that stuck with me for many years. It's something that kept running through my mind: how does she not feel sorry for what we've been through? How come she doesn't feel sorry for not functioning as a mother? All of a sudden, it makes sense to me why she isn't sorry. And why do I need it at all? Now, I can notice my strength in this situation for doing the right thing. I knew exactly what to do and how to do it. I was in control of the situation. I see myself as strong, and not as weak. These are new things I've discovered now during our Inquiry that I hadn't noticed before.

Facilitation #9: She Wants Me to Pay Her

When we have the belief that someone said or is about to say something threatening to us, most of us experience fear and get defensive. When we get defensive, we shut off, our curiosity and openness are gone. It's the I-don't-want-to-know mind at play, not wanting to listen anymore. And so, the other person continues delivering their message, but we have already checked out of the conversation.

Facilitator: Tell me about the situation.

Client: This was about twenty years ago. I was in my early twenties. I was still living with my mother and I was working at some job. One day, when we were standing in the hallway, out of nowhere, she told me she wanted me to pay her for living with her. I don't remember if it was for rent, or food, or utilities. I was surprised by her request. I was working and saving money so I could move out and go and study at a university in another city, so I needed to save a lot of money for tuition and rent and other expenses. So, when she asked me for money, I was afraid. I was thinking that if I gave her money then I wouldn't be able to move out. I wrote on my Worksheet:

#1 I am surprised and feel unwanted by my mother because she wants me to pay to live with her.

#2 I want her to see this idea is absurd. I want her to support me in my first steps as a young adult.

#3 She shouldn't ask me for money. She should understand that this is another sign for me that she doesn't love me.

#4 I need her to invest in me, I need her to invest in our relationship.

#5 She is unloving, interested in money, delusional, doesn't care about me.

#6 I don't ever want to feel like I don't have a safe home.

Facilitator: Read your first statement to me.

Client: She wants me to pay to live with her.

Facilitator: Back in the apartment, your mother asked you to pay her for the bills or food or rent. "She wants you to pay her"—**is it true**?

Client: Yes.

Facilitator: **Can you absolutely know that it's true** that she wants you to pay her?

Client: Yes.

Facilitator: **How do react, what happens, when you believe that thought** that she wants you to pay her?

Client: I'm surprised. I'm scared. I stop listening to her. I'm having a conversation in my head that I'm not going to do this because I already hate living with her and, for years, I've been dreaming of the moment I can leave her house. I was thinking that, if I have to pay, then I'll move out and pay for some place where I actually want to live. I decide there's no way I'm going to pay her.

I hate her. I want to move out but I don't feel ready yet. I don't feel confident and I don't have enough money yet to leave. I'm still dependent on her and I hate it. I resent her for not providing a home where it feels good to be.

I decide that I'm not going to pay to live with her—there's no food, it's messy, it's dirty, and she goes crazy on me every now and then. I don't want to pay for something like that. I believe I'm already doing enough—I'm helping out, I do the grocery shopping, I cook, and I clean. I take care of myself. She doesn't need to take care of me, so the answer in my head is, "No, I'm not going to pay you."

I get defensive and sneaky—I think I need to do something to gain extra time until I'm ready to move out. I feel my time's running out. I need to hurry up and prepare faster so I can leave and succeed, and not fail and have to come back to live with her. I'm scared about the possibility of moving out, failing, and having to come back. It feels like I need to keep a low profile so I can stay until I'm ready to leave.

Facilitator: Your mother wants you to pay her. Are there any images of the past in that moment when she asks you?

Client: I was thinking of all the years when I was younger and waiting for the moment I could leave the house. All my childhood, I'd waited to be grown-up and independent, find work, have money and move out. I hadn't liked her for many years and I wanted to be as far away from her as I could be. In that moment, I was scared. I'd always been scared that, one day, she'd go crazy and kick me out and I wouldn't have any place to go to. I imagined living on the streets and nobody caring about me and not being able to deal with the world—that I'd be a teenage girl on the streets with all the fears about that, of terrible things that can happen like rape, and drugs.

Facilitator: What do you feel in your body in that moment when your mother asks you to pay her?

Client: Right now, I feel like I'm choking. It's hard to breathe. [Cries] I feel sad and sorry for myself back then. Feels like something's stuck in my throat. I see her and myself and everything else in the world stops existing. It's just me and her. I feel stuck with her and I fantasize about a way out. It's like prison and I'm stuck with a crazy woman who doesn't love me and I don't love her. It's supposed to be home but it doesn't feel like home. It doesn't feel like I have a natural birthright to be there.

Facilitator: Your mother wants you to pay her. Is there anything else when you believe the thought?

Client: I think if she's asking me that, it means that she doesn't see me as a daughter. She sees me as some person, and if I'm just a person, a tenant, then she has a right to ask me to pay the rent. It's like we're strangers.

Facilitator: In that hallway, **who would you be without the thought,** "She wants me to pay her"?

Client: Without the thought, I see her. She's been divorced since I was a baby and she's been supporting herself and working all these years. I can see her need for support, her need for security, maybe financial security as well. I can see that maybe she thinks I'm grown up enough and I'm working so I need to pay… it feels like I'm trying to guess what's on her mind. I've been doing that all my life and I don't want to do this. Let me try again.

In my business—in my mind—I see this woman. She's been alone for many years and she has emotional difficulties. She's been working and responsible for her financial circumstances all her life. She's been employed and she provided a place to live, some food. I have a room, I have a bed, I have a table, I have a closet, I have a key to go in and out. Without that thought, I see her and I can listen. [Crying.] Without the story I put on it, I could have listened more and tried to understand her point of view.

[After a pause] I could think without all the emotional drama and confusion. I'd be more grounded when I'm thinking and making my decision about paying her or not. I'd be less shaken and scared. I'd be able to listen to her and I'd try to understand why she's asking, what her reasons are. I'd be less confused and living in the past. I'd be just in that moment, making a decision based on just that moment, without being scared about the future and without all the past history between me and her. I wouldn't bring all this baggage into the moment if I'd had The Work back then.

Facilitator: "My mother wants me to pay her." **Turn it around**.

Client: I want to pay myself for living with her. What comes up for me is that I feel like a victim, I feel sorry for myself for having such a bad mother who doesn't care about me and I don't care about her, so I'm looking for ways to compensate myself. I started drinking when I was sixteen. Drinking, smoking. I tried some drugs, so I was looking for ways to pay myself, to compensate for the emotional distress that I felt and blamed on her. I blamed her for my alcohol abuse.

I want to pay myself. My state of mind was: I need to save enough money so I can leave home and support myself for a while. At least, until I have a steady income and am able to continue to study and live outside home.

I want to pay myself for living with myself. I had some friends in high school and I saw how their families lived—their lifestyle. It showed me life could be better. Seeing how they lived opened a window to a new world and I started to have an understanding that I could create a good life for myself. I needed to pay for my education. I needed to pay for anything I needed to survive and beyond survival so I could be independent like I wanted to be. So I want to pay myself and rely on myself for food and shelter and other things.

Facilitator: She wants you to pay her. What's another **turnaround**?

Client: I want me to pay her for living with her. I helped with grocery shopping and cooking as a way to pay her back. I never felt I had a natural right to be there. It never felt like a home so I felt like I needed to do some things to please her. I had to do some work to earn my right to live there—cook and clean and take care of myself, not cause any trouble, be good at school, not be a burden, and not irritate her. I did all kinds of stuff not to make her angry. She had tantrums. I tried to stay under the radar and not cause any trouble. Of course, it didn't work. I felt like I needed to pay her back, to please her in an attempt to try and control her moods to keep her calm.

After I moved out, I still felt guilty about her because I was resentful and blamed her for what she did. I hated her and I felt guilty about it, so I felt I needed to pay with money to buy my freedom from guilt. I thought that, with money, with gestures like buying her things, I'd feel better about myself.

So, these are examples of how I want to pay her for those years that I lived with her. It's like I owe her. Maybe I still feel this way to some extent—feeling like I owe her, that it isn't my birthright to receive that from her. It still makes me sad. I need to do more Work on this—it's not my birthright to live with her. It still feels heavy. Very heavy.

Facilitator: Your mother wants you to pay her. Do you see another **turnaround**?

Client: She doesn't want me to pay her.

Facilitator: How could that be true?

Client: She wanted to talk about money. She was talking and I wasn't listening. If I'd listened, I could have understood what she wanted but I stopped listening because I was having my own conversation in my head, so I don't know what she really wanted. I wasn't interested in knowing. I was too scared to listen because I'd already put my own story on it and it scared me. I was afraid that if I engaged in this conversation, I'd end up having to pay her. So, I don't know what she wanted or why. I just know my own story about it. I'm clueless.

Facilitator: Maybe she wants to promote you from someone who is dependent to someone on equal level?

Client: [After a pause] Yeah, I can see that. I can see how she might think I'm old enough—ready, working, making money, and it's time to pay my way. I'm beyond eighteen years old, she doesn't have to legally do anything for me. And I did stay. I lived with her for another few months or a year before I moved. She didn't have to let me do that. Maybe she didn't really want me to pay her—because I didn't pay her and she could have changed the lock on the door and thrown me out. She didn't do that.

Facilitator: You said a few times that you were an adult. Maybe she wanted to teach you that you were an adult and you could be on your own, and if you could pay her, you could pay anywhere.

Client: Could be.

Facilitator: Any other **turnarounds**? "She wants me to pay her."

Client: She wants me to pay for myself? Maybe she just wanted me to pay for what I was using, my share of rent, food, and utilities. This situation made me understand very clearly that when I moved out, I'd need to be able to support myself. I had to find a good job. I saved for a year to pay for my first year at university and a few months of rent. This conversation was like throwing me into the pool and telling me to start swimming. I don't know what she wanted but I can see now, from my own business, this was a good push, a call to stand on my own two feet. I needed to be able to pay for all the things I wanted. I shouldn't have expected her to finance my future plans—moving out, education, and stuff.

In retrospect, I'm grateful for that because I'm proud of myself. It made me stronger. Now that I have perspective, I feel thankful that she didn't do all that for me—pay my rent, my tuition, buy me a car… She did support me a little with tuition for my bachelor's degree when I got stuck without money. I asked her for help and she did write a check. For my master's degree, I took out a loan and I needed two people to sign the forms as guarantors and she didn't like that, but she did sign the loan papers. It was the last time I went to her to ask for money. That was a good thing. It didn't feel good back then—it felt like I didn't have support. I was bitter about it for many years, but now that I inquire about it, I can see it was good and I feel happy and proud of myself.

Facilitator: Back in the hallway, your mother asks you to pay her. Which statement would like to work on?

Client: "I want her to see this idea is absurd."

Facilitator: You want her to see this idea is absurd—**is it true**?

Client: Yes.

Facilitator: **Can you absolutely know that it's true** that you want her to see this idea is absurd?

Client: Yes, I do. Even today, I still do [laughs].

Facilitator: **How do you react, what happens, when you believe that thought**, "I want her to see this idea is absurd"?

Client: The first seconds when I hear it, I can't believe it. I get confused. It's coming out of nowhere. Then I feel objection, refusal. I'm not interested in listening to what she's saying anymore. I decide inside myself that there's no way I'm going to do that—I need to save some money so I can move out. I become afraid that if I say no, she'll get angry or even kick me out before I'm ready. I feel like I'm planning my escape and then here she comes with this surprise! I feel pressured, scared, stressed, and I think

I need to be careful and sneaky. Time's running out and I need to speed up to be ready to move. I'm scared I'll move out and fail and then have to come back to her in defeat. I imagine this happening in the future.

I feel trapped and suffocated. Inside my mind, I say to her, "I hate you and I don't want to live with you and I'm saving money so I can move out." That's the truth but I'm afraid to tell her. I'm afraid of her reaction. I see images from the past when she'd go crazy—she has anger outbursts and she can be unexpectedly violent. I even feel it now, how scared I was of her. I always tried to get inside her mind and guess what was going to happen.

I try to find a way out of the conversation. I don't remember what I answered, but all I could think about was how much I hated her and wanted to leave, and if she was going to make me pay her, I wouldn't be able to do it. I felt trapped, like I had to be deceitful to gain some time until I was ready to move out.

Facilitator: You want her to see that this idea is absurd. What happens to the communication when you want her to see it and she doesn't see it?

Client: I no longer listen to her. I have a conversation with myself inside my head, so I've no idea what she says after that. I made my decision and I was talking to myself.

Facilitator: **Who would you be without the thought**, "I want her to see that this idea is absurd"?

Client: Without the thought, I'd be more relaxed and I could listen to her. I could try to understand what she's asking, why she's asking. I'd be interested and curious and more connected with her in the moment and not act out of my fears about the future or my memories of the past. I could listen to her. I could see all the poison that I have inside about her and I see that, in that situation, it's all about me—what I want, what I need, my plans, and I don't care about her needs and wants. I could see I'm living in her house and I hate her. How unfair it is to her to live with someone who hates her and is dishonest about it.

Without the thought, I wouldn't have to be defensive. It brings me back to listen to her… what does she want? I don't know because I shut myself off immediately when I didn't like what I heard; I stopped listening. I could have listened if I wasn't so occupied with justifying myself, defending, and attacking her in my mind. I'd be more open and curious to hear what she had to say. I could agree or disagree after but at least I'd have heard what she had to say.

Facilitator: Ready for the **turnarounds**?

Client: Yes.

Facilitator: You want her to see this idea is absurd.

Client: I want me to see this idea is absurd. It's absurd to pay to live with someone I hate. I'm in my early twenties and I've been wanting to move out for years when she asks me to pay. I decide that I'm staying in that place that doesn't feel like home with this woman that I don't like living with.

I was distracted by the good days we'd had. On the good days, I was carefree and pretended everything was okay and not preparing for the rainy days, the bad days. I wasted valuable time when I could have been making progress with my plans. I only got back to the plan when she went crazy. So I want to see the absurdity in my carelessness and how, on good days, I'm not getting down to business.

Facilitator: I see one example, if you want to hear it.

Client: Yes.

Facilitator: I want to see this idea is absurd… to be twenty and getting a paycheck but not contributing to the expenses I create.

Client: Yeah, I guess. If she's asking, then there's a reason why she wants it or needs it. I can see that. But I always had a fantasy about having a mother who's loving and giving, which to some extent she was. It wasn't all bad all the time. I agree with you that grown-up children who live with their parents should, at some point, start participating and contributing in some way. I justified myself by thinking how I was contributing through cooking or cleaning or shopping, and being a good girl. But paying... I didn't see it at the time because I had this fantasy of being supported by my mother.

Facilitator: And when you say that I'm thinking it's an absurd idea to expect your mother to be supportive.

Client: Yes. She's been a single parent since I was little and all those years she went to work and supported us. She was responsible. My father didn't always contribute with his divorce payments. I can see how maybe it was time that she wanted some support from me—she knew I was working, and I didn't even ask—did she want 100 or 1000? I don't know. I wasn't listening. I was in my head just thinking how I didn't want to do it. It's all about me, me, me, what I want, what I need, my fantasies, my dreams and my plans...

So, *I want her to see this idea is not absurd.* I wanted her to know I hated her but I was scared to show it or say it. In my imagination, I wanted to hurt her back and express my hatred to her. So, it was not an absurd idea to live with someone like me, with my attitude, and expect me to pay for my share. It's not absurd.

I respect her right to ask for support if she thinks she wants it or needs it. She has a right to ask for a financial contribution after all these years she's been working and paying for everything. It's not absurd.

I want her to see this idea is not absurd. It's not absurd because, in my mind, I'm willing to do that... just not with her. I'm willing and planning to do that—live somewhere else where I need to pay rent, utilities, and food.

Facilitator: You don't want her to see this idea is absurd so she can push you to work on your plan. You can't relax and be with her. You have to work on your plan to go away.

Client: Yes. Also, *I don't want her to see that I think this idea is absurd* because I don't want to make her angry. I don't want to irritate her. I'm afraid of provoking bad reactions in her and I don't want her to know what I honestly think about her and her idea in that moment. I'm afraid things will get worse if she knows that I think it's absurd. I have a dishonest relationship with her.

Facilitator: Do you see any other **turnarounds** to "I want her to see this idea is absurd"?

Client: I want her to see this idea is great [laughs].

Facilitator: How can it be true?

Client: It pushed me toward independence. It pushed me not to linger around as I did on the good days with her. It pushed me to stop being oblivious and detached from reality—and the reality was that, for my well-being, I needed to move out. It was a good idea.

Today, when I'm talking about it with you and I look back, I see it was a great idea. It pushed me into action and I'm very proud that, most of the years of my education, I lived and managed mostly on my own. I did ask her for help from time to time and she did help me, but mostly I managed on my own. I worked and supported myself. I lived with roommates, bought my groceries, cooked for myself, and studied and nobody had to save me. I'm proud of myself.

It makes me sad to see how I had to be right and she was the bad one. I thought she was crazy and I was a victim and I wasn't interested in understanding her. I was busy defending myself and attacking her in my mind, so I don't really know what was going on in that situation. I missed the opportunity to know because I wasn't interested in her side of the story. I had my own story.

Facilitator: I missed the opportunity, now it's too late—**is it true**?

Client: [After a pause] No. Thank you for saying that.

Facilitator: What did you write in your third statement?

Client: She should understand this is another sign for me that she doesn't love me. It means to me that she doesn't love me.

Facilitator: Back in the hallway, she asks for money and you have the thought—"She should understand it means to me she doesn't love me"—**is it true**?

Client: No.

Facilitator: **How do you react, what happens, when you believe the thought**, "She should understand it means to me she doesn't love me"?

Client: I'm in her business about what she should and shouldn't understand. I want her to understand it because I'm thinking about consequences, that this is alienating me from her. It feels we're like strangers, not family. She's not my mother if she's asking me for money to live with her. That's why I want her to understand that, for me, it means that our relationship is going to get worse if it comes down to this, that I have to pay her to live with her like I'm a stranger. I want to save our relationship from getting worse. I already don't like her, I already don't want to live with her, and now she asks me for money! It makes me even more frustrated with her and I feel rejected, like she doesn't want me there.

She looks more like a stranger and I feel more like a stranger. It feels less like mother and daughter. I have a thought that parents shouldn't ask their children for money to live with them. It's like a birthright to live with your parents until you're able to stand on your own two feet and you're independent. This whole situation is stressful.

Facilitator: **Who would you be without the thought**?

Client: Without the thought, we're there, we're talking, she asks for money. I would want to know why, how much, what for, what do I get in return for paying money and then it's like a transaction—I give you money, you give me something. If I like it, I pay for it. If I don't like it, I don't pay for it. This could open an opportunity to live with her and be able to set some boundaries, like "Okay, now I'm a tenant, I'm not your daughter, so you'd better behave. Here's your money and now I'm a person who rents a room." So, it could have been better. I never considered it.

Without that thought, there's no attachment to her as a mother, there's no attachment to the thought "she should love me," there's no attachment to the thought, "parents shouldn't ask their children to pay money to live with them," and it's more rational. It changes the relationship to something less personal and less emotional. There's a woman, this is her house, she has expenses, she needs financial help and I'm a tenant who rents a room. We both enjoy the benefits of a landlord and tenant relationship. I never thought about it.

Facilitator: "She should understand it means to me she doesn't love me." **Turn this thought around.**

Client: I should understand it means to me she doesn't love me?

Facilitator: How can it be true?

Client: Well, I don't have a way of knowing if she loves me or not. She could love me or not love me in her own way, which is beyond my understanding or the way I think it should be. In that moment, I should understand it means to me she doesn't love me… I hate her, so why should she love me? I can't expect her to love me if I don't feel love for her. Maybe she does, maybe she doesn't, but I can't expect it if I can't do it. I can't expect her to love me.

I think about all the stories from the past I have in my head about her not loving me. I have a lot of proof, many examples of things she does that mean she doesn't love me. I should understand that this is what I'm doing—I keep finding proof that she doesn't love me.

This situation is another example for a story I already believe in—that she doesn't love me. And it's okay, she doesn't have to love me. It's just another story I believe in. It's unoriginal—my mother should love me and she should do what I want because that would be proof that she loves me. If she doesn't do what I want, it means she doesn't love me.

Facilitator: Let's look at another **turnaround**.

Client: I should understand it means to her that I don't love her. I'm guessing if she needs money and I have money and I don't help her, maybe to her it's a sign that I don't love her or support her. I don't even want to listen to her. I don't even want to understand what she wants. I'm so busy with my "No, no, no!!!" with three exclamation points and I'm so busy thinking, "I hate you, I hate you, I hate you. I don't want to live with you. I'm waiting for the moment when I can leave this place," and a lot of resentment. Yup. So, yes.

She shouldn't understand it means to me she doesn't love me. Because it's me with my mind, my story, my interpretations, my projections, it's all the war that's inside me. It's not her business, it's my business. She shouldn't understand because if she only knew what was going on in my head and in my heart about her... in my mind, I'm tearing her apart... so she shouldn't understand what's going on inside my head for her own good.

Facilitator: What did you write in your next statement?

Client: I need her to invest in me, in my future.

Facilitator: **Is it true**, "I need her to invest in me"?

Client: Yes.

Facilitator: **Can you absolutely know that it's true** that you need her to invest in you?

Client: No.

Facilitator: **How do you react, what happens, when you believe that thought** that you need her to invest in you?

Client: There are a lot of conditions in that thought. It's like—you invest in me, I'll invest in you. You give to me, I'll give to you. You take care of me, I'll take care of you. You invest in my future and, when you grow old, I'll take care of you. There are a lot of conditions. It's a very conditional love. It's transactional.

I'm disappointed, now that I see that giving love is conditional on so many things. From a child's perspective, the expectations I have from my mother... and now that I'm a mother and have children, I see it the other way around: "They do what I want, then I'll be happy. They don't do what I want, I'm not happy with them," and it's the same. So, back to me, where she's the mother and I'm the child, if she doesn't give me what I want, what I need, I'm resentful. If I want food and there's no food, or if I want her to show interest in me and she doesn't, I feel resentful and I don't like her and from situation-to-situation, from day-to-day, from year-to-year, the resentment grows because she doesn't do what I want or expect her to do. It's a childish perspective, very narrow and limited and centered around myself.

I'm selfish and egotistical to treat another person like this: I love you as long as you do what I want you to do. I love you as long as you make me feel nice and cozy. But when you don't, I don't love you in that moment and if there are many moments like that, the unloving grows and I don't see her as a woman with her own needs and wants and should haves…. Who's to say whose needs are more important, her needs or mine? We both need money and my need isn't more important than her need, but when I'm a child, it's all about me, me, me, and there's not a lot of room for her to be weak, to be sick, to be in emotional distress, to be in need. I want a super-mom who goes to work and brings home money, food and shelter, conversation, birthdays, who buys me what I want when I want it. It's a recipe for disaster.

I feel sorry for mothers. I feel sorry for her. I feel sorry for myself as a mother because it looks like it doesn't matter what I do, it's beyond my control when the children want something and I can give it to them and they'll be happy, or I don't give it to them and they won't be happy. I disappear as a human being and I shrink into existing only as a mother but it's only a part of who I am. When I look at my mother like that, she has no right to exist unless she's the mother that I want, the mother I need, the mother of my dreams—and every time she shatters my dreams, I love her less. And now that I look at this, it makes me really sad. She has a right to exist and she has a right to ask for whatever she wants. [Crying] I want to see who I'd be without the thought.

Facilitator: In that hallway, when she asks for money, **who would you be without the thought?**

Client: [After a pause] I'd be a listener and I'd want to hear what she has to say and understand her. I would ask why, how much, what's the reason—is she having a difficult time? Is she running out of money? I'd want to know what's going on with her. I refused to know what was going on with her.

I'd see that I have dreams and fantasies about the future. I think I'd be more interested in having a conversation with her, asking questions before I make a decision. My decision would not be based on the chaos in my head. I'd be more reasonable.

Facilitator: Ready for the turnarounds?

Client: Yes.

Facilitator: "I need her to invest in me." **Turn it around**.

Client: I need me to invest in me. In that situation, invest in my listening skills and care about another person, notice how my mind's going crazy and causing me trouble and distress. So, invest in the good skill of being more present in a situation. I had an opportunity to learn something, like when someone asks me for something, the first step is to try to understand: what they're asking, what they're talking about, what their reasons are… invest in communication.

In other ways, I need me to invest in myself because it's my job to invest in myself. I can't be a child forever, depending on my mother. I don't want to be that kind of person. I need to invest in myself so I can be what I want to be, an independent woman. I don't want to run to my mother with every trouble every time I need something because it's not good for me. Planning for the future was the beginning, the first step in investing in myself. It always comes back to me.

If I want other people to invest in me, I need to invest in myself first so they'll have something to invest in, so I'll be a good investment to invest in [laughs].

[Client finds another turnaround] *I need me to invest in her.*

Facilitator: How can that be true?

Client: She's my mother so she'll always be a part of my life. She'll always be on my mind and in my DNA—love, hate, it doesn't matter. She'll always be there. If I don't want to suffer forever and ever and ever, I need to invest in her and figure out the best way for me to do that. This is a lifelong relationship until death do us part, so I'd better come up with a good investment plan. I hope the Worksheets will help. They surely shed some light on what's going on. In the situation, it would have been better to be a listener, be a student, and I wasn't.

I don't need her to invest in me. She has invested in me so far. She raised me, she fed me, she provided what I needed to go to school, I had a room, I had a bed. She was working, so she's been responsible. I was already twenty-something. That's proof that she invested in me. Other than that, I've reached that certain age when it's time to go into the world and do it by myself—succeed, fail, learn from my mistakes. It's my job. Twenty-something is enough… like the birds that throw the little birdies out of the nest and either they fly or they fall. She's not throwing me out of the balcony [laughs], she's just asking for money.

Facilitator: Only teaching you how to fly.

Client: Yes, she could have tossed me out of the door, but she didn't.

Facilitator: What did you write in #5?

Client: She is unloving. [Client turns the judgments around] *I am unloving.* I resented her, I hated her, I didn't want to help her, and I wasn't interested in what she had to say. I didn't care. *She is loving.* It could be that she was loving but she had no chance in that moment because I wasn't open to accepting that she loved me.

She's interested in money. Well, she was, and that's okay. *I'm interested in money*—for sure. In that situation, I was interested in having my own money. I wouldn't give her my money, it was just for me. My money was for me and my big plans, my big dreams. I wasn't willing to share it with her.

She is delusional. *I'm delusional.* I'm in the stories of the past and the future, my imagination is working, and I only see myself in that moment. It's all about my needs, my dreams. I don't care about her dreams, her needs. I'm delusional. I don't even see her as a person. I only see her as the mother I want her to be and that she isn't. *She is not delusional.* She has a twenty-something daughter living with her and she's realistic—it's time to grow up.

She doesn't care about me. *I don't care about her.* I already gave plenty of examples. *I don't care about me.* At that point in my life, I did a lot of things that were abusive toward myself, like self-hatred. I was unkind to myself with self-criticism. I was very judgmental and didn't love myself, always feeling not good enough and beating myself up. *She does care about me.* I don't know that because I've already decided that she doesn't care about me.

Facilitator: What's in your #6 statement?

Client: I don't ever want to feel like I don't have a safe home and I'm not wanted.

I am willing to feel again like I don't have a safe home and I'm not wanted. Even with my children, I sometimes feel like I'm not wanted in my own home with them. This issue still shows up. Here I am, in my home, where I'm the mother and I'm not wanted by my children. I believe they don't like me, they don't care about me, they don't see me as a person. I'm just a mother to them, there to fulfill their many requests and I've no right to exist besides making them happy by being the mother of their dreams. So, yeah, more Worksheets.

Facilitator: And I'm looking forward...

Client: I'm looking forward to feeling like I don't have a safe home and feeling unwanted. I'm looking forward to feeling unwanted in my home. Yeah, this is why I have kids—my teachers.

The Mother I Want vs. The Mother I Have

"Every time you try to change someone, you are trying to change someone that doesn't exist. They only exist in your head. People are who you believe them to be."
Byron Katie

There is a whole world of unquestioned beliefs and stories about "Mother." When we think of our mother, there are a few images of her running in our mind. The three prominent ones are: the birth mother, the mother (I think) I want, and the mother (I think) I have.

The birth mother

In the physical world, there is a mother who is a woman, person, human, body who gave birth to you (or raised you). There is a piece of paper, a hospital document, that serves as evidence to prove it as a fact. She is the woman others have named "your mother" and you believe it and call her, "my mother."

She is a real, physical person and we have stories about her womanhood, personality, humanity, body. (Notice what stories arise in you as you think about your mother using each of these words?) "The woman who gave birth to me" is a story as well. You can sit in Inquiry and ask yourself the four questions and turnarounds on this thought, "This woman gave birth to me," to reveal what stories, attachments, and identity you have created around this belief.

The mother (I think) I want

"The mother (I think) I want" is a fantasy of an ideal, perfect mother. She exists in our mind. We usually meet her during those stressful moments we have with our birth mother (or the mother who raised us). Depending on the kind of relationship we have, some of us meet her frequently in our imagination, while she only makes a rare appearance to others.

We fantasize that this woman we call "my mother" will be unconditionally loving, caring, nurturing, warm, soft, strong, powerful, tender, healthy, present, grounded, confident, resourceful, talented, beautiful, sensitive, supportive, and protective of us. She will be someone who answers all our wants and needs and puts them before her own. She has magical powers; a kiss, a word, or a hug she gives can heal our wounds, solve our problems, and make the pain go away. She is the mother we want.

We keep a mental Ideal Mother Wish List with expectations like: she should be someone I can depend on, who supports me emotionally and financially. She will always be there for me. She tells me she is proud of me and I am proud of her. She loves me the same as she loves my brother or sister, she never hurts me, she cares for me when I am sick. She is someone who will throw me a birthday party, pick me up from school, come to my school play, help me with homework, bake cookies with me instead of promoting her career, cook me dinner at 10 PM but not tell me what to eat, and buy me a car. She is a wonderful grandmother, she helps me with my kids and is happy to babysit her grandchildren. She stays in her own business, gives me space, hangs out with me when I need her but knows her place when I want to be left alone or don't want her intervention in my life. She can handle all these expectations and their opposites, and she can read me like an open book. ("You want your mother to read you like an open book"—**is it true**?)

The wish list gets updated and changes as our life situations change. Some things remain the same, some things fade away as we move from being babies to children, teenagers, adults, parents ourselves, and so on. From the moment we are born, we want and expect something from our mother. For some people, as long as they are attached to the image of the ideal, perfect mother, they might spend their whole lives longing for her and waiting to meet her.

When Mom dies, this fantasy doesn't necessarily die with her. After death, the physical element is gone but she continues to live in our mind. Death changes things like thinking, "She should call me on my birthday," or "I want her to give me a loan," but it doesn't change all the expectation we had from her while she was alive like, "She shouldn't have ruined my life,"

"She should have loved me the same as she loved my siblings," and "She should have shown an interest me." These thoughts can live in us forever. Your mother lives in you forever.

"The mother (I think) I want" is a creation of our imagination—a fictitious character. The ongoing waiting for her and thinking about her is addictive. The Work invites us to wake up to reality and we can do that when we question all these should haves, wants, and needs we have about Mom. For you to be happy and free, you need her to change, and you want her to be more loving—**is it true**? Katie says, "I-don't-know is my favorite position because that's the place where life has a chance to show me the truth."

The mother (I think) I have

"The mother (I think) I have" is also a fantasy, a subjective awareness, a perception we have about our birth mother. In stressful moments, we might confuse the two images and believe that the birth mother is equal to "the mother (I think) I have." However, sometimes these two images don't match and this can be a cause of confusion. We also get lost sometimes when we compare "the mother (I think) I have" with "the mother (I think) I want."

"The mother (I think) I have" comes with "disappointment flavor" sprinkled on top of her title. She is not as good as the perfect mother image that is playing in the background—the mother that I want her to be, the one I think she should be. As we wait, hope, or try to make the ideal mother show up and she doesn't, we can get frustrated, angry, bitter, sad, disconnected, and depressed, even violent and suicidal. The cause of our suffering is the attachment to the belief that, "I don't want the mother I have" and, "She needs to change," for me to accept her.

"The mother (I think) I have" is what you make her to be. She depends on who you are physically, emotionally, and mentally. "The mother (I think) I have" is an experience, not an object. The Mother-experience is created and affected by pieces of information you gathered about her, facts mixed or confused with selective perception, projection, subjective interpretation, and imagination. She is your personal experience that is influenced by images of the past and the future—you believe you really know her. There are behavioral patterns you developed in relation to her. For example, it could be, "If I say this, she will get angry. She might not talk to me after that. I should be more sensitive and careful (or not)."

What you call "my mother" is what you believe about her. She is everything and all the opposites that exist in you—good and bad, smart and stupid, interesting and boring, strong and weak. As they say, "It takes one to know one." It is a dynamic image. The mother you think you have has the power to shift in front of your eyes in one swift moment from being a beautiful, kind, angelic, and loving mother to an ugly, selfish, horrible, and cruel mother. She changes and evolves as you change and evolve.

As the children that we are, we focus on "I" and "me" and that stands in the way of knowing our mother. As it happens at times, we think, "She doesn't see me, so I'll stop seeing her," or we think, "She doesn't listen to me so I don't want to listen to her." So, who or what is the woman you call "my mother"? Whatever we do know is just the tip of the iceberg.

It is clear to me that I create my own experience of my mother. I notice how I make up stories about her. For example, we exchange text messages, she asks me questions, and I think, "She's interested in me," and it makes me happy. Later, on a phone call, she asks a lot of questions about my daughter and I become impatient as I think, "She's asking too many questions." On another occasion, she's talking about plumbing problems and tensions with the neighbors and I think, "I've heard this before. She already told me last time. She's boring." But, when I get the idea to think of her as "Friend," I notice that my interest shifts and I listen more closely to what she says, as I do with my close friends. When she recommends that I try some product for my health, I think, "She cares about me," I feel warmth and closeness, but when I think, "I don't want her advice," I sense an internal withdrawal and rejection.

Always swinging between the beliefs that, "She cares about me," and, "She doesn't care about me," I explore how it affects my emotions and sensations. I take mental notes of my thoughts and interpretations of what it means to me when she gives me what I believe I want from her and when she doesn't.

I create my mother in so many ways. On top of everything I mentioned above, my mind also runs memories of the past as a reference point to what is going on in the present moment. Sometimes, I travel into the future and see images of her and myself and how it is going to be as we both get older. There are multiple options for how this experience, this story I tell myself about my mother, can develop and unfold. The various ways the mother-daughter plot can twist and turn in my mind is infinite.

Mind game

Notice, when you think about your mother, read her text messages, talk with her on the phone, or sit together with her at the dinner table—are you present? Do you have thoughts that distract you from what is happening in the moment? Where does your mind wonder?

Notice when you…

- compare her with the fantasy of the ideal mother that you want her to be, that she should be, in order for you to be happy.
- are occupied with thoughts like "I want…," "I need…," "When will it be my turn?" "See me, hear me, do for me," "She should…," "She is…." What happens when your wants and needs are in conflict with your mother's wants and needs?
- are in her business, telling her what she should do and be, either in words or keeping it to yourself in your mind. Are you dictating to her what to do, giving her advice, wanting to save her (from herself), believing you know better, deciding for her when she didn't ask you to do any of it?
- are sticking with your story, defending your version, not being open to her story, or to anyone's different story about you, her, or the situation.
- are mentally traveling in time, comparing your mother of the present moment with images of her from the past or images of her in the future.
- compare her to the kind of mother you think she is to your brother or sister.
- compare her to other mothers you know like your friend's mother, aunts, grandmothers, or to your father.

- compare her to yourself or the parent you think you turned out to be or are going to be one day.
- measure your mother against human-made norms, social conventions, and concepts and evaluating whether she lives up to these standards. (For example, "Women have a maternal instinct," "Mothers put their children's needs first," or, "My mother owes me because she gave birth to me.")

Since we are storytellers, we can never fully know who our mother is (assuming we want to). We selectively create our own internal, subjective, selective experience of "my mother" when she says what she says and we hear what we want to hear, when she does what she does and we understand what we are able or open to take in. We spice things up when we add meaning, put on interpretations, we throw in some projections, a pinch of imagination and voila—here's Mom!

As long as she behaves according to our fantasy story, there's no problem. The confusion—the arguing with reality—starts when she doesn't live up to what we expect of her while we (continuously, stubbornly) stick with our story. She has her ways to show us the kind of person she is while we might be occupied with dreaming and fantasizing about the way things should be.

It puzzles me when I try to untangle and separate between "the birth mother," "the mother (I think) I want," and, "the mother (I think) I have," because they all come with stories that I and others have put on them. What is a creation of my imagination, fabricated, untrue? And what is the reality? It seems like there is no objective mother, only images that change with my awareness. Who is this woman? I surrender and accept it as an axiom that there is no way I can completely and absolutely know for sure who my mother is, "The Real Mother." I can only guess and continuously test it as I sit with the four questions and turnarounds about each thought and belief I have regarding, "She is my mother" and, "I am her daughter," seeing the fantasy for what it is.

Giving Advice to Your Mother

You probably have some suggestions for your mother about what she could or should to do to become a better mother or a better person. You have some ideas in your mind, whether you have expressed them to your mother or kept them to yourself. We are generous with offering advice to others even when we were not asked to give it. We have different motives for doing that, like we want to help people, save them, we want them to have a better life, we want the world to be a better place and so on. We have good intentions.

Statement #3 on the Worksheet is about giving advice and putting it on paper: "In this situation, what advice would you offer her?" One piece of popular advice I hear people express about their mother is "She should go to therapy." That's a thought.

After we explore all the advice we wrote on the Worksheet and sit in the four questions, we take them to the turnarounds. In the turnarounds, we test the advice turned around and we try it out to see if it could be as true that the advice is meant for us, maybe even more so, than it is meant for our mothers.

Mind game

Look at the following list of advice (you can add your own) and check if any of the turnarounds feel as true when the advice is turned to the self, turned to the other, and turned to the role.

Meditate on these turnarounds and test them. Notice what brings you peace and what causes internal war. What advice is in your business and which ones are not in your business? What advice is within your control (you can actually do something about it) and which ones are out of your control?

Giving Advice to Your Mother

ADVICE	ADVICE TURNED TO THE SELF
She should take care of me	I should take care of myself
She should help me	I should help myself
She should see my difficulties	I should see my difficulties
She should show me she cares about me (She should call me, visit me, ask how I am not only when she wants something from me)	I should show myself I care about myself
She should take me out to lunch/dinner	I should take myself out to lunch/dinner
She should love herself	I should love myself
She should buy me things, give me money	I should buy myself things, give myself money
She should listen to me	I should listen to myself
She should admit she hurt me	I should admit I hurt myself
She should apologize to me about the past	I should apologize to myself about the past
She shouldn't expect me to parent her	I should expect me to parent myself
She should nurture me	I should nurture myself
She should treat me kindly	I should treat myself kindly
She should keep her criticism to herself	I should keep my criticism about myself to myself
ADVICE TURNED TO THE OTHER	**ADVICE TURNED TO THE ROLE (when you are the parent/adult with children)**
I should take care of her	I should take care of my children
I should help her	I should help my children
I should see her difficulties	I should see my children's difficulties
I should take her out to lunch/dinner	I should take my children out to lunch/dinner

I should show her I care about her (I should call her, visit her, ask how she is not only when I want something from her)	I should show my children I care about them (I should call them, visit them, ask how they are not only when I want something from them)
I should love her	I should love my children
I should buy her things, give her money	I should buy my children things, give them money
I should listen to her	I should listen to my children
I should admit I hurt her	I should admit I hurt my children
I should apologize to her about the past	I should apologize to my children about the past
I shouldn't expect her to parent me	I shouldn't expect my children to parent me
I should nurture her	I should nurture my children
I should treat her kindly	I should treat my children kindly
I should keep my criticism about her to myself	I should keep my criticism about my children to myself

All this good advice that we have for other people leaves us hanging, waiting for them to do something, or to change. You can try to change your mother, teach her, punish her, and use different strategies to show her how to do things right. You can wait and wait with growing frustration, anticipation, agitation, and stress… maybe she will come around, maybe she will go to therapy, and maybe that would make her change. Or, you can go to the source, change yourself.

When all this good advice is turned to yourself, it brings you closer to self-love. When you are able to be kind and gentle with yourself and do the things you offer to others for yourself, one less human being on Earth is suffering—you—and it has ripple effects on the people around you and your environment. You want to make the world, your world, a better place? Start with yourself. Question your stories and beliefs and study your mind.

Facilitation #10: She Focuses on the Negative

Facilitator: Let's get started. Tell me about the situation.

Client: The situation is that I'm at home. It's the middle of the day. I receive a message from my mom in the family WhatsApp group (my sisters, my dad, me, and my mom are in this group). She has sent a scary video about Coronavirus (COVID-19) and I get upset because this is not the first time. I immediately judge her.

Facilitator: What's in the video?

Client: Someone's talking about some government conspiracy related to Coronavirus. I can't remember the details because I immediately realize what's happening there—I don't get any deeper into the content, instead I immediately delete the message. So, I filled out a Worksheet:

#1 I'm disappointed in my mom because she is focusing on the negative.

#2 I want her to understand that she's harming herself.

#3 Mom needs to take care of herself more.

#4 I need for Mom to get rid of negative thinking.

#5 Mother is stressed, anxious, impenetrable, egocentric, delusional, repressive.

#6 I never want to experience watching her harm herself again.

And it's because of an autoimmune disease that she has that I'm of the opinion that she's causing this to herself. Every time she focuses on something negative, she causes herself more harm.

Facilitator: Let's start with the first statement. "She is focusing on the negative"—**is it true**?

Client: Yes.

Facilitator: **Can you absolutely know it's true** that, "She is focusing on the negative"?

Client: No.

Facilitator: **How do you react, what happens, when you believe that thought,** "She is focusing on the negative"?

Client: My initial reaction is that I'm disappointed in her. I'm annoyed with her for contaminating my device with delusional videos. I'm angry. Then I think about how she's harming herself, that she doesn't quit her habits. I'm afraid that she'll continue to hurt herself until she kills herself.

I'm in her business because I imagine her being pulled into these stories and spreading them and I'm angry that she's stressing out everyone in the group. I remember some messages she sent in an extended family group chat—all sorts of fake news, and every time someone responded to her that it wasn't true, that these are intimidations, and yet she still continues to do it. I want someone to call her out on her mistake and I hope someone will because I don't have the patience and energy to see it anymore. In my experience, she's wrong and she's harmful, and not only to me—so I'm also in the family's business. I judge her for not learning from her mistakes, and for really killing herself. It infuriates and scares me at the same time. I don't want to lose her because of this, so all that comes out of me is a push back and disappointment. I feel it in my heart, constricting me and annoying me simultaneously.

Facilitator: Do you see images of the future with the thought, "She's focusing on the negative," in this situation?

Client: I'm in the future about the fact that she continues to wallow in this and that she's damaging her health even further.

Facilitator: In that situation, **who would you be without the thought,** "She's focusing on the negative"?

Client: I'd open the message, play the video, understand what it's about, and stop it. I'd go back to my activities and not be surfing into thoughts of the future, and not justifying them with thoughts of the past. I wouldn't hold anything against her. She has shared something and I'd check if it suits me or not. I'd stay in my own business. I have a choice: do I want to consume this information, or not? I'm not blaming her or attacking her. I'm calm. My body doesn't react in any particular way. My awareness is focused in the present and that's it. It becomes something simple—this is something she wanted to share, without sticking too many harsh labels on it.

Facilitator: Ready for the **turnarounds**?

Client: Yes.

Facilitator: "She is focusing on the negative."

Client: I am focusing on the negative toward her. I interpret what she did as an act of negative coercion and she's forcing some delusional truth on us. I focus on all the negative aspects of it, like what kind of damage she does to herself because of her focus on it. I see her as someone addicted to suffering and fear. I focus on her illness, her reasons, and motives in a negative way. Everything receives a negative interpretation of what this means about her and her future, and how she's treating the group and how she pollutes my phone, all her actions and the consequences of her actions. I'm focused on the negative aspects about her.

Facilitator: Is there another **turnaround**? "She is focusing on the negative."

Client: I am focusing on the negative toward myself. My reaction was negative—deleting the video in anger and being negative about it. It doesn't do me any good at that moment. I'm also delusional about her getting sick, suffering, and her health deteriorating, and it scares me. I don't want her to cause damage to herself. I don't want to lose my mother. So, I have this negative vision of how I'd be left without a mother or I'd have to see her suffer and hear her complain. My negative interpretation of the content of the video... I didn't even listen to the whole thing but automatically focused on how negative it was and I didn't want to be exposed to false information or any kind of scary conspiracy theory that stresses me. I focus on the negative aspects of this situation and how it's going to affect me.

Last turnaround: *She is focusing on the positive*. Yes, while doing The Work, it occurred to me that I can understand that she wanted to share it with us because she thinks it might be helpful to us. I'm sure she doesn't want to scare us. The way I know her, I can see that it can be positive. Her intention could be positive. She may be focusing on a solution to something or information that could give us an answer to a certain question.

Additionally, some time has passed since the situation, and she's in a completely different place. She showed me in reality, this week when I visited her, that she's in a different place with her thinking. She's focused on the positive. So, this is a living example of what's happening now—she's working on it. This is funny because it hasn't yet canceled out the negative perception I have about her.

Facilitator: Let's look at the next statement.

Client: Yes. "I want Mom to understand that she's harming herself."

Facilitator: Your mom sent a conspiracy video about the Coronavirus in the family WhatsApp group. "I want Mom to understand that she's harming herself"—**is it true**?

Client: Yes.

Facilitator: **Can you absolutely know that it's true** that, "I want Mom to understand that she's harming herself"?

Client: No.

Facilitator: **How do you react, what happens, when you believe that thought,** "I want Mom to understand that she is harming herself"?

Client: I'm needy. I need something from her to make me feel safe. I don't see it happening and I'm scared. I push it away and get angry. I'm disappointed and judgmental toward her. I can see that she's not making progress, and even moving backward. It makes me uncomfortable, frustrated, and physically contracted.

I'm disappointed in her and a little disappointed in myself as I practiced The Work with her for a while and we worked on her thoughts. I take it personally to some extent. I feel like I failed. All the work that we've done together, and all the apparent progress we've made—and, again, here she is, polluting her space with negative things. I'm disappointed in our work. I judge her for not being persistent and not practicing or doing The Work, for not working on herself seriously enough. The thought that she's harmful to herself, that she's consciously hurting herself, is very annoying and disappointing to me. "How can you do this to yourself?" In my mind I yell at her. "How blind can you be?" I'm very much in her business. I want to get into her mind, her spiritual process, her personal progress, and her coping.

I think I know what's good for her, that I know what she has to do and how she should cope and how she should think. Because I'm not able to do this, I'm frustrated and it's terribly disappointing. I expect her to be someone who is aware, enlightened. I see her getting caught again and sucked into her old ways that harm her, which cause her spiritual and physical damage. Her body reacts and she ignores it. I'm impatient with her. I dismiss her.

I'm in the future… I don't want to hear her complaints about having a hard time again, about being in pain, because I know it's her fault. I blame her and judge her for harming herself and I believe that, until she understands this, she'll keep doing it until she finishes herself off. I don't want to see her suffering because it's difficult for me. And I don't want to experience her complaints, but she doesn't do anything about it. So, it develops into avoidance—avoiding talking to her and avoiding visiting her so I won't be disappointed again and again. In general, I avoid a physical encounter so I won't have to see her condition.

I also have images and memories from the past. A few weeks ago, she was deteriorating. I see images of me watching her messing with her body, touching and hurting, and her sharing her experience of it can be very graphic and unpleasant. This whole experience comes to mind and it makes me sick. I feel a profound sense of repulsion. "I don't want you to show me. I don't want you to tell me how awful and difficult it is. I don't want to see you messing with it." I see her being non-stop obsessed with the wounds, with the disease. I see her as someone nearly caught in madness. I have flashbacks of this when I watch the video. I think, "What are you doing? See what you're doing! How unaware!" It frustrates me terribly. It annoys me and it all comes together into a pushback. I want to push it away from me. I don't want to meddle with it at all. But I do.

Facilitator: Is there anything else with this thought? "I want Mom to understand that she's harming herself."

Client: It's a burden. I feel the weight of the burden the moment I'm exposed to this nonsense, and also in the future when I have to take care of her or endure her condition and the deterioration in her health, and the difficulty of seeing it, and containing it. Everything drains into a moment of, "You're dropping this burden on me again. Here, it's happening now."

Facilitator: **Who would you be without thought,** "I want Mom to understand that she's harming herself"?

Client: I'd be spared a whole world of suffering. I wouldn't be meddling with it. I'd see what she sent, out of curiosity. I'd decide if I want to watch it or not. That's it, very simple. I don't get into her business and I don't imagine anything. I'm back in my business. Actually, I'm still worried about her, but I'm not anxious. I can allow myself, for a moment, to care about her, love her, want good for her, and want good for myself. If I don't want to see this information, I don't have to. I can delete the video and move on.

When I'm with the thought, in addition to this video I play my own movie in my head with horrific images, much worse than the conspiracy one. I'm really a conspirator [laughs]. I hallucinate about all the terrible things that can happen because I judge her for harming herself. Without the thought, I'm not playing the video. I become very technical; it's very simple. It doesn't take energy away from me. Since I'm not invested in conspiratorial and harmful thinking, I go back to the basis in which everything happens as it should. Everything's fine. I'm not here to manage anything. I'm safer in my world because I don't have a scary movie that shows me that she's going to die in front of me. It's much easier.

I return to my own self. I can respond from a place that cares and worries about her. I can talk with her, not with my thoughts about her. I can ask her what's going on, how she's doing. If I'm so sure that she's harming herself, I'll call her, and we'll talk. Maybe she's having a bad moment right now, so instead of judging and putting her in a corner and punishing her, I can reach out to her. I can be more available in this moment and I do something about it rather than be anxious, terrified, and frightened, which keeps me away; it's the opposite of giving a hand.

Facilitator: Ready for **turnarounds**?

Client: Yes.

Facilitator: "I want Mom to understand that she's harming herself."

Client: I want to understand that I'm harming her. In that moment, in my imagination, she's deteriorating and harming herself. In my imagination, she's hurting herself, and then us. I want to understand that, at that moment, she's not doing anything. I'm the one who's taking it a step forward and imagining the damage she's doing to herself.

I harm her in the sense of the image that I have of her in my head, how I perceive her as my mother, and her responsibility for herself and us. I also harm her in the way that I perceive her later on, in our meetings. It doesn't help when I expect the worst about someone I love. It doesn't support her when I perceive her as a person who focuses on the negative and harms herself. I'm harming her.

Facilitator: When you have a horror movie in your mind and then you interact with her?

Client: Yes.

Facilitator: Do you see another **turnaround**?

Client: I want to understand that I'm harming myself. My present moment becomes a huge nightmare. Physically, I harm myself by bringing fear, tension, stress, and discomfort into my system. I harm myself by imagining how this thing happens and I live it, I see it, I create it in my head, and I get sucked into this movie. At that moment, I'm the only one who's doing it to myself.

I harm myself in my relationship with her, in the way I perceive her and how I treat her in communication and non-communication, in avoidance.

In the end, I harm myself because she's my mom. She's one of the closest people in my life. This attitude ends up harming me, our relationship, how I treat her, and my sense of security in this world, as well. It's my mother. If my image of her is so negative, then something in me loses stability. The primal anchor in my life suddenly becomes something terrible. So, there too, I harm myself, in my inner world and all the key roles she's had and still has in my life.

Facilitator: Is there another **turnaround**?

Client: I don't want her to understand that she's harming herself. No, because I already saw when I answered Question #2 that I can't absolutely know it's true because it isn't my job to know what she needs to understand. In the moment, she does what she does and that's what I want because that's what's going on. I argue with it and then terrible horror scenarios go through my head. I certainly don't want that.

Beyond that, I don't want her to understand anything because that's not my process, that's not my understanding, it's not my way of life, it's not the lessons I have to learn in life. These are lessons she has to learn in life. If she needs to cause herself harm right now, that's what she needs. It's not my business to know the right path for her. I can understand that because I also harm myself in many moments, as well. I understand that, even when I harm myself. I understand it and I still choose to do it. So that's a hallucination to want something like that from her. I can't even stand up to it 100%.

And I also don't really know if she's harming herself. I interpret it as "she harms herself," but who says that's what she's doing at all? It's just a thought. Who said that was true in any way?

And the last turnaround, *I want me to understand that she's doing herself good*. This is her way of sharing something that interests her. The more I understand this, the more I'll stop judging her motives and getting into these terrible, horrible scenarios. Also, I won't be harming the image I have of her in my life. This way is better for me. She's really doing herself good. I'm not in a position to judge what she's doing and her way of doing it. It really is beyond me. So, I want to hold onto the perception that it's a friendly universe and what occurs happens to everyone at the right time, in the right amount, and we all have our place and there's nothing harmful besides what I perceive at that moment. To judge it as harmful is to believe that reality is incorrect, that Mom makes mistakes, and that she brings herself to ruin. I can't know all that for sure.

In my experience, every time I've been in a situation where I've had this thought, "I harm myself," I could see that I had to go that way in order for me to understand another thing about my life. So, I want to see and understand that she's doing herself good in her own way.

Facilitator: Let's look at the next statement.

Client: "Mom needs to take care of herself more."

Facilitator: "Mom needs to take care of herself more"—**is it true**?

Client: No.

Facilitator: **How do you react, what happens, when you believe that thought,** "Mom needs to take care of herself more"?

Client: I criticize and judge her. I imagine her engaging in materials or information that are harmful to her and she can't stop because she's obsessed with it. I'm in her business. It disappoints me, scares me, and frustrates me. I delete the video in an instant and I want to get rid of it and of her. I'm in a world of discomfort and fear of the future because I see pictures of how she harms herself.

Facilitator: Like what, for example?

Client: I see her getting angry, upset or scared, messing with her body and not letting it go. She runs around the house, stressed. I recall seeing it happen in the past, when she looks for help from every direction, like from someone who can remove a spell from her, or all sorts of delusional things like that. From magic to aromatherapy, there's nothing she hasn't tried. I judge her for not turning to her thoughts and consciousness and instead she looks outside and tries to put a Band-Aid on it. She doesn't understand that she's doing it to herself and that she shouldn't worry about what's in the news or these people who have conspiratorial ideas about what's happening. I judge her that she should stay in her own business while I'm in her business. I have a lot of tension and anger toward her and fear of the future.

Facilitator: **Who would you be without this thought?**

Client: More easygoing. Not judgmental toward her. Staying in my business whether I choose to watch the video or not. I won't be going into all sorts of scary fantasies, my body's calmer, and I'm not preoccupied with a negative image of her. I stay neutral. I don't go into what it means about her. It's just information and I choose what to do with it and then move on. I don't need to blame anyone if it doesn't suit me.

Facilitator: Let's try the **turnarounds**. "Mom needs to take care of herself more."

Client: I need to take care of her more. To care about her more is not to project negative perceptions onto her, nor to imagine her as someone who's irresponsible and harmful that doesn't take good care of herself. But, instead, to make sure I stay caring about her and if I think watching the video isn't good for her, then I can do something like talk to her, take an interest, and ask her. To accept that what came to my mind at that moment is empathy for her situation, and it just developed into something frightening and scary. But before that, it was empathy and care. It was a positive and good thing. It's something that comes from a loving, non-judging place. So, I need to take care of her because it's good for me and maybe it also benefits her. Yes.

Facilitator: I saw an example. May I share?

Client: Yes.

Facilitator: I hear from you that you love your mother and you're close to her and you really care about her. You have fears deriving from horror movies about what you see in the future. So, "I need to take care of her more," whenever you see an opportunity, do something you can do to support her. Like in the situation with the video, ask her, "Why did you share the video? Is there anything in it that was interesting to you? Do you want to talk about it?"

Client: Yes, for sure.

Facilitator: And another **turnaround**?

Client: I need to take care of myself more. I shouldn't get involved in these horrors. It doesn't do me any good. Not be anxious and judgmental toward her behavior right now because it really stresses me out and frustrates and scares me, and makes me distance myself—a lot of things I don't want. And because it's my job in life, to take care of myself more.

I can't force anyone to do anything. I need to take care of myself more at times when I'm stressed, in habits I want to change, in making healthier choices—that's my job. It's something I can definitely do more of. That's where my true strength is, not in my attempts to make someone else put in more effort to take care of themselves. What's really behind this whole story is that I want her to take care of herself more because, if she's not okay, I won't be okay. It's all about me. So this is kind of a shortcut. I don't need her to do anything. I'll take care of myself and then she can be who she is unconditionally. Easier.

Facilitator: Is there another **turnaround**?

Client: She doesn't need to take care of herself more. She needs to take care of herself less also works. When I hear this turnaround, I see her obsessive fussing and her over-worrying and her fear about her health. She doesn't need more of it, for sure. She's already doing her best. And, maybe, like you said, with the video she's sharing something that interests her with the family and that answers the definition of caring and being empathic about herself. Technically, factually, she is super, super-caring about herself. I see lots of examples of how she maintains her comfort and her health, and she does as much as she can to make herself feel good. She really does a lot—she's on it. She doesn't have to do more.

Facilitator: Is there anything else you want to say about this thought?

Client: Something I've discovered many times is that the initial intention I had, before it turned into a monster, was to be caring about her, to be empathic, or to make contact. I can be more alert that, if it makes me feel any emotion toward her, I could do something about it. I don't have to turn to the video library of horror movies in my mind. I can pick up the phone, make contact, talk, ask. First of all, it's a shortcut and it'll save me a lot of alienation, fear, and frustration that seem to protect me at that moment but actually prevent me from the goal, which is closeness and caring and love and all the things I'm afraid of losing when I watch this imaginary horror movie. So, instead of scaring myself about all these things I'm afraid of losing, I can be close to her right now. It's so available when I'm not sucked into a scary movie.

Facilitator [after a pause]: What did you write in statement #4?

Client: "I need Mom to get rid of negative thinking."

Facilitator: "I need Mom to get rid of negative thinking"—**is it true**?

Client: No.

Facilitator: **How do you react, what happens, when you believe that thought**, "I need Mom to get rid of negative thinking"?

Client: I'm frustrated and judgmental toward her. I say to myself, "She's doing it again. She's putting herself in a negative place again." I'm disappointed with her. It makes me angry. I act recklessly, deleting the message and tossing the phone away from me. I'm left with a sense of righteousness. I'm expecting her to not be exposed to negative thoughts, to not be exposed to negative videos, to not watch the news. I'm disappointed she's consuming news, that she's consuming fear, and harming herself. I'm very much in her business.

Facilitator: How do you treat yourself with this thought?

Client: I'm defensive. I defend myself from negative content. I treat myself like I'm in danger of being exposed to another nonsense because of her, like I'm being forced to watch a lie that can scare me, so I must immediately defend myself, shut it down, delete it to protect myself.

Facilitator: **Who would you be without the thought,** "I need Mom to get rid of negative thinking"?

Client: Without the thought, I'm more in control of my world. It doesn't shock me and I can choose whether to watch it or not. I can delete the video, not out of anger, but out of choice. I don't need to attack her or defend myself from anything. I'm calmer. I go about my business and it becomes a marginal, short episode. I don't invest much time judging her, what she needs to do, what she does to herself. I feel better. I don't need anything from her.

Facilitator: **Turnarounds**?

Client: Yes.

Facilitator: "I need Mom to get rid of negative thinking."

Client: I need to get rid of negative thinking about my mom. It does me no good. I'm haunted by images. It makes me distance myself from her, this thinking that imagines how her health is deteriorating and she's doing herself no good. Negative thinking is that, in the moment, I judge her for spreading lies. Negative thinking is of my disappointment in her for not choosing the things she consumes. I perceive her negatively as a human being, not just as a mother, and it's pulling me away from her. It doesn't support me—it adds a lot of tension to me and I need to get rid of it. [Pause] It's a story I tell myself. I need to get rid of the negative thinking about my mother.

Another turnaround is *I need to get rid of negative thinking about myself.* In the moment, I believe it's hurting and threatening me. I see myself as someone unable to control his thinking or what he's consuming—it's the same claim I have against her. The way I perceive myself is that it's being forced on me and I'm being wronged. I'm thinking about the negative experience of how I'd feel when she suffers, my experience of how I'd feel when information I don't want to see is forced on me, when someone invades my sterile space.

Also, there's my negative thinking beyond the situation about self-judgment and criticism—a lot of fake news. It doesn't matter if I turn off the TV or ignore the newspapers, I still have fake news. I'm still exposed to information that can be negative, corruptive, and scary without opening any news.

Facilitator: You mean the fake news that you create for yourself?

Client: Yes.

Facilitator: Do you have another example or another **turnaround**?

Client: I don't need her to get rid of her negative thinking because it has nothing to do with her. I hold my thinking in that moment. Even if she'd sent something else, I'd have perceived it negatively. It's not my business where her thinking is and what she's telling herself. Maybe that's what she needs at the moment.

I don't need it because I can't know if her thinking is negative or not. It always depends on how I see it. If I see it as negative, then it *is* negative. It will always be what I make of it. I interpret this as a negative way of thinking because it annoys me, so I turn it into a negative story.

Facilitator: Let's look at the next statement.

Client: Mother is stressed, anxious, impenetrable, inaccessible, egocentric, delusional, repressive.

Facilitator: **Turn it around** to yourself or to her.

Client: I'm stressed. *I am really stressed, anxious, impenetrable, egocentric, delusional, and repressive* in the situation. I push the video away from me. It stresses me out. It makes me anxious about her and about the future. I become closed and I shut down. I'm worried about my well-being. She hurts my space. I am delusional, I'm really in my own illusions, I'm in my fake news.

Mom is calm, not anxious, open, sharing, realistic and coping. Definitely. I can't know she was stressed. She just shared a video. She's open and sharing. She's not impenetrable because she's open to other ideas that may sound very strange and conspiratorial to some of us, but she's open to them. She's not egocentric because she shares this with us. Maybe she wants to hear what we think? Maybe she thinks it can help in some way?

She is connected to reality, hers. I can't know. I've no idea what her reality is.

She doesn't repress. She's coping. In general, she's a strong person and she copes with a lot. At that moment, she was dealing with the information in the way she knows how, by sharing it. Maybe she wants to hear feedback, or just share.

Facilitator: What's next?

Client: Statement #6. I don't want to experience and see her harming herself again. [Turns it around.] *I'm willing to experience and see her harming herself again.* Because I don't know if she really is harming herself. When I think this, then I'm harming myself. So this is a refreshing reminder to myself that I've entered into a harmful judgment. It doesn't trigger resistance in me. Even if she's harming herself, it's her way.

I'm looking forward to experiencing this and seeing her harming herself again. Yes, I'll see where I stand about it. I'll see if I still interpret it as causing harm. I can find myself in this spot again, because I know there are places where I harm myself.

Facilitator: What was a significant turnaround for you?

Client: I need to get rid of thinking negatively about her. It means that I'll always see it as negative when I have that thought, "I need Mom to get rid of her negative thinking," since it doesn't depend at all on what she does.

It's a reminder that can help me see that *I'm* thinking negatively, *I'm* not seeing things objectively, and then go back to my business.

Also, the fact that I create fake news for myself—it was an important insight for me, understanding this, because I hold this position of righteousness. I haven't watched the news for years. I'm not exposing myself to any of this—how enlightened I am. And that just showed me how much I do watch the news myself when I create my own fake news in my mind. I'm not watching the TV's fake news, but I'm busy with making my own fake news.

Facilitation #11: Mom is Mean to Dad

Client: The situation is from three weeks ago, on Mother's Day. We were sitting in the kitchen—me, my mom, and my dad. The backstory is they'll most likely be getting divorced. My dad says to my mom, "I asked you to wake me when Jane got here," and my mom shakes her head and says, "No, you didn't." And my dad says, "I did," and my mom says, "No, you didn't." And every time he says something, she shakes her head and goes, "No, you didn't."

Facilitator: What did you write in your Worksheet?

Client [Reads her Worksheet]:

#1 I'm disappointed with Mom because she's mean to Dad. She is dismissive of him. She doesn't care about him. She's lying. She's taking this too far. She treats him badly. She's abusive to Dad.

#2 I want Mom to treat Dad like a person. I want her to treat him with kindness and gentleness. I want her to treat him with respect. I don't want her to humiliate him. I want her to answer kindly. I want her to apologize for the miscommunication. I don't want her to shut him down.

#3 Mom should not take her hurt out on Dad. Mom should be kind to him. She should separate her personal grievances toward him from the moment. She should see that she's being hurtful toward him.

#4 I need Mom to answer Dad kindly. I need her to validate him and admit to misunderstanding him. I need her to redirect and appreciate that we're all together now. I need her to not treat Dad like a stranger. I need her to see that he's been her loving husband all these years.

#5 Mom is angry, mean, rude, unfair, unkind, hostile, unmovable, bitter, resentful, arrogant, cruel, violent, abusive.

#6 I never want Mom to treat Dad like someone she doesn't care about ever again. I never want Mom to feel justified in being violent toward Dad ever again. I never want her to isolate herself from people who love her ever again.

Facilitator: Choose one of the thoughts you'd like to work on from Statement #1?

Client: She is dismissive toward him.

Facilitator: I invite you to go back to the situation in the kitchen on Mother's Day. "She is dismissive toward him"—**is it true**?

Client: Yes.

Facilitator: **Can you absolutely know that it's true** that "She is dismissive toward him"?

Client: Yes.

Facilitator: **How do you react, what happens, when you believe the thought**, "She is dismissive toward him"?

Client: I feel caught in the middle, like I have to choose sides. I'm disappointed. I wish it was different. I see my dad as being so mistreated and I'm trying not to hate my mom in that moment because I'm blaming her. I'm also feeling like I need to be supportive and kind to both of them, so it's very confusing to me. I'm very angry with Mom. I wish she'd change the way she's reacting. I'm going crazy. I think she's acting like a child. I'm scared and worried. There's the savior that comes out in me that feels like it needs to help Mom see the truth. I feel like I have to say something or do something to fix this desperate situation between the two of them to make it better.

I'm judging them for living in the past. I wish they could put that shit aside for a minute. I see past images of being in a room with my mom and dad when they start fighting and my mom starts getting that way with him. I feel angry at my brother for supporting my mom's behavior.

I feel sorry for my mom as I imagine a future where she'll divorce him and be living in a condo by herself and then she'll be totally miserable and realize it was her fault all along. And, oh my God, I see future images of my dad getting old alone and living in a nursing home and it makes me sad.

I'm compulsively eating bread in that moment. I feel overwhelmed and I try to keep it together and pretend it's not affecting me. I feel like I have to be the mediator, that I'm not allowed to show I'm upset.

I feel scared about my own ability to be in a healthy relationship with someone. I have future images—horror movies—of my boyfriend meeting my parents and seeing me as being part of this weird family. We're the family that's not like everyone else's and we have problems that no one knows about. I feel trapped and alone.

I think about getting high. I'm waiting until I can leave so I can implode and collapse in my apartment. I want to get home and smoke pot and eat junk food. It feels like a nightmare. I think about my boyfriend and I feel shame and guilt about times that I've been unkind or unfair toward him. I feel so much pressure to make the relationship with him work to prove that I'm not going to end up like this.

There are images of talking to my therapist, by myself or with my parents, and them pointing out this triangle where me and my dad have a team against my mom. I'm seeing images of all those times when I felt so offended by the way my mom treated my dad and I talked to him in private. My mom's the bad guy, my dad's the victim and I'm the savior. I'm believing that thought.

Facilitator: Anything else comes up with this thought?

Client: I see past images of her walking into the kitchen and snapping at him. She doesn't let him eat any of her food now—she keeps it separate. I feel like I have no space to process this. It's hard. I feel like a victim.

Facilitator: Back in the kitchen, **who would you be without the thought,** "She is dismissive toward him"?

Client: I see how I could sit there and observe. I see how my comments are unnecessary. I see how the love and appreciation I feel for each of them is not dependent on how they get along or don't get along. I'm with two people who really support my life and both want to spend time with me, even though they don't want to spend time with each other.

I'm not seeing either of them as the victim or the perpetrator anymore and I notice that I listen to a lot more of my mom's side of the story than my dad's. I'm more curious about what's going on with her. I see that she continues to engage with him in her own way after she already answered his question. She answered it multiple times.

I might notice my own body sensations, my own feelings. I might ask Mom and Dad if we can hang out one at a time and say, "This is really hard for me. I'm still trying to make sense of what's happening in your relationship."

Without all the stories I have about how they're going to divorce and my dad getting old and sick, I notice I've been watching this between them for many years—this isn't new. Without all the added stories, I see two people who've known each other for a long time disagreeing with each other [laughs]. Where's the surprise? It's even kind of funny. I'm grateful for being connected to both of them still.

Facilitator: Are you ready for the **turnarounds**?

Client: Yes.

Facilitator: "She is dismissive toward him."

Client: I am dismissive of myself. Yeah, I'm forcing myself to be the middleman, the savior, when I feel completely uncomfortable with the situation. I pretend I feel okay when I don't. I dismiss my sadness, confusion, and hurt.

I tell myself that I'll never have a healthy relationship. I dismiss that desire to have healthy relationships, like it's not for me. I'm noticing how I dismiss myself in my own intimate relationship. Yeah.

I'm dismissive of the part of myself that can relate to my mother.

Facilitation #11: Mom is Mean to Dad | 215

She is not dismissive toward him. She answers his question. She continues to respond when he continues to engage. She doesn't tell him to stop. She stayed in the kitchen when he came in—she didn't leave.

Facilitator: Do you see another **turnaround**, "She is dismissive toward him"?

Client: I'm dismissive toward her. I blame her and I make it her fault. I think she's abusive to Dad. I don't believe her side of the story. I don't see her feelings as valid. I think she should be different. I try to be the savior and intervene, gloss over their differences and paint a different picture. I clearly make her the villain in that situation.

Facilitator: What about the **turnaround**, *I am dismissive toward him*?

Client: Oh. I don't trust Dad to handle the situation either. I see him as pathetic and decrepit and hurt. I'm thinking, "Oh, yeah, poor Dad." I don't think he can handle the situation or my mom. I pretend it was a misunderstanding as I try to stop him from arguing with my mom.

Facilitator: What did you write in the next statement?

Client: I want her to treat him with kindness and gentleness. We can shorten that to, "I want her to be gentle with him."

Facilitator: Going back to the situation in the kitchen on Mother's Day, look at the three of you. "I want her to be gentle with him"—**is it true**?

Client: Yes.

Facilitator: **Can you absolutely know that it's true** that "I want her to be gentle with him"?

Client: Yes.

Facilitator: **How you do react, what happens, when you believe that thought**, "I want her to be gentle with him"?

Client: I feel offended. I take it personally. I feel victimized. I'm disappointed, blaming. I see my dad as a victim. I wish she'd see the sweet man that I see. I see images of him hurting. I'm in my mom's business. I want to wake her up so badly. I feel lost. I have an image of what a loving, caring scenario should look like—and then there's this reality.

My world is rocked. I want to leave but I feel like I need to stay. I'm eating the bread. I think about smoking. I'm imagining that there's going to be a nasty divorce and I worry that I won't get some money I'm supposed to get.

There's this infantilization of my dad and a concern that he's not well and incompetent. Can't Mom understand that she's killing him? I'm concerned about how much stress she's putting on him. I'm imagining that my dad's going to have a heart attack and die, and my mom will have to live with that. I imagine my mom getting lost in a story that she made him get sick and die. I want to protect my mom.

My family feels so wrong. I think I've got the worst family ever. We're fucked up. Other people's families aren't like this. In that moment, I fantasize about a scenario where everyone's validated and okay. It breaks my heart. My heartbeat increases. There are uncomfortable feelings in my stomach because I'm eating too much. It's like I'm trying to numb myself. I feel guilt. I need to be the clear-minded one who does The Work all the time. I need to be the one who can show up and be strong and reliable.

Facilitator: See yourselves back in the kitchen. "I want her to be gentle with him." **Who would you be without the thought** in that situation?

Client: I could see myself being an observer without all the judgments. I can breathe along with what's happening. I see myself there with the bread and the dips and it's like I'm eating popcorn while I'm watching this movie going on [laughs].

Without the thought, I'm grateful for them. I see two people who love me very much. I see the reason he's upset is that he thought she was supposed to wake him. I see Mom standing her ground. She says she doesn't want to take responsibility for him anymore. She's being true to herself. I've never seen her like this before. Who am I to say that her being authentic is not a gentler way than holding in all of her feelings and then exploding, like I do? She's actually teaching me how I can be. My mind goes, "I didn't want to say that." [Laughs.]

I feel a lot more forgiving toward myself for how I treated my boyfriend last night when I look at my mom. Without the story, I see her as being honest. She's not taking care of Dad's emotions anymore. She's not going to wake him up from his nap. She's sure that's not for her to do. Damn. Wow, she's so clear. She wants to be separate. She doesn't want to be responsible for waking him. She doesn't want to buy him food. She doesn't want to do these things. She moved into another room. She's like, "We're roommates right now," and he's, "You're supposed to wake me," and she says, "No." Wow! Go, Mom! [laughs]. I'm ready for turnarounds.

Facilitator: Okay. "I want her to be gentle with him."

Client: I don't want her to be gentle with him.

Facilitator: How could this be true?

Client: She doesn't let him play the victim. She stands up for herself. She's being as clear as clear can be. She says, "No, you didn't." I don't want her to be more gentle because that wouldn't be authentic for her. She's tried to be gentle for everyone else and she's suffered a lot over the years and, obviously, it's not the time for that anymore.

Facilitator: Can you see some examples in this turnaround that are about you and how you don't want her to be gentle with him?

Client: I don't want her to have to be gentle to someone that she feels this way about. How could she? I notice it's hard for me to say it's not my business here. I'm fighting with reality when I think I know how she should be with him. When I'm not feeling responsible or taking it personally, or not worried that my dad will die of stress, it's really not my business.

It's a hell of a thing for me to expect her to be gentle toward him when they're going through a divorce and are forced to live with each other still.

Hell, she was civil! [laughs]. It was actually my dad who gave her the look and said, "Thanks a lot!" [Laughs.] It's entertaining.

Facilitator: What's another **turnaround** to, "I want her to be gentle with him"?

Client: I want me to be gentle with him. Yeah. I don't want to put any expectations on my dad. If he's angry at Mom, I don't want to hold him to the image of my spiritual dad, where nothing phases him and he's such a rock. That's not gentle. I want to be more gentle with him in allowing him to unfold in that moment and not try to redirect him, or correct him, or dismiss him, or change the situation.

I want me to be more gentle with myself. I don't want to blame myself for this situation happening. I don't want to get all in my head about it and make this a reflection of me and my relationship with my boyfriend. I could be a lot more gentle with myself in that moment instead of blaming myself, like I manifested this, I deserve this, I'm the one from the dysfunctional family. Putting all those identities on myself isn't gentle.

I don't want to put so much pressure on myself to fix the situation and make it better. If I need to cry in that moment, I'd like to let myself do that. It's very rigid when I think everyone needs to play a role a certain way. What can be more perfect than a divorce for dismantling these roles and people starting to get real? Wow. Divorce is like a whole new marriage [laughs]. I see my mom beginning to marry herself. I guess some people can do it while staying married and some people can't, and that's okay, and to be gentle with that. The fact that they made it together through thirty-five years is nuts. I can be more gentle. If they aren't getting along and they're actually going to do something about it this time, I trust them. They're sure about it [laughs]. Oh, my God, it's not my business.

I want to be more gentle with them and let them be people, and not just parents, and it's so funny because my first statement was, "I want Mom to treat Dad like a person," and I'm treating them like Mom and Dad and what that means to me. They're supposed to be everything to me, they owe me, they brought me into this world and I'm theirs, they're mine, and it's forever… it's like a marriage. And nothing like a divorce to make us end with ourselves [laughs]. Oh, man. There are rules and assumptions around parents. There are lots of ideas that create suffering when life happens. Do you see anything?

Facilitator: What about *I want me to be gentle with Mom*?

Client: I want to stop blaming her for this. I've pinned her as the perpetrator, as the one who's in the wrong, and my dad's the good one who loves her and she just doesn't see it… she doesn't get it.

Me and my dad even spiritualize it together sometimes and he'll say stuff like, "I hope one day she'll wake up to herself," and I'll say, "Yeah, yeah." I use spiritual concepts to dismiss my mom. Like Dad and I are on this awakened path and my mom's in the dark.

I want to be more gentle with her. I need to stop making her responsible for my dad's feelings and experiences. I think that's what she wants anyway. She said he didn't ask her and it's not her responsibility to wake him. In that situation, what if it's totally true? What if she was never asked by him to wake him? I'd like to be more gentle with her. She has the man she wants to divorce blaming her for not doing something, saying it's her fault, and she says, "No," and she's not willing to engage and I want to respect that. Damn. This is so confusing.

Facilitator: What did you write in the next statement?

Client: For statement #3 I wrote, "Mom should not take out her hurt on Dad."

Facilitator: "Mom should not take out her hurt on Dad"—**is it true**?

Client: No.

Facilitator: **How do you react, what happens, when you believe that thought**, "Mom should not take out her hurt on Dad"?

Client: I put the blame on my mother. I feel pity. I profile my dad as an old person and expect her to see that. I'm comparing them and determining that, given their attributes, my mom's younger and more in a position of power than my dad. I'm in her business. I blame her for making things worse.

I feel defeated, frustrated, disappointed. I think Mom should do The Work. I see my mom as having so much potential to rise above this. In my mind, I think if she could do some Inquiry or some kind of awareness practice, she could turn this whole situation around. I put a lot of responsibility on my mom to be kind to my dad, be kind to me, hold it all together and that's exactly what she's rebelling against right now and I'm putting that expectation back on her. I'm trying to keep her as "Mom" and "wife of Jack." I'm wanting to maintain this idea of family. Definitely.

I see my dad as the victim and I'm also upset with him for not standing up for himself. I see him as lame and pathetic. I see images that suggest he's going to die of stress, and it'll be her fault and she'll regret it.

I feel shocked. I feel she's hurting me, too. I see her as hurtful and unreasonable and unmovable. I see images of phone conversations with her where she tells me she's keeping her food separate from his and she's told him he can't have any of her food. I'm seeing my mom as beating up on dad, this poor, helpless victim. I think she's wrong. This is abusive and dysfunctional. I judge that what's happening is inappropriate and shouldn't be happening. There's a part of me that's traumatizing myself because I'm stuck in non-belief. I don't want to believe this is really happening.

I feel uncomfortable. There's tension in my butt cheeks touching the chair. There's stiffness in my shoulders. I'm worried. I start reacting, seeing where I can interrupt, where I can put a word in to try to bolster Dad without putting Mom down. I'm taking sides but I try to pretend that I'm not. I have definitely determined that my mom's up to foul play in this situation—she's the one causing the problem.

I want to protect my mom from doing more damage to the relationship than has already been done. I'm scared. I see a future where my dad dies and my mom's hit with so much guilt and grief and confusion and I don't want her to experience that.

I'm scared that there's no love there. I'm scared to reach out and comfort my dad in front of my mom. I'm scared for her to think that I'm choosing sides. I feel I have to suppress an authentic reaction to seeing her being mean to my dad. I'm scared to leave because I imagine that, as soon as I leave, she's really going to let him have it. I imagine she's being restrained around me and I see her yelling at him later: "You shouldn't have done that!" and her face is angry. There are plenty of past images of that. I see an image of my brother and my mom aligned against my dad, and I see him as a very poor man.

Facilitator: In that situation, look at yourselves again. **Who would you be without the thought**, "Mom shouldn't take out her hurt on Dad"?

Client: I notice two people having a disagreement. I see the moment when my dad turns to my mom and he goes, "Thanks a lot!" and in that moment I'm totally confused and the story flips. What happened for me when I considered the question was an image that came up of my dad treating my mom like that. I started to feel guilty about villainizing my dad.

I see that I'm allowed to have my own experience. I'm allowed to observe, I'm allowed to feel, I'm allowed to not intervene. I feel more connected to myself with all the feelings. I'd be open and I imagine that if I felt like I wanted to cry, I'd just do it. If I wanted to tell them I was sad or scared, I'd just do it. It would make a lot more sense for me to admit those feelings than to sit back and pretend that everything's okay. I could tell them it's hard for me to see them fighting and ask if we can see each other separately.

Without the thought, I can see how it's not my business. I care about them both. I'm curious to see how it's going to play out. I'm grateful to be observing an interaction like that. I get a chance to see there's something about me that thinks this is unacceptable for people to communicate that way. Where in my life do I communicate this way? It's like I'm being given a gift, I'm being shown something and it's playing out in front of me.

Facilitator: Are you ready for the **turnarounds**?

Client: Yeah

Facilitator: So, **turn it around**. "Mom shouldn't take out her hurt on Dad."

Client: I shouldn't take out my hurt on Mom. I've no idea what she's going through. I've no idea what's going on between the two of them. I don't know what each day is like for them since I don't live there. If the stories that she tells me about him are true, I wouldn't blame her. And if she believes these stories, regardless of whether they're true or not, how could I blame her? If I have that kind of awareness, I shouldn't take out my hurt on Mom.

Facilitator: What do you mean by "that kind of awareness"?

Client: I can hear her experiences without writing her off and thinking, "Oh, these are just her beliefs and she could or should change that." When I understand that her experience is that this guy's rude and malicious to her, then I shouldn't take out my hurt on her. She's already hurting a lot. Me beating up on her more isn't going to help. Also, that's my hurt. I'm blaming her for projecting onto my dad and I'm projecting onto her. Oh my God.

In that moment, I'm seeing that she isn't even Mom. She's just a woman. My idea of Mom isn't who she really is. There's a woman, and there's what I'm laying on her because of who I think she is, and how she should be. That causes me to project my hurt toward her. My expectations aren't being met, my stories aren't being confirmed... I'm being faced with reality and I'm confused. I'm thinking that's not how Mom's supposed to be [laughs]. All she's saying is, "No, you didn't," to my dad. Three words. She's allowed to feel the way she does, and it's Mother's Day and she's going through a divorce while living in a house with the man she's divorcing. [Pause] I just see how my expectations of Mom are causing me to take out my hurt on her. And I see how it's so unwarranted. They're both in the kitchen and if she's feeling hurt and it's about him, then how could she not? She should take out her hurt on Dad.

I'm noticing the thought, "I wish things were different between them," because the Mom that I'm wanting her to be is a completely fictitious character based on a story where she and my dad get along more than half the time, and that's not her experience from what she's communicating with me.

I have the belief that he's her personal punchbag. What I notice is that she's doing her best not to interact with him because she's feeling hurt.

And he's contesting her answer—he's continuing to engage her, so yeah, she should take out her hurt on Dad. She's not all of a sudden going to turn into this peaceful woman who loves her husband and considers his feelings. No, her *modus operandi* is to separate from him at this point. She wants to be out of the house. She should take out her hurt on him because she believes he's the cause of most of it. When I believe that someone is the cause of my hurt, I should take it out on them. What else can I do? Well, I try to take other measures [laughs].

Facilitator: Do you see another **turnaround**?

Client: I shouldn't take out my hurt on myself. I'm sitting there, overeating, watching the whole thing. I'm taking out my hurt on my body by eating beyond fullness. When I construct that identity—I'm the daughter, I'm the one in the middle, I have to keep the peace, I have to intervene, I need to redirect, I'm taking my pain and trying to mobilize it into a solution instead of just being with it.

I shouldn't make myself responsible for their relationship. I see the times in the past when they fought because my dad wanted to let me have something that my mom didn't want me to have. I have this identity and blame toward myself and my brother and sister. There's a belief that when the kids are so fucked up, their mom and dad's marriage also gets fucked up—that's my story. If they weren't under the stress and pressure that me and my siblings put them under, they'd have had a nice relationship. I should notice what my mind is doing. I should notice that stories are being spun here. My mind goes, "It's hard." [Laughs.]

In that moment, I'm thinking that when I get home I'm going to make some junk food to eat, I'm going to smoke pot. I'm already thinking about what I'm going to do to myself to take the pain away, which happens to be things that can bring more pain—pain to the lungs, pain to the stomach. I also see how I drag the situation all the way home. I can't let it go. I play those images over and over again. I make myself into a victim and consolidate that. I blame them, I blame myself, and make myself guilty somehow.

Facilitator: Do you want to look at another **turnaround**? "Mom shouldn't take out her hurt on Dad."

Client: I shouldn't take out my hurt on Dad. Yeah, I'm imagining the hell and torture of being in my own stories as his reality. I'm projecting that the hurt I'm experiencing is the hurt he's experiencing. It could be kind to let him feel how he feels without me interjecting anything. I'm painting a picture where my dad hurts all the time and I hurt both of us when I believe that.

I shouldn't take out my hurt and disappointment that he isn't this... I have this caricature of my dad in my head that he's heroic, he's an epic man and, in that moment, I see him as physically weak, fighting with my mom, I'm seeing images of her telling him what to do, and I'm projecting all of that on him.

Facilitator: Let's look at the next statement.

Client: After noticing how I could have reacted differently, these statements are all for me.

Facilitator: Which one would you like to work on?

Client: "I need Mom to answer Dad kindly."

Facilitator: "I need Mom to answer Dad kindly"—**is it true**?

Client: No... it's amazing how those "no" answers start to come quicker when you do an Inquiry.

Facilitator: **How do react, what happens, when you believe that thought**, "I need Mom to answer Dad kindly"?

Client: I feel like she's ruined the day, but it's Mother's Day so I have to pretend to be okay with her acting this way. I'm angry and resentful toward my mom. I blame her. It's her fault we're all in a bad mood. I put all the responsibility on her.

I feel sorry for my dad. I see images of the future and the past and think of her being unkind to him, talking to him in a certain tone with a stretchedup face, addressing him, and pointing. I want to change my mom. She seems untouchable, like you can't say anything to her, and she's set in her ways.

I'm disappointed and angry, stiff, tense, wanting to leave, wanting to eat and smoke. In my mind, I'm arguing with her, "You don't have to talk to him like that! Was that really necessary?" I believe she could do it differently but she chooses not to. She's being malicious. Dad is the innocent victim. He's the one who's been controlled and manipulated and emasculated by my mom all these years. I feel like I've also been controlled and manipulated and emasculated by my mom all these years.

I imagine other families and other parents talking nicely to each other. I imagine my family is abnormal. There's a comparison and there's the assumption that my dad's kind and civil, and my mom's the problem. I'm starting to understand how painful it must be to be a mother and have so many people put so much stuff on you.

I'm also scared that if she becomes empowered, she'll stop supporting me financially. I'm scared she'll find her truth and be like, "Nope, I'm not supporting you." There's probably a payoff for each family member who projects her as the small one or the one at fault. Me, making my mom the perpetrator, has a payoff for me. I get to secure some sense of money. I'm scared of what I'll lose by my mom switching the roles after I blamed her all these years. She's finding something else for herself now, and it's time for me to find something else for myself. She's not the woman I think she is. I probably missed out on getting to know her a lot of the time, and her going through this divorce, I'm finding I like her more and more. I'm starting to see her.

Facilitator: **Who would you be without the thought**, "I need Mom to answer Dad kindly"?

Client: I'm supportive of both of them. I'm present and grounded and kind and not in my stories. Mom seems to be doing just fine. Dad looks a little confused and upset and I can check in with him. I can check out my stories to see if they match up with reality. I'm interested in their experiences. Wow. It's like, with the thought, to inquire about their experiences feels like I'm confronting them, but without the thought, it feels so natural for me to ask how they're feeling, to check instead of dismissing it. Ohhh...

Without the thought, I'm in my own business. I see my mom's doing okay. She's holding her own. I notice I have a fear of talking kindly to my dad with my mom present. It's an ongoing thing where I've always felt she was jealous of the connection I have with my dad, or she felt left out. Me and my dad connect in ways that sound impractical and woo-woo to my mom. When we're all together, I feel insecure for my mom to see me like that with my dad. She thinks she's grounded in reality while Dad and I are out in space and we talk differently. And so, without the thought, it would be okay to ask for some one-on-one time with each of them.

I notice I'm rubbing up against the belief that my parents are supposed to stay together, be happily married, and get along. When I expect it to be different, I hurt myself so much. Without all of that, I'm not a victim anymore. I'm with two people who are choosing to divorce and who also choose to spend time with me.

My mind goes now, "The Work is witchcraft. What's happening? I don't really believe that. I made it all up. Take it back." [Laughs.]

Facilitator: Let's check it in the **turnarounds**. "I need Mom to answer Dad kindly."

Client: I need me to answer Mom kindly. I need to respect her feelings and not only be concerned about how my dad feels. I need to include her. I need to not dismiss her and see her as less of a person in that situation. She could definitely use some kindness instead of me coming at her with all my stories.

I need to answer her with real kindness, not fake kindness. I put all my focus on my dad and how he's the victim. I need to answer her kindly by not putting expectations on how she should be treating a man who she's divorcing kindly—that's crazy.

I need to answer myself kindly. To not blame myself for being responsible. To not eat on auto-pilot. I need to not shame myself for eating the bread or for wanting to smoke. Just to notice this is a hard moment for me. I should answer kindly to myself instead of scaring myself with images like I'm going to get fat, I'm going to be an addict and I'm going to blah blah blah… I need to connect with myself—I'm scared right now—and answer my own feelings kindly: "Okay, I see you want to eat more and smoke. You can do those things. That's okay. What other ideas do you have right now that will help the situation?" I should be there to parent myself. I never understood that I was supposed to be my parent. I thought that they were supposed to be my parents. I see how this divorce is helping me to realize that it's not what I thought.

I need to validate my feelings, to notice. I could ask myself, "Jane, what's the kindest thing you can do for yourself in this moment?" and that question can bring me back to my own business. That's kind.

I need me to answer my dad kindly. It wasn't kind when I tried to manipulate and change his feelings and experience. I was trying to talk him down so we could avoid an escalation of the situation between them. I wanted to move on and, if I was answering kindly, I'd have just been present with what was happening and not trying to change it. Wow.

Is there another turnaround?

Facilitator: I don't need Mom to answer Dad kindly.

Client: Yeah, she made it clear she doesn't want to be in the same space as him. When they're in the house together, she wants to go to her room and close the door. She doesn't want to share refrigerator space with him. She wants it separate. She shouldn't answer him kindly. He's engaging her and she doesn't want to engage with him.

Facilitator: It's, "I don't need…" **Turn it to the self**. "I don't need Mom…"

Client: When I stay in my own business, I don't need her to be that way. I don't need her to be any way. The reality is, I don't need her to answer him kindly and I can't know for sure if that's unkind. She answers clearly and simply without getting into a dispute about it. She's just saying, "No, you didn't." It could get a lot more unkind if she felt she needed to justify herself.

Facilitator: Go back to yourself.

Client: I see it's just a thought. Me believing I need that is the cause of my suffering in that moment. I don't need her to answer Dad kindly. I need to be kind to her, I need to be kind to him, I need to be kind to myself. I only have control of myself and I don't need anyone else to be kind.

Facilitator: What's in your next statement?

Client: Mom is angry, mean, rude, unfair, unkind, hostile, unmovable, bitter, resentful, arrogant, cruel, violent, abusive.

Facilitator: Alright. So, start **turning** them **around** one-by-one to yourself and to the other.

Client: I am angry, mean, rude, unfair, unkind, hostile, unmovable, bitter, resentful, arrogant, cruel, violent, and abusive toward Mom in the way that I think about her, in the way that I blame her, in the way that I invalidate her feelings and turn my dad into the good guy and her into the bad guy. And in the way that I hold images from different times throughout my life against her. I'm unmovable in my unwillingness to understand her, and quite frankly, in my avoidance of doing The Work on her. I see that she's a much cooler Mom than I thought, and how I hold all these things against her. I'm certainly cruel and abusive when I imagine a future where my dad dies and my mom gets struck with how fucked up she's been to him. It's so cruel of me to hold that image about someone who's stuck with her husband for the last thirty-five years. Who the hell am I to judge her? My mind goes, "That's a good question!" [laughs].

[Turning around to the opposite.] *Mom is not these things.* She stays in her own business. She answers my dad's question. She isn't escalating an argument. She's in a difficult situation and she's willing to be in the same space with my dad at the same time. That's *flexible* for a woman who wants to get her own apartment. *She is not violent, she is peaceful.* She's there in the kitchen, she gives her answer, and she's being clear and direct—that's *kind*.

When I believe she's angry, it's because I'm seeing all the images from the past—her with a sour face—and that's not actually happening. *She is not rude.* She has a right to her own experience—that's fair. It matches up with the rest of her story—she says she's not doing anything for him anymore, that she's not communicating with him, that they're living separate lives so, to her, it's fair that he shouldn't ask her to wake him up. She's putting up boundaries and she's all excited.

What's the opposite of bitter? *She is excited* about life. She's learning how to take care of herself. She's not bitter, she's getting better. That feels good.

What I see is that most judgments that I wrote, if not all of them, are based on images that my mind is overlaying on the situation. It's not based on her.

Facilitator: And the last statement?

Client: I never want Mom to treat Dad like someone she doesn't care about ever again. [Client turns it around.] *I'm willing for Mom to treat Dad like someone she doesn't care about.* I'm willing, because I haven't seen that yet. Even in that situation, she isn't sure she can leave him yet because she wants to make sure that he's safe to live alone or that he can get help. So far, I've seen a woman who cares about the husband she's divorcing. She cares about him a lot. They've been thinking about divorcing for at least a decade. It's a good thing that I have The Work when it actually goes down.

I look forward to Mom treating Dad like someone she doesn't care about. I look forward to her living this life she wants for herself that doesn't include him. I look forward to seeing the woman she becomes without spending her life caring for him. That would be awesome and it'll probably be more fun to hang out with her, too.

I never want Mom to feel justified and be violent toward Dad ever again, which is assuming she's being violent toward him. *I am willing for Mom to feel justified and violent toward Dad…* yeah, respect her feelings that the things she says are true or that's her experience. I could totally understand why she'd be violent toward him if she believes he's violent toward her. So, who's the good guy and the bad guy there? I don't know what's going on. I only know that this is her experience and she's going to live out her experience however she does.

I look forward to Mom feeling justified and violent toward Dad—when I can see it as a step toward her own empowerment and I don't see my dad as a victim but as someone responding to his own inner experience to this woman. [Pause] What I found in doing this Worksheet is that I'm capable of being at peace no matter what's going on between them, so I look forward to it.

And the last one I wrote is—I don't ever want her to isolate herself from people who love her ever again. *I'm willing for her to isolate herself from people who love her again* if it's the best choice for her. Just because someone loves you, it doesn't mean you have to marry them and it doesn't mean you have to live with them. It doesn't mean you have to do their laundry.

I'm glad I'm doing this Worksheet. I feel compassion for my mom. I feel inspired by her. She's showing me some cool stuff right now.

I look forward to her isolating herself from people who love her again. She's taking care of herself. That's a great thing. I don't know what's going to happen, but I know that when I tell my story of what I think should happen, it's not true and it hurts. I've got to write this down.

Facilitation #12: She Repeats Herself

Even as we become adults, in an instant we can feel like little children again who need their mother. The longing for the ideal, gentle and caring mother, "The mother (I think) I want", doesn't fade away—it is a fantasy and it is painful. Then, as we question our thoughts, we wake up to reality and notice that we are not little children and we do not need our mother the way we thought we did.

Client: I called my mother yesterday just because I haven't talked with her in a long time. I've been upset with her about some things that went on during the holiday. I decided to call her. She was happy I called and we talked for thirty-five minutes. I noticed that she kept repeating herself by telling the same stories over and over again and I got frustrated. I wrote a Worksheet on that situation.

[Client reads from her Worksheet]:

#1 I am frustrated with my mother because she repeats herself.

#2 I want my mother to wake up, to get clear, to be present, to say new things, to listen to me, and to ask me questions.

#3 My mother shouldn't be so boring to listen to and talk with. She should be more interesting.

#4 I need my mother to keep the conversation short, I need my mother to not repeat herself, I need my mother to remember she already told it.

#5 My mother is boring, annoying, not present, forgetful, old.

#6 I don't ever want to feel so disconnected talking to my mother.

Facilitator: Thank you. So, you were talking on the phone with your mother, and it's been a long time since the holiday and you notice she's repeating her stories. "Your mother repeats herself"—**is it true**?

Client: Yes.

Facilitator: "Your mother repeats herself"—**can you absolutely know that it's true**?

Client: Yes.

Facilitator: **How do you react, what happens, when you believe the thought** that "She repeats herself"?

Client: I feel heavy in my head, with pressure in my forehead and around my eyes. I feel dizzy and it becomes more difficult to breathe. I feel my whole body aching and becoming uncomfortable. I'm bored. My mind starts drifting, I start typing on my computer while she's talking. I keep saying to myself that I need to listen to her and be present, otherwise it'll get worse; she'll tell more and more stories if I'm not present. I get a headache. There's a little voice inside of me that keeps saying, "Why do expect me to listen to all your stories when you're not asking about my life, when you're not listening to me?" I distance myself from her.

At the beginning of the call, I had this warm feeling, "Oh, I'm happy I'm finally calling my mother." I wanted to feel close to her. I wanted to hear how she was... and then as the call went on, I disconnected from her and judged her more and more. I felt bored, like I was wasting my time talking to her. I kept noticing how she kept trying to gossip about my brother, how he isn't raising his children the right way and she kept returning to that gossip, which also annoyed me.

I see all these past situations when she talks about herself, her life, her friends. It's like a blow of words in my face without considering if I'm interested in hearing it, without asking about me, and I see it's just the same as always. It's her talking and me listening. She feels less and less like a person to me and more and more as this voice that's very persistent in telling all these stories.

I see future images of it getting worse as she gets older. It was the same with my grandmother when she'd tell the same stories a few times in a row, one after another. When I listen to my mother, I see the same future with her, getting worse and worse. There's this anger toward her, almost as if she's wasting my time on purpose.

I notice how I promise to come and see her to get out of the conversation, just to find a way to end the conversation. I'm not being honest or authentic to myself or to her.

There's also some sadness. When I started the call, I had this image of my mother, beautiful images in my head: my sweet, kind, caring mother, but then, during the call, I'm sitting with this person who I believe to be selfish, narcissistic, old, and boring. These are two images that don't match. I feel my mind getting tired. It's too much to cope with, too much to deal with. There's disappointment. Where did this caring, loving mother go? She isn't there.

I feel sorry for myself. This ugly victim role pops up and I feel sorry for myself: "Why am I stuck with her?" And then I feel bad for thinking that way, almost like I'm going to be punished for having that thought. There are other thoughts like: "I'm not a good daughter", "I'm not a decent human being". I keep having this headache. There's pressure in my entire head almost like my head's going to blow up.

Facilitator: Anything else comes up for you with this thought, "She repeats herself"?

Client: It's interesting that I'm not able to identify what it is that she repeats. It just feels like everything she says is a repetition. It's something that I heard before. There's nothing new.

Facilitator: Let's go back to yesterday when you were talking on the phone with your mother. **Who would you be without the thought** that your mother repeats herself?

Client: I'd feel more calm, more present with her. That's where my focus would be. It feels like the Morning Walk exercise when I listen to her. It feels like the first time I hear her saying that and I feel like I want to ask her questions like, "How did that happen?" or, "How did that make you feel?" I feel more curious about what she's saying. There's no comparison of past and present, it feels like right now, just like doing the Morning Walk and naming things for the first time. I hear her talk about my brother and how she doesn't believe he's a good parent and I want to ask her questions like, "Where did that come from? Did you speak to him about it?" and this conversation requires all my focus. I'd be very focused on what she's saying and I'd want to hear all of it. I want to listen. She feels more neutral. She feels more like a person sharing her life with me and I want to make sure I get it all. I feel open in my body and I notice I'm free to finish the call any time. I'm free to excuse myself. I don't have to stay on the line for a certain amount of time. That feels peaceful, knowing I can hang up whenever I want to leave. It feels like it's efficient to say, "I want to hang up now. I'll talk to you another time." It's all I need to say. I don't have to promise her anything or come up with an excuse, so there's more room to breathe.

Facilitator: Are you ready for the **turnarounds**?

Client: Yes.

Facilitator: "She repeats herself."

Client: *I repeat myself.* It's very true, I can see it's the same judgments that come up about her. That she's boring, that she has a boring life, that nothing new happens, that she never asks me about how I am. This isn't even true. It's like the same thoughts, same judgments about her in my mind that I repeat myself.

Yes, I actually often tell her the same stories about my life because I don't feel like sharing something deep with her, so I often talk about my work or my apartment, or my boyfriend. It's the same things that I tell her. I don't tell her that I've been depressed in the past few months. I don't tell her about something where I felt vulnerable. I also repeat myself in the sense that, each time before I call her, I see an image of this lovely, caring, loving, warm, beautiful mother that I'm calling. I don't know where these images come from, maybe from movies. I see her in front of me and I'm so open and I call her but after a few minutes of conversation, I'm like, "Oh, no, back to reality," and I'm disappointed. It's the same thing I do every time, and I keep disappointing myself. So I keep repeating myself.

I also repeat myself in the sense that there's a part of me that keeps thinking it's going to change. One day, I'm going to call her and she's going to be that mother who's there for me. I keep having that thought no matter how much proof I get that she's herself. She is true to herself, she is the same.

Facilitator: "She repeats herself." Is there another **turnaround**?

Client: I repeat herself? Yeah, I can see how after five minutes, I have a firm picture of my mother, my real mother, and then I stop listening to her. Then I'm like, "Oh, there she is. She's narcissistic. She's only thinking about herself. She only wants to talk about herself," and then I don't hear what she's saying. So, I repeat herself. I pull out that image that I have of her each time and I don't listen to how she tells me about her friends and her new boyfriend, I just have this stuck image of my mother in my head.

I repeat herself. I see that I keep having the same judgments about her that she's mean, narcissistic, and only thinking about herself. In that sense, I keep repeating the labels I put on "Mother." The labels don't change, they're the same labels. I notice I put them on other females as well, like colleagues. I take the Post-Its off my mother and reuse them. So, I repeat herself, I keep seeing her, the one that I have so many opinions and judgments about, in others. I don't remove the labels and see the "her" that is in front of me. I see all the "Mother" Post-Its everywhere.

Facilitator: Do you see another **turnaround** to "She repeats herself"?

Client: She doesn't repeat herself. Actually, when I was in question three, I tried to remember what it is that she repeats and I couldn't think of a single sentence she repeated. I mean, she mentioned my brother several times but, each time, it was with a new story about him so it wasn't the same story. I'm not able to identify a single sentence she said twice.

And she doesn't repeat herself. Truly, I wouldn't know because I don't listen. After ten minutes, I start writing emails on my computer and I'm just like, "Yeah, yeah, yeah," so I wouldn't know.

And she doesn't repeat herself. Each time she tells me something, she tells it with new energy like she's telling something new. Like, "Oh, I need to remember to tell you this," or, "Oh, did I tell you about that?" She uses different words. It's not a complete repetition of what she already said—there are nuances.

I can see that she's happy that I called her and she's sharing her life with me. She kept saying, "I've been thinking so much about you and I didn't know if it was okay to call you."

Facilitator: Read to me your next statement.

Client: I want my mother to wake up, be clear, be present, say new things, listen to me, and ask me questions. I want my mother to listen to me.

Facilitator: Okay. So let's go back to the phone call. You want your mother to listen to you—**is it true**?

Client: Yes.

Facilitator: You want your mother to listen to you—**can you absolutely know that it's true?**

Client: No.

Facilitator: **How do you react, what happens, when you believe that thought** that you want your mother to listen to you?

Client: I'm frustrated. I feel disconnected from her. I want her to listen to me in the sense that I want her to be able to feel how depressed I've been feeling lately. I want her to be able to connect to that part of me and be there for me. I don't want her to just listen to stories about my work or my apartment. I want her to be able to hear how I truly feel at the moment. I want something from her. I want her to have so much empathy that she can hear how I am just by listening to my voice and I want her to say that everything's going to be okay.

I have this need, this want, this craving from her. I want to shake her to wake her up so she can come out of all her stories and look at me and listen to how I'm feeling.

I see this past situation when I was so stressed and depressed with my work and I decided to tell her about it. It felt like it was the first time in my life I truly told her something emotional and vulnerable about myself—and she couldn't listen. She immediately interrupted me when I started crying and then she started telling me about a situation from her workplace twenty years ago, and I felt so alone and so betrayed that she wasn't able to listen to me and tell me it was going to be okay. I felt like a little child in that situation. Also yesterday, when talking to her, I felt like a little child who needs her mother. That's painful.

Facilitator: How do you treat her when you think, "I want my mother to listen to me"?

Client: I treat her as if she has something I need, like a golden key and she's the one who can make everything better. Almost as if she can say the magic words and I'm going to feel good. I put her on a pedestal like she has something I need, and so I need to be sweet to her before she can give it to me. I need to please her, I need to smile, I need to ask her a lot of questions, and listen to all of her stories.

Facilitator: How do you treat yourself in that conversation when you want her to listen to you?

Client: I treat myself like a little child who isn't capable of taking care of herself. I also put myself in this waiting position—waiting for her to say the magic words. It feels like I'm freezing. I'm stuck in that situation. I treat myself as if I don't have any power myself. I give her the power.

Facilitator: **Who would you be without the thought** that "I want my mother to listen to me"?

Client: It would be easier to breathe. I'd feel more like a grownup, stronger. I notice that I'm in my apartment and this is just one of the things I'm doing. It doesn't take over everything. It's just one thing that I'm doing: calling her. It feels like the energy around the call is more relaxed, peaceful. She seems smaller, less important, less powerful. The whole conversation seems less important. It just feels like I need to call her and listen to her and talk to her and then move on with my day. It's not a huge issue. I'm sitting in my apartment, I'm warm, I'm cozy, I've just eaten some chips, I have everything I need, and I have a kitchen full of food. I don't need anything in that moment.

Facilitator: Are you ready for the **turnarounds**?

Client: Yes.

Facilitator: "I want my mother to listen to me."

Client: I want me to listen to myself. I want me to remember that I'm a grownup. She's an old lady and I'm forty-six. I have my own life and she has her own life. I also want me to listen to me and to see that I still think I need something from her. It's almost like I'm a little girl still.

I want me to listen to myself. I want me to take care of this depression I've been feeling in the past few months and not wait for someone from outside to come and fix it. And start to notice what it is that I'm believing that's making me feel this way. That's very true.

I also want me to listen to myself and see that thirty-five minutes for a phone call is too much for me. Maybe twenty minutes is better.

Facilitator: "I want my mother to listen to me." Do you see another **turnaround**?

Client: I want me to listen to my mother. Yeah, because I'm not listening to her. When I don't call her for a long time, she thinks about me and she doesn't know if she can call me or if I'm angry, so I create a lot of frustration for her. I just realized that.

I want me to listen to her. So what if she says the same thing twice or three times? She's an old lady. It's not like anything's taken from me. I can just say, "Oh, you just told that," or, "Oh, I believe I've heard that already."

Sometimes she even says, "Tell me if I told you this before…" She is open. I want me to listen to her so that it matters when I call her.

Facilitator: Do you see another **turnaround** to "I want my mother to listen to me"?

Client: I don't want my mother to listen to me. Well, I don't listen to her, [laughs] and I tell her the same easy stories that aren't really important. I don't tell her anything important or stuff that really matters to me. I keep telling her these unimportant things, and why should she want to listen to that? It's a waste of her time.

I don't want my mother to listen to me. It feels like it's her business how she sees me and what she hears. I can see how busy I am on my side so, if she's just as busy on her side, then it's the way it is. I don't want her to listen to me if she finds it hard or difficult.

Facilitator: Can I offer an example?

Client: Yes.

Facilitator: I want to listen to her because it's been such a long time since the last time. So at least now I should listen to her for half an hour or twenty minutes because it's been weeks or months since the last time we talked.

Client: It's very true.

Facilitator: And I don't want her to listen to me. I heard you say that, on the one hand, you're repeating the same, boring, ordinary stuff and, on the other, when you try to tell her something more vulnerable and meaningful to you, you feel she can't take it, for whatever reason; it's her business. So, it's another example of not wanting her to listen to you if she can't handle it.

Client: Yeah, that's very true. She's actually being very true to herself.

Facilitation #13: My Mother-in-Law is Not the Warm Person I Thought Her to Be

Substitute Mother

When the longing for "The mother (I think) I want" to show up is not being met and the relationships with "The mother (I think) I have" is a cause of ongoing frustration and disappointment, it can send us searching for a replacement, a surrogate, a substitute mother in other female figures. If we cannot get what we want and need from our birth mother, we might go looking for a mother somewhere else, in a teacher, aunt, grandmother, boss, neighbor, or our mother-in-law. Sometimes, we might find what we're looking for and the search will be over, and sometimes we won't.

Can a substitute mother give us what we are looking for? Is she the key to our happiness and freedom? Is it a mother that we find in a substitute figure, or is it ourselves that we find? Is she the one who can give us a home, or is it still up to us to find a home within ourselves? Could it be that, even with a loving and kind substitute mother, we still project our internal story on an external person?

Client: This is about my mother-in-law. The situation is from two years ago. I picked up my daughter after school and brought her to my mother-in-law's place. Her other two grandchildren were already there—my daughter's cousins. Once a week, they go to my mother-in-law, they have lunch, they play, and spend a few hours together. So, my mother-in-law is in the kitchen, making lunch. Some of the food is already prepared and sitting on the counter. She and I are standing by the stovetop, talking. It's around 2 PM. I'm hungry. She's frying chicken nuggets. And then it hits me and I'm being flooded with thoughts and emotions—I want her to invite me to stay for lunch. I want her to ask me if I'm hungry. I want her to ask me if I want to eat. I want to feel like the children, like I naturally belong in this scene. I'm jealous of the kids. I want to stay and have lunch together as if this is my home. I'm looking for a mother in her. It's that kind of moment but she doesn't say anything like this. I wrote a Worksheet. [Reads her Worksheet]:

#1 I am deeply disappointed with my mother-in-law because she is not the warm person I thought her to be.

#2 I want her to invite me to join them for lunch. I want her to make me feel like I'm part of the family, like I'm some kind of daughter to her.

#3 My mother-in-law should invite me to join them for lunch. She should ask me to stay.

#4 I need my mother-in-law to be warm and loving to me, to invite me to join them, to love me like a daughter.

#5 My mother-in-law is frigid, distant, reserved. She will never be like a mother to me.

#6 I don't ever want to feel like an orphan, alone, abandoned, unfed, unnourished, motherless, like I have no family.

She's not the warm person I thought her to be. I can already see that I'm not the warm person I thought myself to be.

Facilitator: Don't race ahead. So, you're at your mother-in-law's house. She's cooking all this food and you're hungry. She doesn't offer you anything. Get still in that moment. "She is not the warm person I thought her to be"—**is it true**?

Client: Yes.

Facilitator: **Can you absolutely know that it's true** that "She is not the warm person I thought her to be"?

Client: Yes.

Facilitator: **How do you react, what happens, when you believe that thought**, "She is not the warm person I thought her to be"?

Client: I'm disappointed. I'm waking up to reality. I feel emotional pain. I feel needy, desperate, and craving a mother's love. I want to ask her if I can stay or if I can grab a bite, but I'm too proud. I believe it will put me in a vulnerable position and I prefer to hold on to the image of "I'm tough and strong and I don't need anybody." It makes me sad. I'm jealous of the grandchildren, who go there once a week to be fed after school.

I see past images, and they're making me feel sorry for myself, of when I was a child coming back home from school to an empty house. There was nothing to eat, there was no mother. She was at work. There was no one. I feel like a little child, lonely. There's a feeling of emptiness. My happiness in that moment depends on her invitation, her saying a few words like, "Would you like to stay for lunch?" I depend on those few words and they don't come. I can't bring myself to tell her that I'd like to stay and have lunch with them.

I see a past image of when I came to visit her once by myself and I stayed for the night and she fed me, she made me coffee and gave me a piece of cake. It was like visiting Disneyland for me. I thought, "I'm so lucky, I have the best mother-in-law," and I thought this was how it was going to be forever and ever. It's hard for me to say it, but what I really wanted was a hug. A big, long, close, mother's hug and to feel like this was home. But my mother-in-law doesn't do that; she's not like that.

[Client asks herself a sub-question.] How do I treat her? I get colder. Something in me gets frozen. I take a mental, emotional step back from her. I judge her to be a person who takes the kids once a week only because she believes this is what she's supposed to do and because my sister-in-law forces her to do it, but not because she really wants to. I see her as someone who's pleasing others. It's important to her to do the "right thing" all the time—she's avoiding conflict by doing this, not because she really wants to cook and have the kids over. I criticize her about that. It makes me appreciate her less. I want to leave as soon as I can. Instead, I play nice. I stay, I'm polite, I chitchat, but what I really want to do is leave. I'm behaving the same way that I judge her to behave—being nice and kind and polite, chitchatting with her because I believe this is what I'm supposed to do when I bring my daughter over.

Facilitator: **Who would you be without the thought**, "My mother-in-law is not the warm person I thought her to be"?

Client: I see a woman. She's nearly seventy. She's in the kitchen, cooking, wearing an apron. She has three energetic grandchildren she needs to feed. I see that she's getting older and slower and I feel respect for her that she makes this effort to have them every week, make lunch, let them stay for a few hours. She's making an effort and trying to be helpful. She's supporting her family. In that case, I feel more appreciation for her, more respect. She keeps a nice house, it's clean, it's full of light, she makes their favorite food, and she's sensitive to what they want to eat—she's making pasta from scratch! I see she's a nice woman.

I'm happy about the opportunity to get a little break from my daughter. I'm happy that my daughter can spend some time with her family—her grandmother and her cousins—for a few hours a week. With the thought, I think "it's not enough." Without the thought, I appreciate what I have and the situation has nothing to do with me. The arrangements never included me staying and having lunch, too.

Facilitator: "She is not the warm person I thought her to be." **Turn it around**.

Client: I am not the warm person I thought myself to be. Before we moved closer to them, I'd planned to make an effort to be closer to them. For a while, I made an extra effort but then I fell back into old habits. I say I want to be close but I realize that I'm not willing to put the effort into what it takes to be closer to family. I want my peace and quiet. I prefer to allocate my time to other things like work, reading, and resting, rather than making big family meals and inviting relatives to come over. So I realize I'm not that kind of person.

I also found that I prefer to skip the hugging and kissing when I meet her and my father-in-law. With some people, it comes to me naturally, but not with them. So, I can't say I'm warm to everyone. I'm not the warm person I thought myself to be toward her.

In that moment, when I realize she isn't going to offer me anything to eat or ask me to stay, I mentally withdraw. The criticizing and judging kick in. I want to escape the situation but I'm afraid to be perceived as rude, so I stay and chat and play nice while, inside, I'm restless.

When I see that my expectation that she'll be closer to my children, her grandchildren—see them more often, invite them over more often, everything more—isn't happening, I get colder toward her. I call her less often. I invite them over less frequently. I have thoughts like, "She's not really my family. She's my husband's mother," and I let my husband do the job. He should call her, he should show interest in her, he should do all these things. As long as he does these things, I feel I don't need to do it.

She is the warm person I thought her to be. Well, compared to my mother, she is. I compare them. She's better than my mother—warmer, kinder. It feels nice to be in her house. I feel comfortable. I feel welcomed. I guess it's something she projects, or I project onto her… anyway, in that moment, she's a living image of what I had in my imagination: she's standing by the stovetop, wearing an apron, frying chicken nuggets, and she's exactly the image of my dream of a warm, loving mother or grandmother. In my dream, this is what she does—cooking and nourishing her family and the children are safe and happy to be there.

I see that I have a strong story about what a nourishing, loving, caring, warm mother or mother-in-law or grandmother should be like. It was built on parts of different women—my aunts, my grandmothers—that I put together to create this picture of a woman in the kitchen, cooking, and that's what she's doing in that moment, and on other occasions too. By the script of that dream, she *is* the warm person that I thought her to be.

Facilitator: What did you write in the next statement?

Client: I want her to invite me to join them for lunch.

Facilitator: "I want her to invite me to join them for lunch"—**is it true**?

Client: Yes.

Facilitator: **Can you absolutely know that it's true** that you want her to invite you to join them for lunch?

Client: Yes.

Facilitator: **How do you react, what happens, when you believe that thought** that you want her to invite you to join them for lunch?

Client: I'm desperate. Needy. My happiness depends on her. I look for a substitute mother in her. I'm expecting her to fulfill my childhood fantasies of home and a mother who is present, and home-cooked meals. The dream of a female figure, warm, loving, nourishing. I forget I'm a grown-up woman. I'm like a child again, wanting a mother. My happiness and well-being, in that moment, depend on her saying those few words, "Would you like to join us for lunch?" When the words don't come, I take it personally and I'm hurt, feeling a little bit rejected. I want to leave as quickly as possible. She only seems available and caring for the grandchildren, but not for me. I'm only the grandchild creator. I'm only wanted and needed for the purpose of bringing my daughter to her, staying for a while to chitchat, playing the game of niceties and then leaving.

I'm in the past, remembering those childhood years when I came home from school and there was never a meal or anyone waiting for me. No food, no mother. I feel sadness about that, and pain. It brings back the memories and sense of loneliness, some hunger, and feeling sorry for myself. All this comes to life in that situation and I want her to solve this issue for me by inviting me to stay and eat together.

In the back of my mind, I make comparisons between her and me. I make it a point, when someone comes to my house, to offer them a drink, to offer them food, whether it's a cleaning lady or a handyman, a neighbor, or the children's friends. To me, it has developed into a way of showing people I care about them. Food and love, love and food, they go together for me. I feel I'm better than her, superior to her.

In that situation, I'm in a dream. I see in the past that there have been similar situations like that with her when I thought I needed her to give me that "thing" and when she doesn't give it to me, I lose interest in the relationship and withdraw. She becomes just another person I'm connected to because I'm married to her son—that's the only thing that connects us. Otherwise, she's just like any other random woman. When I look for a substitute mother in her and it's not happening, I think she's cold and I become cold. I think she's reserved and I become reserved. I judge her by thinking that she does what she does just to keep up that image of a good grandmother, and I do the same. I'm doing what I think I should do to keep up my image as a good daughter-in-law, good wife, good mother, good person. I want her to think good things about me so I do what it takes to keep that positive image. But deep down, I'm not that interested in a relationship with her anymore.

I'm so jealous of those kids who feel naturally entitled to be there. I think, "I hate my mother. I'm broken because of her. I'm feeling like this because of her." This thing runs so deep. It creates a strong identity. A strong and sticky story.

Facilitator: **Who would you be without the thought**, "I want her to invite me to join them for lunch"?

Client: I'd see that we never discussed the option that, when I bring my daughter, I'd stay for lunch. I'd be happy about the opportunity my daughter has to spend time with her grandmother and grandfather and her cousins. I'm doing this for my daughter. It's not about me. I'd be happy about the few hours that I have to myself, not taking care of my daughter and knowing she's being taken care of by my mother-in-law, who loves her. This was my purpose with this arrangement in the first place—to give my daughter that experience.

I'd see that my mother-in-law is a kind woman. I like her. There isn't anything to resent about her when I'm not putting all these expectations on her to be a substitute mother to me. Without the dream, there's nothing wrong. She's a good person and I'd be able to say something like, "Oh, this chicken looks really good and I'm hungry. Can I have a bite? Can I stay?" or I could say, "I'm hungry. I think I should go," instead of staying and lingering there while my mind gets confused.

Everything's less complicated without all these expectations and putting that role of Mother on her. I'll work on my issues instead of dropping all this baggage on her. She didn't do anything wrong. She's not even aware of all this stuff going on in my mind.

Without the fantasies, my mind's clearer about what I want in that moment, and that is food [laughs]. So, I can find a way to get some. I can ask her or I can leave and take care of myself instead of criticizing her for not guessing what's on my mind. There's no notion of "she should know." I'm being unfair and unkind to judge her for not being able to read my mind, or for not having that natural tendency to offer food. It doesn't mean she's flawed in any way.

Facilitator: "I want her to invite me to join her for lunch." **Turn the thought around**.

Client: I want me to invite myself to join them for lunch. If I wasn't so proud, I could have asked to join them. That's what I thought that I wanted but I didn't do anything about it besides thinking crazy thoughts in my head. So, reality shows that I didn't want to join them for lunch. I believed she was only interested in my daughter. I chose to be a victim, to take the identity of the little girl that I was with a mother who didn't cook and didn't nourish me emotionally or physically. I chose to be in that identity instead of taking a risk with my mother-in-law because of the fear of rejection although I'm pretty sure she'd have said yes, if I'd asked.

I don't want her to invite me to join them for lunch. I don't want to because I see her there at nearly seventy and, in my mind, she looks tired. If I stay, she'll have to cook more food and work harder. I don't want to create more work for her that would make her more tired and then I'd feel like I'm creating another chore for her, making extra work for her.

I don't want her to invite me because, if she invites me and I accept, I'll be exposing how needy I am. I don't want to reveal to her how desperately I crave a motherly connection. That would make me vulnerable and I'm not willing to open a crack to the soft spot inside of me. It would be like putting my heart in her hands for a few seconds and I'm afraid to do that. It would show that the image I try to portray of myself as strong and independent—the "I don't need anybody" identity—is a facade.

I want me to invite her to join me for lunch. In that situation, I don't see anything. I do ask her to come over sometimes or meet in a coffee shop. I do invite them over, not as often as I used to, but I do. I threw her a birthday party and it made her happy but, since then, we've grown apart. We don't talk or meet very often. When I want to invite them over, I tell my husband to call them and invite them over. So, I guess I should be the one who makes the call.

Did you see something?

Facilitator: Yeah. "I want me to invite her to join me for lunch", if you want to have lunch with her, you can ask her. It's your job to ask. In that situation, you can say, "I'd like to have lunch with you. Would you like to have lunch with me?"

Client: Yeah, when I ask her, she usually comes… after she's asked many questions to make sure that she isn't a bother.

Facilitator: It's alright. She can say that. That's her business. She doesn't know you want to have lunch with her. Maybe she thinks you just want to drop the kids off and get the hell out of there.

Client: Yeah. I don't know. I'm imagining my sister-in-law; she'd probably just take food from the plate that's on the counter and eat without asking but I don't feel free to do that. I don't feel like I naturally belong there. I don't have that sense of entitlement.

Self-facilitation

The rest of this Worksheet was completed by the client in self-facilitation.

#3 My mother-in-law should invite me to join them for lunch.

Is it true? No.

How do I react, what happens, when I believe that thought? I depend on her invitation to feel happy. I believe I don't belong there. I imagine feeling what it would be like to feel, naturally and easily, that I belong there. This makes me feel frustrated, lonely, family-less, and that no one truly cares about me. It hurts. I envy the kids. They seem so carefree in that picture and, in comparison, I'm not—I'm an outsider. I don't feel part of this happy picture. I want to leave as soon as I can without being perceived as rude.

I resent my mother-in-law and I judge her for not being more big-hearted, more generous, more loving. I criticize her for being calculated and frugal with food. I judge her for not being closer to my kids, as well. I'm unhappy about her but I put on a smile.

In the back of my mind, I blame my mother that I feel this way because of her. I hate her for never creating this kind of home that I see in the situation at my mother-in-law's house. I'm sad because I believe it's only available to the grandchildren, but not to me.

I feel like a small, abandoned child that no one remembers exists. It hurts. A lot.

Who would I be without the thought? Without the thought, I don't really care. There we are, standing by the stovetop, talking. She's cooking. She doesn't invite me to stay. I don't invite myself. I'm hungry. I say, "I'm hungry. I should leave. When should I come to pick up my daughter?" I could go to a coffee shop. There are plenty of options for where to eat. I can treat myself. I'll be more present and less in a fantasy world, reliving the past and dreaming about another future. I'll be grounded.

I won't expect her to read my mind or believe, "She should know," "She should be motherly," "She doesn't have a mother's instinct," and all that stuff. I'll be able to drop these stories.

Turnarounds:

My mother-in-law should not invite me to join them for lunch. That wasn't the plan. We never discussed it. I know she's always frugal with food. I take into consideration, based on how I know her, that she might not have enough food for everybody if I join them for lunch.

If I wanted it, I could ask for it. I shouldn't expect her to read my mind.

I was happy about having a few hours to myself without my daughter. It was rare that these opportunities happened. So, she shouldn't ask me to stay.

I should invite myself to join them for lunch. If I wasn't so proud, I could have asked and been open to hearing a no. I didn't do that. I didn't want to take a risk. I was afraid of rejection.

I should ask, I should try something new. A new behavior, a new approach. Test it, challenge myself. Be curious to see what happens as a result. Be fearless.

I should be honest, open, and ask for what I want. She might say no, she might say yes. I should be authentic if I want an honest and authentic relationship with her.

I should invite my mother-in-law to join me for lunch. Only if I mean it. I didn't invite her. I was focused on my need to be fed and nourished. I was selfish and self-centered. I didn't consider that she might need that, too, and that she has no one who cooks for her, either.

#4 I need my mother-in-law to love me like a daughter.

Is it true? No.

How do I react, what happens, when I believe that thought? I dream about falling into her arms and being hugged as I've never been hugged before. I so crave this kind of hug. I make myself smaller. I become a little child, helpless, less powerful, and forget that I'm an adult.

I resent that she isn't like that. I resent myself that I'm not like that. I hate my mother for not being like that. I want the dream to come true. There's an unwilling acceptance that it will never come true. I will never have that kind of mother—loving, hugging, open-hearted, safe, open, nourishing, caring for me, her child. I hate my life. I hate myself. I want to escape from that kitchen. I can't bear it. I feel lonely and isolated. I'm jealous of the grandchildren for getting that kind of attention and love, and food—it's so natural and easy for them.

Who would I be without the thought? Grounded in reality. In reality, she's not my mother. In reality, she's my mother-in-law. I've known her for two decades. I see her as a kind, gentle woman. In reality, we have a polite and reserved relationship—it's mutual. I don't expect her to do anything special for me.

She's a woman wearing an apron in a bright white kitchen, frying chicken. She's making lunch for the children. I am not "children." The arrangement is that I bring my daughter, stay for a chat, and leave. It's not becoming foggy and complicated by fantasies and hallucinations.

Turnarounds:

I don't need my mother-in-law to love me like a daughter. This arrangement was about my daughter having a grandmother, not about me having a surrogate mother.

In reality, she's not my mother and arguing with reality makes me weaker, not stronger. Living in a dream is not supporting me. So I don't want that.

I was doing fine until that moment and I'm okay in that moment as well. If she's like a mother to me, I will have to be like a daughter to her and I don't know what it means. I might not like that new arrangement.

I need me to love my mother-in-law like a daughter. It could make her happy. She has sons who don't call or visit her as often as she'd like them to. She has expressed her frustration about it to me a few times throughout the years. She might enjoy a more loving attitude from me. She made some comments to me a few times that she'd like to hear more often from me.

I need to show up for holiday family meals and not find ways to avoid them.

In the situation, I could have rolled up my sleeves and helped, joined in the cooking, as I would when visiting my aunts, where I feel like I belong. That's very true.

I need me to love myself like a daughter. That's the most true and powerful turnaround. Any person has the potential to not live up to my expectations and needs, dreams and fantasies. It feels the best way is to love myself, to go back to myself, to stay grounded in reality and be present—it's the best feeling. That's the most loving act to myself and others when I'm able to be in that space.

I should treat myself like I'd like my mother or mother-in-law to treat me. I can fulfill all my dreams of what it's like to treat my children when I'm fulfilling my potential as a mother and direct that toward myself. The reality is that even my children don't want all the goodies I have to offer them. It's best to give that to myself. That makes me the happiest, to give all that good stuff to myself. I'm always happy to receive it—how funny.

#5 My mother-in-law is frigid, distant, reserved. She'll never be like a mother to me.

Turnarounds:

I am frigid, distant, reserved. I treat my mother-in-law that way in the situation in the kitchen. I'm withdrawn, I get colder when I don't get what I believe I want. I am an adult, I'm not a child anymore.

She is not frigid, distant, reserved. She's standing there, cooking, talking to me. She's friendly, the kids are loud in the background, the place feels happy and bright. She's interacting with me. She's smiling while talking to me and she's kind.

I will never be like a mother to myself. I'm working on being a mother to myself after realizing so many times that only I can understand and fulfil my wants and needs exactly the way I dream them and make it happen—no one outside can do this for me.

#6 I don't ever want to feel like an orphan, alone, abandoned, unfed, unnourished, motherless, like I have no family.

I am willing to feel like an orphan, alone, abandoned, unfed, nourished, motherless, like I have no family. It brings me back to being my own mother, to caring for myself and that's something I look forward to. I know how to make myself happy. It feels good to mother myself—there are no disappointments. It's a solid place to be, and it's very powerful. And sane.

I look forward to feeling like an orphan, alone, abandoned, unfed, unnourished, motherless, like I have no family. I think the universe created husbands and children for that purpose—that's funny. I feel that way with them sometimes, as if I have a family but I don't have a family. Like when they're not present, when they're cooped up in their rooms, each person in their own little world and we mostly meet in the kitchen when they get hungry, it's like we're roommates. I feel lonely and alone when they're in their rooms for hours, or at times when there's limited interaction, or when they're annoying. It sure does bring me challenges and pushes and I already know that, after a push, I can do The Work and there's more freedom to be found on the other side. So, I look forward to the next push that will bring me another Worksheet and then clarity.

Storytellers

It can be challenging, even intimidating, to imagine ourselves and what our lives would look like without our story.

Have you ever felt offended by something someone said to you? How many times did you get upset about a text somebody wrote to you? Does a day go by without experiencing stressful events of this sort? In my experience, such incidents occur daily and it's not only words that can cause tension or spark a conflict. Have you ever been upset about a gesture someone made toward you? Have you been irritated by the way someone looks at you? Facial expressions, smells, sounds that people make, and even their silence can trigger us when we put a story onto what it means. We react to the triggers so quickly, sometimes even before we become aware of what we were thinking about them. These stressful situations happen when we attach an interpretation and hold on to a story about the meaning of what happened; we react to a story that is running in our mind.

We are storytellers. More than that, we are the scriptwriters and the leading actors in the movies that we are directing. An innocent moment can turn into drama or comedy depending on our state of mind. For example, your mother could have said to you, "You're such a special child" and you felt offended by it. Your interpretation was that it means you are different from other children, unique in a negative way. You thought she meant that something is wrong with you, while her intention was to compliment you and this was her way of telling you she appreciated you. In such a case, it was your imagination making up a story that was working against you—you were the one hurting yourself.

When we meditate on Question 3, we get to explore the story we made up around a belief and how it affects us. In Question 4, we get to see what it would be like without our story. Here's another example: my friend was reading his mother's lengthy text message on his phone relating to a stressful incident between them that had bothered him for months. He had a whole story about it. We worked on one thought: "She didn't address the issue in her answer". In Question 3—"How do you react, what happens, when you believe the thought," he said he felt separated and withdrawn from his mother. He accused her of using "flowery" language (New Age words) as a diversion and a way of avoiding the topic. Additional thoughts attached to that one such as, "She should apologize," "She is inauthentic," "She should acknowledge her part," "She created the problem, she should fix it"—all these judgments came up from a mind that was adding interpretation and meaning to the words she wrote.

In Question 4—"Who would you be without the thought," without the story of, "She didn't address the issue," he said he would be engaged, and he would have empathy. He acknowledged his stubbornness and was willing to move on. There were other thoughts such as: "She is making progress," and "She is bringing up issues that bother her." He said that, without his interpretation of what she wrote, "I'd be watering the garden instead of putting pesticides on it and I wouldn't let the issue cast a shadow over our relationship." So, same situation—nothing has changed—same text, same mother and son, but without adding meaning and making up a story, my friend had a different experience of his mother's words.

We create our own experiences of other people by imagining and adding meaning to what they said or did. We are projecting our internal world on the external world. We are confusing and scrambling facts with interpretations, we're getting lost in the past and the future. We are constructing stories about everyone and everything. We do this innocently, automatically, spontaneously; we can't help it. The mind can be as busy as a beehive and our imagination can run wild. Therefore, it is our job to question the thoughts that construct a story especially when that is causing us mental confusion and emotional turmoil and, as a result, separates us from ourselves and others.

Facilitation #14: She is Criticizing Me

Facilitator: Tell me about the situation.

Client: The situation was that my family and I went to visit my parents. We knew we'd also see my husband's family during that visit because they live not too far away. I told my parents this more than once. And then when we were there, my mother was sitting at the kitchen table, it was morning, and I started to explain to her our plans for visiting my husband's family. Then she said, "I knew you'd just run away," and I was surprised. I wrote, "I felt surprised with my mother when she said, 'I knew you'd just run away.'" I'd like to work on that, including the emotion, "I am surprised."

Facilitator: So, you're in your mother's kitchen and you tell her your plans to go visit your husband's family and she says, "I knew you'd just run away." You're surprised by what she said—**is it true**?

Client: Yes.

Facilitator: You're surprised by what she said—**can you absolutely know that it's true**?

Client: No.

Facilitator: **How do you react, what happens, when you believe the thought**, "I am surprised by what my mother said"?

Client: My mind goes blank. My jaw drops. I freeze. My eyes grow wide. I can't think. I'm frozen in time. Feeling some hurt and confusion because she knows it was the plan. I judge her for being wrong, for saying what she's saying and not remembering. I'm confused by why she says this. I'm shut off from her in that moment, I judge her negatively and I feel tense. I'm not open to talking about it or responding to what she's saying. I feel, "Oh, here we go again. My mom plays the victim," and I see other times when she acted this way. I see that this is how it's going to be between us in the future now that my dad has dementia. Whatever I do is never enough for her. She always needs more, wants more. I'm feeling sad, disappointed, and guilty. I think, "This trip should have been longer. Maybe we should change our plans and spend the whole time with them. It feels like she needs me here. My parents are getting older, I don't get to see them very often." I create pain for myself, judging myself, judging her, being shut off from what she said.

Facilitator: In that moment in the kitchen with your mother, you're surprised by what she says, "I knew you'd just run away"—**who would you be without the thought**?

Client: I'd be more relaxed. I can see myself reaching out for her hand and feeling love for her and I feel love from her. I'm smiling. I'm open to either responding to her statement or curious to find out more about what's behind her statement. I'll be more empathetic and understanding, accepting that in this moment this is what she's thinking and I'm happier, more relaxed in the sweetness of that moment. The sweetness of, "She doesn't want me to go. She loves that I'm here. She's been looking forward to this visit and spending time together." There's no problem. There's love and sweetness and connection. It's not a threat. She's not attacking me. She's sharing her feelings.

Facilitator: How do you **turn this around**—"I'm surprised by what my mother said, 'I knew you'd just run away'"?

Client: She's surprised by what I'm saying. That's in her business, I don't really know her experience but I'd like to try and give her the benefit of the doubt. I can see that she's forgotten about our plan and so she's surprised by what I'm saying.

Facilitator: And in your business?

Client: I'm surprised by what I said. My reaction in that moment is about the judgment that my mind is making about what she said. Therefore, I'm surprised by what I said in my mind.

Facilitator: What did you say in your mind?

Client: It was probably, "She's wrong, I'm not running away." I'm defending myself. "This was the plan. I'm not running away." I'm surprised by what I said in the sense that I was ignoring her. I wasn't giving any attention to what she just said. Do you have any ideas?

Facilitator: What thoughts that came up caught you by surprise?

Client: "It's a bigger deal than I thought." I'm reacting to that thought. In Question 3, I was surprised to see there was some guilt. I was surprised that I was expecting a different reaction.

The other turnaround is, *I'm not surprised by what my mother said.* I'm not surprised because this is who she is. It's not uncommon for my mom to say things like this. And at the same time, it feels like it's obviously a big issue for me. The second level that comes up for me is that I'm surprised by my reactions, my thoughts, and judgments about what she says. I make it mean that she's saying I'm wrong and so, in that moment, I say she's wrong. We're both doing the same thing, in my mind—we're wronging each other. I'm surprised to see all this stuff that happened. I didn't realize this at that moment.

Facilitator: What do her words mean to you?

Client: She's criticizing me. She's saying I'm bad. I'm a bad child [laughing].

Facilitator: When you talk to your mother about your plans and she says, "I knew you'd just run away," your mother is criticizing you—**is it true**?

Client: Yes.

Facilitator: **Can you absolutely know that it's true** that your mother is criticizing you?

Client: No.

Facilitator: **How do you react, what happens, when you believe** that your mother's criticizing you?

Client: I'm surprised and hurt. I defend myself in my mind: "It's the plan. She knows this is the plan. She's feeling hurt." I feel guilty and think maybe we shouldn't be going. I'm shutting down. There's guilt. I'm not considering changing our plans. I'm going full steam ahead. "This is our plan whether you like it or not." There's a lack of consideration for my mother, a lack of connection. There's judgment of her and then I see in that moment that she's criticizing me or she's criticizing my plans so I react by being critical of her and defending myself. I'm making it all about me and that creates pain for me and for her. I don't feel cared about, I don't feel heard. I'm no longer the good child [laughs].

Facilitator: Is there anything else about this thought, "She is criticizing me"?

Client: I can see images from the past where she's criticized me, been disappointed in me and I can see it happening in the future more and more.

Facilitator: **Who would you be without the thought,** "She is criticizing me" when she says, "I knew you'd just run away"?

Client: First thing I'm seeing is reaching out to hold her hand and feeling relaxed and connected to her. I'm not taking what she said personally. I'm able to sit with her and hear her and maybe reflect on what she said. I'm more curious about what she's feeling. I'm open to being there with her, being willing to hear her statement and address it with care and consideration. I'm feeling love for her. It's more about her, not about me.

Facilitator: Are you ready for the **turnarounds**?

Client: Yes.

Facilitator: "She is criticizing me."

Client: I am criticizing myself. I'm the one having the thought that the statement she said means that I'm wrong, my plans are wrong, I'm not good. All these thoughts are in my head. Therefore, I'm criticizing myself. She doesn't say any of those things.

I take it further. I'm believing those thoughts when I question my plans, and I'm telling myself I shouldn't leave, I'm wrong for leaving. It's all these thoughts in my head in the moment. Besides, after that statement, she's totally quiet. She doesn't even look at me.

I'm making what she said mean all these different things about me, all these negative things about me—"bad child," and "she doesn't love me." I'm making her statement all about me, in my mind. I'm the one criticizing me.

She is not criticizing me. I can see that she's sharing her feelings. I see her disappointment. She's being authentic. She's communicating with me the best she can. She says what she says based on her experience, her world, and it's not about me. It's a reflection of her experience.

Facilitator: Was there any pinch of a little bit of running away for you?

Client: Sure, yes. So, she's stating the obvious [laughing]. Yeah, I think in the circumstances, I'd say that's true. I *am* running away, yeah. Yeah, so, therefore she's stating the obvious—I am running away [laughing]. Part of the reason that we visit my husband's family is to get a break from being around my parents. So, in that sense, I'm running away. She's stating the obvious. We're leaving. Thanks for that one.

I am totally criticizing her, for sure. In my mind, I have these negative judgments about her. I wrote in statement #5: She is needy, she is overreacting, she is wrong, she shouldn't be saying this, this is the plan… There's nothing right about her in that moment.

Facilitator: Let's look at the next statement.

Client: "I want her to stop overreacting."

Facilitator: Back to the situation, "I want her to stop overreacting"—**is it true**?

Client: Yes.

Facilitator: "I want her to stop overreacting"—**can you absolutely know that it's true**?

Client: No.

Facilitator: **How do react, what happens, when you believe the thought**, "I want her to stop overreacting"?

Client: I blame her. I'm not looking at my actions and I'm making it about how she's wrong and I don't see how I'm overreacting. I'm not connecting with the truth of what she's saying. I'm angry. I'm judging her. I'm the victim. I see images of this is how it is with my mom—she's always overreacting. I see all the gazillion times when she overreacted in the past and she's not going to change and this is how it's always going to be in the future and why am I not used to this by now? I'm causing myself pain. I'm helpless and hopeless. And then, I see my brothers and my father thinking the same thing. I'm superior, better than her. I'm letting her down. It's costing me my relationship with her, it's costing me my relationship with myself. At the same time, it feels like it gives me more ease… blame an external factor, it's nothing to do with me, it's all about her. The blaming feels like an addiction, a very common pattern.

Facilitator: **Who would you be without the thought**, "I want her to stop overreacting"?

Client: I wouldn't overreact [laughs]. I'd be relaxed and calm. Loving her, loving myself even though what she says is the truth, and I'm okay anyway. I'm doing the best I can. We're both doing the best we can in that moment. I can smile at her. Just be grateful we're there together, in the sweet moment. Grateful she's being honest. I can agree with her. It's not about me, I'm not taking it personally.

Facilitator: And the **turnarounds**?

Client: I want me to stop overreacting. I can clearly see how, in that moment, it feels like the world's ending. I can see how there's nothing wrong in that moment, we're both safe, we're both warm, we're sitting in the kitchen having a sweet moment together, and yet here I am freaking out, I can't even think straight. I overreact so much that my mind goes blank, I'm overcome with emotions, shocked, blaming her, being angry, and feeling guilty. It's like a bomb exploding in my head when there's nothing wrong. She's being honest, she's telling the truth and I'm totally freaking out and creating a war zone in myself and acting like she's threatening my life. I'm defending myself: "This is the plan. She's wrong. She shouldn't be saying this." I'm totally fighting in the moment and making it something awful when it's just me and my mom in the kitchen, communicating with each other.

Facilitator: "I want her to stop overreacting."

Client: I don't want her to stop overreacting. She's not overreacting; therefore, she doesn't need to stop what she's doing. She's being honest. She's sharing her feelings. I want me to stop overreacting because that's what I have control over—myself.

Facilitator: You want her to continue overreacting?

Client: Yeah, *I want her to continue overreacting* if that's what feels authentic for her. I want her to be honest and comfortable with me, be herself with me. This is what a relationship is all about and I want to be the same way. I want to be myself, be honest, be authentic, so, I want to extend that to her as well. And if telling the truth and being honest is overreacting then, yes, I want her to overreact. And if I see it as overreacting, it means I still have work to do on this issue and it leads me to more freedom if I do Inquiry… if I do The Work.

Facilitator: What's in your next statement?

Client: "She should remember this was the plan all along."

Facilitator: "She should remember this was the plan all along"—**is it true**?

Client: No.

Facilitator: **How do you react, what happens, when you believe that thought**, "She should remember this was the plan all along"?

Client: With the thought, I'm defensive. I blame her. I'm not seeing her and not really hearing what she is saying. I'm tense, not breathing. I create war with that statement and I'm arguing with her. I'm arguing with the present moment. I'm confused. My hackles are up. This is a problem. I'm a victim.

Facilitator: **Who would you be without the thought** "Mom should remember this was the plan all along"?

Client: I'd be present in the moment with her. I can see with that statement she's saying, "I knew you'd just run away." Yes, she knew because I told her so. She does remember that was the plan! It's funny to see that. She *is* actually remembering the plan. So, we're on the same page. We're allies [laughs]. She knows the plan.

Facilitator: Then, who would you be?

Client: I'd be relaxed, loving her, being in the sweet moment with her, grateful we're together, nothing's wrong, connecting with the kindness of the universe. My mind's clear. I'm just hearing what she said and not adding to it.

Facilitator: "Mom should remember this was the plan"...

Client: I should remember this is the plan. Yeah, I can see how myself remembering that this is the plan creates confidence, clarity, a more clear mind. I can do this for myself, I don't need her to do anything. It's what I can do to help myself feel more centered and clear in that moment. Hearing what she said, that's the plan, and I should remember [laughs], and there's no problem.

Facilitator: She just wants to spend more time with you, and this is the plan.

Client: Yeah. There's an acceptance of her and me in that, when I remember this is the plan. No second-guessing, just more clarity.

She should not remember this is the plan. It's not her responsibility, it's not necessary. She remembers what she remembers. She's obviously remembering, like she said she already knew I'd be running away. There's no reason why she needs to remember. I'm there. I can remind her. We all have a lot of things on our minds and there's no reason why she should remember. She forgets things, I forget things, it's the human condition, so she shouldn't remember.

Facilitator: Read your fourth statement.

Client: "I need her to be supportive."

Facilitator: So, when you're in the kitchen talking about the plan and she says, "I knew you'd just run away," you need her to be supportive—**is it true**?

Client: No.

Facilitator: And **how do you react, what happens, when you believe** that you need her to be supportive?

Client: I'm not seeing where she's being supportive. I'm just looking for proof of where she isn't supportive and for images from the past where I determine she hasn't been supportive, and I see it happening in the future. I'm blaming her, making her wrong, not seeing the best in her in that moment. I'm the victim. I'm selfish. I'm at war with her... not really with her. I'm at war with the mother that, in my mind, I think she is. It's causing me pain; we're not connected. I'm tense, I'm not breathing, I'm deflated.

Facilitator: **Who would you be without the thought**, "I need her to be supportive"?

Client: I'd be okay. I'd see how I'm supported by the universe, by her, the floor's supporting me, the ground, the chair, my body's supporting me. I'm breathing, my heart's beating. I'm perfectly fine, I'm totally supported. I'm there with my mom, we're together in a sweet moment.

[Client is moving to the turnarounds.] So, *I need me to be supportive of myself* by being connected to the moment, not believing my thoughts, staying connected to myself and her. It would change the whole situation if I gave myself the support I needed. I could be taking a breath, realizing something's going on, realizing something's been triggered, taking a breath, reconnecting to the moment by seeing what's in the moment, finding what I can be grateful for in that moment, trying to connect with what I definitely know is true in that moment. Start over, shake it off. There are so many things I could have done to support myself that would have made it more pleasant for me and for her. So, I needed to be supportive of myself, and I can do that.

I need me to be supportive of her. I see how this could have changed the energy, seeing she needs care and attention, listening to her, to what she said, to her words. That would have been supportive of us both. Reaching out to her, not making it all about me at all, but about her. Being curious about her and where she is in the moment would have been supportive of her and me, more enjoyable for both of us. I can do that. I'm more in control of my actions than her actions.

I don't need her to be supportive. I can see how I don't need her to be supportive because I'm totally fine. I can give myself support. There's nothing I need at that moment because I'm fine. Sitting in the kitchen, talking. We're both okay, we're fine. And by what she says, she's supporting me. She's telling me, "Yeah, we're on the same page. You're going away. You're running away, I know that." So, she's supporting me [laughs] and reflecting back. Do you see anything else?

Facilitator: She wants to spend time with you. She's not kicking you out.

Client: Yeah, right, she's very supportive.

Facilitator: What's in your next statement? Read it **turned around** to "I."

Client: She is a drama queen, anxious and needy. *I am a drama queen, I'm anxious and needy.* Yeah, I can see how much I overreacted to what she was saying. I can totally see where I was, being a drama queen. Maybe she couldn't notice on the outside but, certainly, when I see what was going on in my mind, I can see I was overreacting, all drama. Along with that, all this anxiety because I'm making it mean, "I'm wrong. She's blaming me. She's saying I'm bad." It's all these negative judgments I tell myself she's saying to me that create a lot of anxiety. And then the guilt creates anxiety and it's all going on inside my head. So, I'm definitely anxious at that moment. And all that needing from her, needing her support, needing her to stop overreacting, needing her to remember, needing her to be different, needing her not to say what she said. I was incredibly needy at that moment. I can see how I can be a drama queen, anxious and needy in other situations too. It's definitely as true, or truer.

Facilitator: And can you see the **turnarounds** turned to her?

Client: I don't know what her experience is, but as far as I can tell, *she seems calm, she's relaxed, she's just sitting there and she said the truth*: "I knew you'd just run away." It's funny how different it sounds when I listen to it literally, aside from what I was making it mean. She was just calm and stating the obvious, and telling me, "I remember, you're going away. You're running away." Looking back now, after this Inquiry, it's obvious she was the sane one, she was the calm one, she was connected to the moment. She was honest, telling the truth.

Facilitator: Read your next statement.

Client: I don't ever want to experience my mom overreacting again [laughs]. I have to say that *I am almost excited to experience my mom overreacting again* because I've realized during this Inquiry that I'm the one overreacting. I'm excited to have that thought because, hopefully, I'll remember whenever I think she's overreacting, that it's really me and I can do something about my overreaction. It'll be like a flag showing me the path to freedom, happiness, and peace.

So, *I look forward to it* and *I am willing to experience my mom overreacting again*. Even if it leads me to another Worksheet, then that's great because I can get to this space again. Once I do a Worksheet, I'll realize, I'll remember, I still have work to do, creating new patterns for myself. I'm excited [laughs]. This feels a lot better.

Facilitation #15: She Didn't Say Goodbye to Me

Facilitator: Tell me the situation.

Client: A few years ago, in my mother's last days, when we knew she was going to die, she asked to have personal conversations with specific people like my father, my brother, my sister, her sisters, her friends—those who were important for her. I arranged all the meetings she asked for. However, she didn't speak with me [crying]. For weeks in the hospital, I was there all the time and she didn't have a private talk with me. This fits my entire history with my mother. Why didn't she want to talk to me? Why didn't she think it was important to talk to me?

About a week after she died, when I had time to sit and think, I started to process it. "There, again she had another opportunity and she chose not to take care of me, not to do something for me." It was another experience where I was disappointed with her. This thought came up after she passed away—"It happened again." While she was still alive, I was very busy caring for her at the hospital. It came after that, while we were mourning, after she had died, and I was sitting in the living room at my father's house.

Facilitator: What did you write in your Worksheet?

Client: [Reads her Worksheet]

1 I'm angry with my mother because she didn't say goodbye to me.

2 I want her to spend time with me like she did with all the others.

3 Mom should say goodbye to me, to pay attention to me too, to know I am also worthy of her attention.

4 I need Mom to acknowledge that I'm also her child.

5 She is behaving like she always does, I'm the responsible adult and she is the child.

6 I don't ever want to be unseen, without presence, to be neglected.

Facilitator: I invite you to go back to the moment, about a week after your mother passed away. "Your mother didn't say goodbye to you"—**is it true**?

Client: She didn't say goodbye in a clear way. No, that's not true. She did say goodbye in her own way.

Facilitator: Is it a "yes" or is it a "no"? In one word. "My mother didn't say goodbye to me"—**is it true**?

Client: No.

Facilitator: **How do you react, what happens when you believe the thought** "My mother didn't say goodbye to me"?

Client: I feel neglected, unimportant, unseen. It's the same story I've been telling myself most of my life [crying].

Facilitator: What's the story you've been telling yourself?

Client: That I'm not worthy, that I'm not loved. That I have to do everything for myself by myself. That if I don't do things for myself, no one will do them for me. It always goes back to that.

Facilitator: Do you see images of the past when you believe the thought that she didn't say goodbye to you?

Client: I see small things that trigger a lot of emotions. Like when I was four and I wanted her to pick me up in her arms and she wasn't comfortable with it so she put me down. Small things that seem absurd but express the feeling that being close to me made her uncomfortable. There are more significant things like when I told her a family relative raped me. She asked me, "Are you sure you saw what you think you saw? Are you sure you understood what happened there?" She was unable to contain or to accept that it happened to her daughter because she had difficulty with her own sexuality. Or, for example, when I was in the military and everyone got packages of home-cooked meals and cookies from their moms, and she didn't send me anything. These are small things that connect with this pain. When I did a drawing she wouldn't say, "How nice! You tried". Instead, she'd talk about how it didn't look good because she was more talented than me. It was her jealousy of me that didn't give me space. When she was stressed, she'd hit me. This is what immediately comes to my mind, more the neglect than the abuse. The neglect hurts me more. She made me wear shirts she wanted me to wear as opposed to what I wanted to wear. I know, it's nonsense, but it represents this general feeling that I could see her but she couldn't see me.

Facilitator: How do you treat her when you believe the thought, "My mother didn't say goodbye to me"?

Client: I don't see her. I speak from a childish place. I assume she didn't want to say goodbye to me, but that's not necessarily true. She felt very poorly physically. The very fact that she was able to have these conversations, that she could pick herself up and say something pretty much amazed me. I treat her like I'm a baby, like it's still her job to cradle me. I don't see her as a person, as a woman who's suffering at that time. One of the things that came to mind in the previous question is when we came to visit her before her hospitalization, and I physically helped her with all sorts of things, like getting up from her chair. She said she didn't want me to leave because it was so pleasant and comfortable for her that I was there. On the one hand, she complimented me, but on the other hand, I felt like she needed me there as a nurse because I did things better than my father. This is the part where, as long as I took care of her, it felt like we had a relationship. So, I don't see her. I don't see her when I want something from her, there isn't room for us both. Why is there this black-and-white, and the relationship can't include the other person as well?

Facilitator: Let's see **who you would be without the thought**, "My mother didn't say goodbye"?

Client: [Crying] I'd be mourning her death, that she's no longer with us. Sad. Taking care of my dad. Without the thought, I could be more an adult, more myself. The thought weakens me. If my mother didn't say goodbye to me, then who will? Without the thought, I can take care of myself when I need to. I'm a woman sitting in the living room, that's what I am. And that, too, has a lot of stories around it. [Pause] I'd be a woman mourning her mother. I'd be softer, not combative. Without the thought, I'd see her, her pain. It pulls me down less, takes fewer resources away from me.

Facilitator: Let's try the **turnarounds**. "My mother didn't say goodbye to me."

Client: She did say goodbye to me.

Facilitator: Give me three specific and authentic examples how this can be true.

Client: She said a very authentic goodbye, very true to how our relationship had been all my life. So I accept that this is what was between us. So she did say goodbye to me and that's the goodbye she could say to me.

Facilitator: What goodbye is that? What does it mean?

Client: It means that, not formally calling me for a conversation, is the goodbye she could say. This is the sort of contact she could have with me. That in the end she couldn't or didn't want to do anything different. It's accepting that this is what she could have done at the time.

Facilitator: Are there any ways she behaved that you could say meant, "Goodbye"?

Client: There was a certain moment in this process, when she told me, "This is the end" and it was the only moment when she had direct communication with me. Beyond that, it was just what she needed and asked me to help her with. That was her goodbye. There wasn't a moment when she said goodbye to me personally or acknowledged my need. She said the goodbye she could say.

She did say goodbye to me by asking me to help her. That was her way. My expectation of anything else is unrealistic. It was different from what she did with the others, but it was real.

I didn't say goodbye to her. It's true. I didn't initiate a moment with her. I was busy taking care of her, and not only her, but also my brother and sister and my children. I didn't bother to find myself time with her—it's important for me to hear myself say this.

I didn't say goodbye to myself sounds weird but it connects to what I just said. I need to pay attention to what I need in this process. It feels more empowering.

Facilitator: What does this mean to you, I didn't say goodbye to myself?

Client: On the one hand, I want her to do it, for her to initiate it. On the other hand, I'm not a baby, I'm not helpless. I want her to make it happen, I want her to be responsible for our relationship, and it's disappointing and it never worked—it rarely worked. I can count on one hand the times it worked. And there's the part of paying attention when I'm taking care of someone else, to what I need, and how I protect myself in the process. It's something I didn't do with her. If she didn't know what I needed or wanted, it wasn't good enough and I'm disappointed.

I love the turnarounds [smiling].

Facilitator: Let's look at the next statement.

Client: "I want her to spend time with me like she did with all the others."

Facilitator: **Is it true**—"I want my mother to spend time with me like she did with the others"?

Client: After we talked ... let's say yes. It's hard for me to say yes or no.

Facilitator: "I want Mom to spend time with me like she did with all the others"—**is it true**?

Client: Yes.

Facilitator: **Can you absolutely know that it's true**, "I want my mother to spend time with me like she did with all the others"?

Client: Yes.

Facilitator: **How do you react, what happens, when you believe the thought**, "I want my mother to spend time with me like she did with all the others," and, in your opinion, she didn't?

Client: I feel less important to her, less significant. I'm less worthy.

Facilitator: How do you treat her when you believe this thought, "I want my mother to spend time with me like she did with all the others"?

Client: I believe that she's capable of more than she shows. That she's stronger than she chooses to be with me. I treat her like she did things consciously and that she chose not to pay attention to me at the time. I think that she's responsible for the relationship between us, for how I feel about the relationship. I give her a lot more power than I want to give her.

Facilitator: Do you see images of the past with this thought?

Client: What comes to mind is that, in the past, I didn't want her to spend time with me because her behavior toward me was violent, so, personally, it's better that she didn't spend time with me. Interesting, no? But with the others... she wasn't violent with my brother. He doesn't remember her being violent at all. With my sister, I remember my mother tried to get closer to her and made an effort to do so and I helped the connection between them, so there's also a longing for, "Why couldn't she do this with me?"

Facilitator: How do you treat yourself?

Client: I hold the role of being the responsible adult. It disconnects me from my feelings, from my needs, as if it's impossible to have both, to have my feelings and needs and to take care of myself, and also to take care of her. It's hard to manage both. I disappear. The more I want her to spend time with me, to see me, the more I disappear. I don't show up because I'm waiting for her input, for her engagement.

Facilitator: So, in the same situation, **who would you be without the thought**, "I want Mom to spend time with me like she did with all the others"?

Client: A mature person, a person in my own right. A woman in my own right. Whether she's devoting time to me or not, I'm okay, it has nothing to do with her. I feel calmer and more neutral.

Facilitator: Let's try the **turnarounds**. "I want Mom to spend time with me like she did with all the others".

Client: I want to spend time with myself like with all the others.

Facilitator: What examples do you have in the situation, or around that time?

Client: At the time, especially when family and friends came to visit us, it meant connecting with what I felt instead of being a host and making sure all the people who were visiting us were okay. Sitting with my pain and letting others take care of me. On some level, I did do that. I think there was a balance. Even being with my mother at the hospital and taking care of her helped me say my goodbye to her. Taking care of others is also devoting time to myself in some way.

I would have preferred to not help my dad with my mom's belongings, but I still did it, like deciding what to do with her clothes instead of letting him do it. It wasn't my place, but it helped him and that's how the relationship between us is. [After a pause] I would choose the wars I fight and not be fighting by default.

Facilitator: Do you see another **turnaround**, "I want Mom to spend time with me like she did with all the others"?

Client: I don't want my mom to spend time with me like she did with the others. It reminds me of what we talked about before, when I didn't want her to be with me or spend time with me. When I think of that specific time, I think I wouldn't have believed her if she spent time with me. There's a part of me that didn't want the formality around it, that wouldn't have believed it. Because it's just words. It's not who we really are. A part of me didn't want her to spend time with me. I preferred to spend time taking care of her rather than talking with her that way. A part of me didn't want her to spend time with me because I wanted her to be focused on healing, even though she was already beyond that stage. A part of me wanted her to do it for the others, my brother, my sister, and my dad, for them to have time with her and that's really what happened. This is an insight I didn't have before.

Facilitator: What insight?

Client: That I also didn't want her to spend time with me, not in that way at least.

Facilitator: [After a pause] That's good to know. What did you write in the next statement?

Client: "Mom should pay attention to me, too." [Crying]

Facilitator: Back to the week after your mother passed away. "Mom should pay attention to me, too"—**is it true**?

Client: No. That's not true. She didn't have to.

Facilitator: **How do you react, what happens, when you believe the thought** that your mother should pay attention to you, too?

Client: I'm judgmental, I'm disconnected from what's happening. I'm weak, I'm waiting for her to do something. I'm waiting for her to pay attention to me. I'm left anticipating, wanting. When I expect it from her, I reduce my ability to do something about it or take care of myself, or even interact with her.

Facilitator: **Who would you be without the thought** that your mother should pay attention to you, too?

Client: I'd be able to say to my mother, "Hey, I'd love to spend some time with you," or something like that. I would take the initiative. I'd also pay attention to myself, what's happening with me, what I need. I'd take care of myself regardless of her. I'd provide myself with what I need. The power and ability to do these things would come back to me. I'd connect with myself. It seems easy and simple but it's not, otherwise we probably wouldn't be here today.

Facilitator: Let's try the **turnarounds**. "Mom should pay attention to me, too."

Client: I should pay attention to myself. Eat, sleep, deal with what I feel in the process itself and not set it aside because now we're taking care of Mom. It doesn't have to be this or that. Give myself time by myself, to not engage in what I know will help someone else but won't help me, like with my dad.

Facilitator: Can I offer an example?

Client: Yes.

Facilitator: I should pay attention to myself, when moments before her death, you're still waiting for your mother to show up, like you did your whole life in your dreams and fantasies. It still exists even at this age (forty plus). In that place, at that time, you go back to being a little girl waiting for her mom to finally become the mom she always wanted.

Client: True, absolutely.

Facilitator: This is a great cause of pain.

Client: True. Exactly.

Facilitator: And soon, there won't be a chance. She's about to die and that's it.

Client: True, this is the great mourning. The fantasy is over. The potential for her to appear as the mother I wanted no longer exists.

Facilitator: What's another **turnaround**? "Mom should pay attention to me, too."

Client: Mom shouldn't pay attention to me. Yes, that's true. This is exactly what I was thinking when I answered "no" to the first question. She doesn't have to. She doesn't have this need. And as much as it pains me to say it, this was the reality for her.

Facilitator: Go back to your business. At that time, "Mom shouldn't pay attention to me."

Client: I'm okay, I'm strong, I'm capable. I didn't need her attention on an existential level. I was fine. I was, of course, hurting that this was happening, but I didn't need her attention to be okay. What you said was important—what's my business and what's hers. It's significant here.

Facilitator: Can you find more examples of when you thought she should pay attention to you, and when you look at it from your business you see that she shouldn't pay attention to you?

Client: Yes, most of my life. When I came to her with that situation with our relative, I think it would have been great if she'd been able to, but it didn't change what happened to me or how I dealt with it afterward. Even if she'd shown up there for me, it wouldn't... the event happened and, even though I often think about it from the victim's perspective—how difficult it was—I think that, because of that, I'm able to do what I do today, be independent and be capable and able in many areas of life.

The fact that, when I was four, she wasn't willing to pick me up in her arms, that made me go and play and be in the world more than I would if I had stayed in her arms. I was fine.

Facilitator: And the third **turnaround**?

Client: I should pay attention to her. This makes a lot of sense to me. On a physical level, there was also my need to take care of her. It was important for me to do the things I did. I consciously remember making that choice.

Facilitator: What does it give you?

Client: It gives me a good feeling, a feeling that I'm a good person. I remember saying that no matter what she did, this was the way I wanted to say goodbye. It didn't matter what our history was. In that moment, she could have been a stranger, and I'd still behave the same way. It was my need to pay attention to her needs. It's important.

Facilitator: Can I offer an example?

Client: Yes.

Facilitator: I need to pay attention to her. Pay attention to who she is and what your fantasy is.

Client: Yes, I'm still working on it. Yes. [After a pause] It was very significant to look at what was my business and what was her business. It helped me get clear. That's where I'm stuck. The part of taking care of her and seeing her needs, seeing what she could and couldn't do instead of coming back to myself and what I needed—if I needed it at all—that's the story I'm telling myself about what I needed. It's helpful and very liberating.

Facilitator: Let's look at the next statement.

Client: I need Mom to acknowledge that I'm also her child. I need her to not ignore the fact that I'm also her child. I didn't need her to take care of me.

Facilitator: Go back to the time after she passed away. "I need Mom to acknowledge that I'm also her child"—**is it true**?

Client: I feel like it is. When I drop my psychological analysis, yes.

Facilitator: **Can you absolutely know that it's true**?

Client: No.

Facilitator: **How do you react, what happens, when you believe the thought** "I need Mom to acknowledge that I'm also her child"?

Client: I feel weak because I... this neediness, this wanting... the old wounds hurt again, the feeling that I'm not getting what I need, I'm waiting for her and I depend on her and my ability to be satisfied and happy in my life depends on how she reacts or doesn't react. I get angry and oppose this idea that I need something from her, that I'm not able to do it by myself, that I can't take care of myself. It's a childish part of me that really wants a mother who was never there when I needed her, or to be more accurate, the times when she was there were rare. When I believe this, I feel weak and helpless.

Facilitator: How do you treat her when you believe the thought that you need acknowledgment from her that you're her child during the time of her hospitalization and before her death?

Client: I only see her as filling a role, not as a human being. I'm like a baby. She doesn't exist as a human being for me, she only exists to me as filling a specific role in my life—a mother. And also, she's the one who influences me, whether I feel good or bad. If she doesn't do what I need, it makes me feel bad.

Facilitator: Are there memories from the past or thoughts about the future with this thought, "I need Mom to acknowledge that I'm also her child"?

Client: Mostly from the past. The question about the future is interesting. It feels like if I keep believing it, then I'm stuck in a place that doesn't allow me to live my life.

Facilitator: The relationship with a mother continues even after she dies.

Client: Oh, yes, even more.

Facilitator: So, what's the future of your relationship when you believe the thought that you need her to acknowledge you as her child?

Client: If I keep believing it, it's an impossible place for me. The mourning is supposed to help give up the desire that things will change and bring acceptance that we got this far and that's it, we're not able to go beyond that.

Facilitator: So, **who would you be without the thought**?

Client: I'm a woman who came to help her mother get through this process. It doesn't weaken me. I live my life. I do what needs to be done and that's it. Interesting. I continue to live my life. I don't need anything from her. What was going on between us is over.

I will mourn that it's over and how we experienced this process. Maybe I could have been more present than being with the specific grief about what

I didn't receive from her. I'd have fought less for her attention and my boundaries, for my own way. I'd have acted as I did, only without war. It frees me from the need to fight for my boundaries when facing her because, on the one hand, she's disconnected, but on the other hand, she's very intrusive. Interesting. I never thought about it that way, about the intrusion and the emotional detachment. It would have freed me to be more present without getting upset over nonsense and saying how people should be.

Facilitator: Let's try the **turnarounds**. "I need Mom to acknowledge that I'm also her child." How do you turn it around?

Client: I need myself to acknowledge that I'm also her child.

Facilitator: Meditate on that. What examples come to you?

Client: In the situation itself, I have to acknowledge that I'm a fighter because I was her child. I need to acknowledge this and give myself grace in this matter. It explains to me why I'm like this without blaming myself. It makes sense to me.

Facilitator: In this situation, how can you give yourself acknowledgment that you're her child?

Client: I'll allow myself to mourn her death. I'll allow myself to feel what happened and not just relate to it as something that needs to be managed. What also comes to me are my roles. If I'm her daughter, then it's not necessarily my job to help my dad clear away her clothes from the house. It's a matter of the boundary of what I'm supposed to do and what I'm not supposed to do—acknowledging that I'm allowed to feel that it's not appropriate for me to handle her underwear. I'm allowed to say that it's not appropriate for me to deal with her jewelry right now because I'm mourning, I've lost my mother.

Facilitator: Can I offer an example?

Client: Yes.

Facilitator: I need acknowledgment from myself that I'm her child... it's easier for you to escape and do the tasks for her than to feel the burn of the pain of wanting love from her and feeling disappointed by her.

Client: True.

Facilitator: Acknowledging that "I'm her child," is much more painful for you to be present with than to run around and do all kinds of errands for her.

Client: Yes. In general, this is very true to my life. The mourning period, in this respect, was a good time to not do this even though I was still the one who was the caretaker, but I also allowed myself to let others take care of me. In this respect, it was supportive when I was mourning that someone else took care of me and fed me, and so on.

Facilitator: Like a child.

Client: Yes, exactly.

Facilitator: "I need Mom to acknowledge that I'm also her child." What other **turnarounds** do you see?

Client: I need her to not acknowledge me as her child. I think that, for most of my life, I did everything I could to not be her daughter. Most of my life, I tried to stay away from being her child, like she did. During this event, one of the things I felt was that, the second she died, for me it was over, done. After that, I didn't have the need to see her clean and tidy, before the grave. The body didn't interest me. It wasn't her anymore.

Facilitator: Give me an example for "I need her to not acknowledge me as her child."

Client: I don't have an example.

Facilitator: Can I share one?

Client: Yes.

Facilitator: I need her to not acknowledge me as her child because then it frees me from the sense of obligation or responsibility for her. There are things that I'm supposed to do for her and I don't want to do them. If I'm not her child and she's not my mother, then I don't have to do them.

Client: This is true in many respects. It's also the guilt that I felt. You know, it was much easier to take care of her—that was easy to do—than to sit with the pain. Taking care of her and her body was easier for me than dealing with her as a mother. Yes.

Facilitator: Is there another **turnaround**? "I need my mom to acknowledge me as her child."

Client: I don't need my mom to acknowledge me as her child.

Facilitator: How is this true?

Client: I don't need anyone to tell me that I'm her daughter. I experienced it. I still experience it. In that situation, an example of this is that I almost got into a fight with someone at her funeral because I wanted to carry the coffin but someone in the crowd was rude enough to tell me that it's not right for a woman to carry the coffin. I didn't even argue with him and I continued to carry the coffin, the body, to the grave. I don't need anyone to tell me. It's my mother.

Facilitator: And from your mother, "I don't need my mom to acknowledge me as her child"?

Client: At the hospital, the way I chose to take care of her—I don't need her to agree or disagree. I wanted to be her daughter. I chose. I don't need her to acknowledge this because, in reality, I was there in a childish place. She didn't have to do anything and I was there. It's very philosophical. It doesn't feel right in my stomach.

Facilitator: I have a **turnaround** for you.

Client: Yes, please.

Facilitator: I need my mother to acknowledge herself as my child.

Client: Oh, that's been my entire life! I think she gave me this acknowledgment, which I needed, "Here I am, doing this for you again, like we used to in the past."

Facilitator: Do you want her to acknowledge this?

Client: Yes, acknowledge that it was wrong [crying].

Facilitator: "I need my mother to acknowledge herself as my child"—isn't that what you want from her when she invites everyone to personal conversations, and she dictates things as the adult one?

Client: I did get this from her, without talking about it. If she's my child, then she's asking me to take care of her again, to help her, or asking me to feed her… she did express it in her behavior, but not in words. Again, it goes back to the fact that she didn't actually say what was happening there. She didn't acknowledge what was going on between us.

Facilitator: And this is what you wanted? It was the last opportunity, in the last conversation, to hear those words?

Client: Yes. It was more correct to hear that than to hear that I was her child. This sounds like something I need to sit with longer.

Facilitator: Would you like to sit with it now?

Client: I'll sit with it later. This feels like something that requires getting there slowly, little by little.

Facilitator: Well, here it comes, in the next statement. "She is behaving like she always does. I'm the responsible adult and she's the child." **Turn it** to "I."

Client: I am behaving like I always do?

Facilitator: Yes. What does that mean?

Client: I fulfill my role and she fulfills her role. Exactly.

Facilitator: And more specifically?

Client: I take care of her. I don't let her take care of me. I don't really let her talk to me. I keep my distance from her.

Facilitator: And, turned to "*She isn't behaving like she always does*"?

Client: She... actually, there was a moment when she didn't behave in the usual way, even toward me. Once she knew it was the end, she chose exactly who she wanted to talk to, and to everyone else she closed her eyes and fell asleep. Or when she said to me, "Enough, it's not good for me. Send them away." So in this respect, she didn't behave as always. This is something that stays with me very strongly, that it's allowed.

Facilitator: What's allowed? Being selective?

Client: Yes.

Facilitator: "I'm the responsible adult." What is a **turnaround**?

Client: I'm not the responsible adult?

Facilitator: Yes.

Client: What strikes me is that I didn't have to take this responsibility on myself. If I hadn't filled this role at the time, I wonder what would have happened. My father was the responsible adult, if anything. And I also remember that I did have a desire to make decisions about what would happen and how.

Facilitator: I'm the responsible adult and I love it?

Client: Yes. Something like that. I see the benefits in it, and I don't want to give this position away. It feels better to choose a role than to have a role forced on me.

Facilitator: She is the responsible adult.

Client: This raises resentment. It goes back to the beginning. There's a voice that says this is the adult life that she decided to have for herself. Whether she decided or not, it's her life. If she's the responsible adult, then she's responsible for deciding how it looks, what her end looks like, as much as possible.

Facilitator: "She is the child"…

Client: There are elements of that, yes.

Facilitator: …**turn it around**.

Client: I'm the child. Yes, there's a part of me that really wants there to be room for this.

Facilitator: I'm the child. You mentioned several times the little girl who wants to act like a little girl.

Client: Yes, this too. I wanted to feel, to have room for these things, a recognition of what's really happening. Can we move on?

Facilitator: She isn't the child.

Client: This is the reality. She knows what she needs and doesn't need, it's not according to my perception that I know what she needs better than she does. I'm climbing down from this tree and acknowledging that she's responsible for her life. At the age of seventy-two, she's supposed to know and decide what she wants in her life. It relieves me, removing my responsibility from this matter.

Facilitator: What did you write in statement #6?

Client: I don't ever want to be unseen, without presence, to be neglected.

Facilitator: **Turn it around** to "I'm willing..."

Client: I'm willing to be unseen, without presence, to be neglected.

Facilitator: And the **turnaround** "I'm looking forward..."

Client: It's hard. But when I think about it, what comes to mind is, if I separate the negligence from the non-presence, it has aspects of power that I've come to know over time. Even during the mourning period, the fact that I could put my needs aside and be there for her was also a choice and it also speaks to my ego in certain ways.

Facilitator: Is this an example of how you're willing to be unseen and without presence?

Client: Yes.

Facilitator: How do you wish to be unseen again, without presence, and neglected?

Client: What comes to me is that I've been doing it throughout my life, and I'm willing to do it again. Today, I'm willing to do it only when I choose and not when it's forced on me.

Facilitator: You can find yourself again in such situations where it's forced on you. What else is left there for you to be ready to be unseen, without presence, and neglected when it meets you again?

Client: I'm okay. Even if someone doesn't appear the way I want, I'm fine. And I also choose more where I don't neglect myself, where I don't allow myself to disappear, and how much I show up. When it's a choice, it's different from when it happens to me. It helps me a lot in my sense of ability in the world.

Facilitator: Can you repeat the sentence, "I'm looking forward to..."?

Client: It's hard. *I'm looking forward to...* Where do I look forward to being neglected again? What comes to me is giving control to someone else, when someone else is the caretaker. This is exactly how I feel about visiting family. I'm there but I'm not there. I'm back in the family nest, and we do what we always do.

And there's also the element of me neglecting myself and not taking care of myself on a daily basis, when I don't sleep properly and don't eat properly. On one hand, I don't feel good about it, and on the other hand, there's the teenager in me who sits in front of the TV until 2 AM and eats junk food in defiance, because I'll do what *I* want, and that's something I'd like to work on. [Pause] It's interesting that "I'm looking forward to..."

More Work to do!

When you are done with an Inquiry on a whole Worksheet, you can read it to yourself and turn the whole thing around to find more gems. Reading the Worksheet this way can give you additional insights about the situation and yourself—it's a wonderful exercise once your mind opens up to new possibilities after Inquiry.

The turnarounds tell us how to give to ourselves what we want others to give us. They show us how to live the advice we give to others. It's the prescription to happiness, a gift from us to ourselves.

Try writing or reading the Worksheet,

1. Turned to the self
2. Turned to the other
3. Turned to the opposite

Slow down, let yourself take it in, see what comes up, and what is still left to be worked on. The tension you might feel about a turned around statement is a sign that there is more Work to do.

The original Worksheet:

1 I'm angry with my mother because she didn't say goodbye to me.

2 I want her to spend time with me like she did with all the others.

3 Mom should say goodbye to me, pay attention to me too, know I am also worthy of her attention.

4 I need Mom to acknowledge that I'm also her child.

5 She is behaving like she always does, I'm the responsible adult and she is the child.

6 I don't ever want to be unseen, without presence, to be neglected.

For example, **the Worksheet turned to the self:**

1 I'm angry with myself because I didn't say goodbye to myself.

2 I want me to spend time with myself like I did with all the others.

3 I should say goodbye to myself, pay attention to myself too, know I am also worthy of my attention.

4 I need me to acknowledge that I'm also my child.

5 I am behaving like I always do toward myself, I'm not the responsible adult, I'm the child.

6 I don't ever want me to be unseen, without presence, to be neglected by me.

Try it yourself turned to the other and to the opposite.

Facilitation #16: I Worship My Mother

Client: Right now, I have no judgments against my mother. Our relationship in the past few months has been blissful. It was hell before that; now it's heaven. I can't think of any problems with my mom right now. I have problems with myself related to my mom. For example, I believe, "I should always be there for my mom," and that creates stress for me. I feel guilty about putting her in a nursing home. Because I worship and adore my mother, I don't have any negative judgments against her.

Facilitator: We can do Inquiry on a positive thought. What do you worship and adore about your mother?

Client: She's fierce. She's been a passionate spiritual seeker her whole life. In my mid-twenties, she came with me to an Osho Ashram. How cool is that? How many moms are going to do that? She read all the spiritual teachers' books. Unlike my siblings or anyone else in my family, who are very materialistic, she's always been a spiritual seeker and widely creative. She's a beautiful singer and composer. She made beautiful things. What can I say? She's just magical in so many ways.

Facilitator: So, do you want to do that? "I worship and adore my mother because..." and sit with it and see which situation you might want to do an Inquiry on.

Client: The problem has been, it's mostly my own beliefs. I'm a rescuer by nature and I neglect myself. With respect to Mom, I can't fault her.

Facilitator: Would you like to do Inquiry on a positive thought about your mother?

Client: We can try. Do you recommend that?

Facilitator: I don't recommend anything. I heard you say how much you adore and worship her, and you have so many good things to say about her.

Client: I do.

Facilitator: You gave many examples.

Client: I could be critical of her. She clearly has a lot of shortcomings.

Facilitator: Would you like to meditate on it? Sit and see what comes up about your mother that you'd like to do The Work on.

Client: It might be helpful to go back six months to when my mom was beating on me to take her home. Part of me didn't blame her but I felt so guilty and depressed about it. It could be valuable to do a Worksheet on that even though it's not happening right now.

Facilitator: We do Judge-Your-Neighbor Worksheets on situations from the past. If you have only 1% that you haven't forgiven, you can do The Work on that, too. Anything that's still stressful is worthy of Inquiry, as well as positive thoughts.

Client: I can't say that I haven't forgiven her because I never blamed her. I understood her. I thought if I was in her shoes, I'd probably do the same thing—try to get the hell out of there 'cos that wasn't a very nice nursing home to be in. I can't say that I held ill will toward my mom. However, I'm still a little bit burdened with guilt for putting her in there in the first place. But that's not on her. I don't have judgments against her so maybe I'm the wrong person to do Inquiry on my mother.

Facilitator: What's the thought? "I feel guilty about my mother because…"

Client: Yes. I feel guilty about putting my mother in a crappy nursing home for five years.

Facilitator: You put your mother in a nursing home for five years, and you thought it was crappy. Now, what does it mean? What makes you feel guilty?

Client: I feel guilty because my mom was suffering there and she wanted out.

Facilitator: "I feel guilty about my mother because she was suffering there," and because, "She wanted out"?

Client: Yeah. She desperately wanted out.

Facilitator: You want to do Inquiry on that?

Client: How about, "She was suffering in the nursing home"? This would be very good because it lasted for a long time.

Facilitator: I invite you to close your eyes and go back to a situation when you visited her. Look at you and look at her, look at what's around you, be there now. "Your mother is suffering in the nursing home"—**is it true**?

Client: No. No.

Facilitator: **How do you react, what happens,** to you **when you believe the thought,** "She is suffering in the nursing home"?

Client: I get very tense. I argue with her and tell her everything's okay. I don't want to hear it. I shut down. I get antsy. I offer her comfort but she won't accept it; she wants to go home, now. I don't know what to do. I clench up inside. I try to take deep breaths. I'm struggling. I'm trying to find peace in the moment without any success whatsoever. I feel like I need to fix her. I can't leave her in this distress. I feel powerless, helpless, and hopeless and deep down, depressed. I don't know how to get out of it.

Facilitator: How does it feel in your body?

Client: I feel tense. I feel myself contracting, all my muscles getting tighter. I'm getting smaller, wanting to disappear. My head is lowered. I look at the ground because my mom looks so fierce and angry. I'm scared of her, intimidated. Oh, Lord. I want to leave. I want to get out of there, but I don't want to leave my mom in an angry state. So, it's another frustrating visit.

Facilitator: Do you see any past or future images to do with this thought, "She is suffering in the nursing home"?

Client: I see myself imprisoned in our home when I was a youngster. There was nowhere to go. We lived in the country with my father, who was very cold. We couldn't go anywhere except by car and he wouldn't drive us. I felt abandoned living in the house. I identified with my mother. I felt like I lived with a bunch of strangers as a child. I felt like Mom was in the same situation in the nursing home. She was living in a house with crazy strangers and she couldn't escape. I identified with her, living with loss and chaos, uncertainty, and powerlessness. I realize now that I probably identified with her in the situation and I didn't know how to fix it.

In the future, I see Mom, after my visits, languishing in misery and suffering pain, feeling frightened. I see her feeling alone and abandoned and depressed.

Facilitator: Is there anything else that comes up for you with this thought, "She is suffering in the nursing home"?

Client: I feel guilty because I could take her home and she could be home with me, but I think I couldn't handle it. My mom said, "You haven't even tried." I did have her in my home for nine months and it was almost impossible. She didn't remember that; it was a while ago. So I thought maybe I should try it again, but it could be difficult to look after someone who's bipolar. I didn't feel strong enough to do it. I was already exhausted and my health has been going downhill and has been badly neglected. But a part of my mind was thinking, how would I feel if I was just dropped in a nursing home with people screaming all day, where they don't really care if you live or die? How would I like that? They do some bad things to you there. Like, they over-medicate you and if you get sick, they never notice. They let you suffer from your symptoms and stuff. How would I feel if my kids put me in a nursing home like that after all I've done for them? And my mom did a lot, but my siblings can't see it at all. It's pretty sad.

Facilitator: During that visit, when you believe she's suffering, how do you treat yourself?

Client: Like crap. I contract. I shrink into myself. When it comes time to go, I sneak out the back door because, if I try to say goodbye, she'll throw a tantrum. Then I go home, and I eat too much for the next few days. I watch too much TV. I feel down and depressed about abandoning her. I constantly think about her, how I can improve her medical situation, and I completely forget about my own medical situation. I don't take care of myself at all because I'm worried about her suffering.

Facilitator: Close your eyes and go back to the situation. You're visiting your mother. **Who would you be without the thought**, "She is suffering in the nursing home"?

Client: I'd be a different person. I can't imagine who I'd be because, unfortunately, I have a lifetime habit of always worrying about other people's suffering instead of my own life. Being a caretaker and rescuer and co-dependent and all that good stuff, I can't imagine who I'd be without worrying about her suffering.

Facilitator: I invite you to meditate on that. The Work is meditation.

Client: I'd be fierce. I'd be fit, creative, bold, and daring. I'd be self-assertive. I was like that as a child. If anything, I was a bully as a child. I wasn't a doormat at all. I don't know if I'd visit her as much. I'd be more selfish. I wouldn't be thinking about other people's suffering all the time and thinking that they need me to rescue them.

Facilitator: Let's focus on your mother and you in that specific situation.

Client: I'd be detached, observing with detachment. I'd be asking my mom, "Is it true? Is it really this awful here?" I'd be asking her to tell me more about it—what she feels, what she experiences. I wouldn't be defensive. I wouldn't contract. I'd be open to anything she tells me. I'd know that she's telling me what's true for her, what she believes, but isn't necessarily true in an ultimate sense.

I'd take deep, deep, deep breaths to center myself in the midst of my mother's agitation, knowing it's her agitation, not mine. It doesn't need to be mine. I don't have to suffer with her. I don't have to contract. I can observe her suffering and possibly find a way to help her with it better because I'm not identifying with her. I'm not emotionally affected in a negative way. I'm not resisting her agitation and her beliefs, and I'm not resisting it. That's how I'd be without the thought.

Facilitator: You want to try the **turnarounds**?

Client: Yes. Absolutely.

Facilitator: "She is suffering in the nursing home." What **turnaround** do you see?

Client: I am suffering in the nursing home.

Facilitator: Can you find examples?

Client: When I go to the nursing home, I dread going. And when I'm there, I feel I need to put on armor to be able to withstand the onslaught. I'm not flowing, I'm not calm, I'm not peaceful. I'm diminished. My heart is contracted. I'm protecting myself. I go there expecting an onslaught and I'm taking it personally. When I leave, I carry that forward between visits. I continue to punish myself at home, imagining all the ways she's suffering in the nursing home. I embellish that story. Oh, God.

What's another turnaround? Let's see. *My mother is not suffering in the nursing home.* Well, she's not suffering every minute. I can give some examples. Sometimes she laughs and plays with the other residents. She's charming when she's in a good mood. She'll go around and be charming and make jokes and put smiles on other people's faces, even when she's going through difficult times. She looks for the positive—that's in her nature. She's very strong. She found peace through prayer. She was having singing lessons and she was feeling happy and peaceful.

Sometimes the aides and the nurses—who are, to me, the greatest heroes in the entire world, the best people—can be very kind to her so she wasn't suffering much in those moments. She even might have been enjoying herself and being happy in those moments. She wasn't suffering all the time.

Sometimes when I was visiting her, she was hell-bent on showing me how miserable she was there. I didn't really know that she was miserable like that all the time. It might have been partly a show to get me to take her home. I don't know. This is such a hard question.

Facilitator: Which one?

Client: Was Mom suffering in the nursing home? I think she believed she was suffering. She was suffering because she didn't want to be there. This is a really deep question.

Facilitator: You found examples that, part of the time, she was suffering and other times she wasn't.

Client: Does anybody really suffer? What is suffering? Does Mom really exist? Her truest nature is incapable of suffering. You can go so deep with that question. I stumble a little with this one.

Facilitator: Let's stay with the questions of Inquiry instead of getting sidetracked onto something else. Stay with the questions.

Client: When I was there with her in the nursing home, was she suffering? The turnaround is, *She is not suffering.*

Facilitator: We're just looking for a few authentic examples.

Client: Well, when I was with her, she wasn't suffering every minute. Sometimes I could get her to giggle and stuff or listen to music with me or sing with me, and in those moments, her suffering was lifted. So yeah, there were times when she wasn't suffering in the nursing home.

Facilitator: And you also gave the examples that she had singing lessons and she talked with other residents and was charming.

Client: Right. Those are good examples. She had some happy times.

Facilitator [reads statement #2]: In this situation, how do you want your mom to change? What do you want her to do?

Client: I want my mom to fully embrace the situation as it is and not ask me to take her home.

Facilitator: These are two thoughts. Which one?

Client: I want my mom to fully embrace her living situation as it is.

Facilitator: Go back to that visit, see yourself there. "I want my mom to fully embrace the situation as it is"—**is it true**?

Client: No. No. I want her to be herself, whatever that is. She should determine how she should be.

Facilitator: It's a yes/no question. "I want my mom to fully embrace the situation as it is"—**is it true**?

Client: No.

Facilitator: **How do you react, what happens, when you believe the thought**, "I want my mom to fully embrace the situation as it is"?

Client: When I believe that thought, I feel miserable because it ain't gonna happen. I'm fighting, I'm arguing with reality. It's me who has to fully embrace the situation as it is.

Facilitator: Let's not jump to the turnarounds. When you're there, and you want her to fully embrace the situation as it is, and you don't believe that she does, **how do you react, what happens** to you?

Client: I feel aggravated, impatient, stressed out, pissed off. Defensive, down, depressed. Guilty, not good. I don't feel anything good when I have that thought when I'm visiting her.

Facilitator: How do you treat her?

Client: I'm impatient. I'm not receptive. I'm not honest, I lie to her. I'm not open to her self-expression. I shut down, I don't want to hear it. I want to have a happy visit. I want to have a good time together and she's not giving me that. It makes me mad. I want her to accept her situation and be happy and she refuses. It pisses me off. Seems like every time I come, I take a beating. And I keep coming. I keep hoping she's going to fully embrace her situation on the next visit, and I keep coming with that hope in mind. I want her to change. I don't come up with better solutions to her situation.

I don't treat her as well as I might because I want her to be happy so we can have a happy visit but it always blows up in my face and so I'm impatient with her and frustrated. Sometimes I even get mad. I feel the poison of her anger inside me sometimes.

Facilitator: How do you treat yourself when you want her to embrace the situation?

Client: I treat myself badly. I neglect myself, I neglect my health, I overeat, I don't take the time to exercise or go to the doctor. Sometimes I'm crabby with the cats. I don't take care of the house properly because I'm too obsessed with my mother. I want my mother to be happy, dammit [laughs] and she refuses to cooperate. I'm going to punish myself until she is happy.

What am I getting out of that situation? A feeling of being needed, wanted, of being super-very-important. Being the most important person in her life. Having the delusion that I am. That makes me feel like I'm somebody… I'm powerful. Oh, God. That's hard to look at. I'm powerful. I have power over somebody. I have the power to make somebody happy or unhappy. That's what I'm getting from believing that. But she doesn't cooperate with that belief. But I still believe it, despite the evidence to the contrary.

Facilitator: **Who would you be without the thought**, "I want my mom to fully embrace the situation as it is"?

Client: I'd be free. I'd be carefree. I'd be able to listen and be sympathetic instead of resisting and fighting her outpouring and her agitation. I'd be able to think of other options to help her rather than closing my ears to her and wanting to fight with her—"You must be happy. Be happy, dammit!" [Laughs.]

I'd be able to sympathize with her and that might make her happier, to just be heard. I wouldn't take it home with me. I'd leave it there. I'd be in the moment. I'd know that her happiness is not my responsibility. At this point in her life, it's God's responsibility to feed her happiness. I realize it's not something I have the power to do and I would accept that fully. Therefore, I wouldn't come home feeling responsible. That's really a huge one for me. It's massive.

I wouldn't obsess about Mom so much, so I could take care of things in my life, or at least take the time to acknowledge that I'm not taking care of myself and investigate that. Why am I obsessing about her? I'm distracting myself from all my problems that have piled up. My health problems, my financial problems. I'd be forced to face my own problems and, by doing so, I'd find freedom and self-love and self-kindness. The quality of my life would be so much better by coming to terms with my own issues.

And in that moment, when I'm sitting there, not wanting Mom to embrace her situation as it is, but accepting her beliefs and her experiences, and her agitation, I'd be kinder to myself. I wouldn't be getting tense or defensive. I'd be seeking deeper levels of peace by breathing more deeply and being centered. I'd see it as a challenge to myself to reach deeper levels of staying centered with a person who is highly agitated and aggressive toward me. It wouldn't be about her, it would be about me, and about me being kinder to myself and expanding on that concept. Learning to love myself.

Facilitator: Are you ready for the **turnarounds**?

Client: I am.

Facilitator: "I want my mom to fully embrace the situation as it is."

Client: I want to fully embrace the situation as it is. Oh, my God, that's so true. I want to stop fighting reality because it's so exhausting. I can't force Mom to embrace the situation. I can't force Mom to be happy. I want to realize that whether Mom's happy or not is up to God, not me. Even if she was at home and I showered her with riches and satisfied her every desire, she might still be unhappy and I couldn't make her happy, because that's the nature of happiness. If a person can't do The Work or some other kind of spiritual practice to improve their own happiness, then it's up to God whether they're happy or not. That's not within my power. I tried and tried, and I didn't succeed.

It's so hard to try to make other people happy that it makes life like self-torture. It's like beating your head against a wall all day long and then you might see an instant of happiness and think, "I did it!" [Laughs.] But you know what? You didn't do it, or you'd have succeeded the rest of the times if it was in your power. So, duh. You can't do it.

Facilitator: How can you fully embrace the situation as it is?

Client: I can embrace the fact that I can't make people happy by stepping back and looking at reality, looking at my life. A lifetime of desperately trying to make people happy. Everybody but me. It's so exhausting and my whole life falls into disrepair in an effort to do it. It's crazy. I definitely want me to fully embrace reality and move more deeply into it by continually doing The Work on a deeper level. I want to look at the reality of my life, how bad it's gotten. I'm neglecting myself and my own well-being so much—my emotional, physical, financial, and spiritual being—by being obsessed with my sick mother. There's something in me that still resists it, maybe a fear of facing my own life situation. [Pause.] I can increase my own happiness by doing The Work and looking clearly at my life situation.

Facilitator: Try the **turnaround,** *I don't want Mom to fully embrace the situation as it is.* See if it fits. Go back to the visit and see if you can find examples.

Client: I don't want her to because I don't want her to be any particular way. If she's happy, she's happy; it has nothing to do with me. If she's depressed and angry, that has nothing to do with me either. I just want to be there for her, to hold her, to receive her feelings, to practice remaining at peace and staying centered even in the midst of her aggression and stress and to ask her questions and for her to explain more about what she's experiencing. I'll be focused on embracing her attitude and emotions as they are, whatever they are. Does that make sense?

Facilitator: Does it make sense to you? It's your Work.

Client: Yes, it does.

Facilitator [reads statement #3]: In this situation, what advice would you offer her? "She should…"

Client: She should embrace the situation as it is—**is it true**? No.

Facilitator: **How do you react, what happens, when you believe the thought**?

Client: I feel frustrated and stressed out because she's not embracing it. I'm fighting with reality. I'm thinking, "Why can't she be happy? Why can't she just accept the fact?" I feel irritated and pissed off at Mom. I feel guilty, and after I leave and go home, I feel down and depressed. Like a really bad hangover. I'm obsessing about how I can make her happy in the nursing home. I feel like I can't be happy outside the nursing home if my mom's miserable inside the nursing home.

Facilitator: **How do you react** during the visit?

Client: I'm impatient, stressed out. I want her complaints to stop. I don't want to hear what she wants to say so I shut down. I'm tense. I feel guilty. My breathing's shallow. I feel a tightness in my chest. I want her to stop begging me to take her home so I look away, I look at the floor. I try to change the subject and that makes my mom really pissed off. I give her a back rub to distract her. I feel hopeless and helpless. I try to sing a song for her, but she stays right on the subject. I feel defeated, beaten. I can't make my mom happy.

I see that I'm trying to overpower her and make her happy and maybe she doesn't want to be happy in that moment. She has every right not to be. I'm not happy all the time. Who am I to force her to be happy? Not realizing that's what I'm doing, I want her to be happy for me. I'm seeing that now. I'm not at peace with her unhappiness. I also can't bring myself to say, "Mom, I'm not going to take you home anytime soon." Sometimes I lie to her and say, "Maybe down the road." I'm not being completely honest with her. I feel super guilty about that.

[Client moving to Question 4] **Who would I be without the thought** "She should embrace it"? That would change everything. I'd be open to her complaining and getting angry. She's scary when she gets angry. She only weighs 100 lbs. but she's 100 lbs. of dynamite. She's very strong-willed and fierce. She's so intimidating and I'm like a two-year-old standing in front of a behemoth when she gets angry.

If I didn't have that thought, I'd be more understanding and I'd be able to be present with her anger. I wouldn't have the thought that it should be any different. I'd focus harder on taking deep breaths and remaining centered and calm in the midst of her storm. I'd listen and take it in and try to learn more about how she's feeling and thinking in that moment. I wouldn't want to escape because I'd know this is about me changing myself, not changing her, and this is my Work: learning to calm myself in the midst of someone else's agitation.

Facilitator: **Turnarounds**?

Client: Alright. *I should embrace the situation.* Definitely. That would be better. I should accept the fact that she's not happy there, in the moment. In fact, she's very, very angry. She's crying. She tells me she has nothing left to live for. She tells me she's afraid. I should listen to that with an open heart and absorb the totality of her apparent suffering. I shouldn't judge it. I should ask her questions to learn more about it. I should reflect back to her what she's saying so she knows I'm really hearing her.

Facilitator: Is there another **turnaround**? "Mom should embrace the situation."

Client: Mom should not embrace the situation. If she's not embracing the situation, that's what she should do. That's the way of it. I honestly feel she's learning and moving more deeply into acceptance and becoming stronger as a result of that.

Facilitator: That's her business. You don't know if it's true. You're guessing. Look at the situation and at her from your business. Why shouldn't she embrace the situation as it is?

Client: Because in her mind, she can convince me to take her home. If she can convince me, her life would be so much better. She'd be empowered again because she'd be living with her dutiful daughter and she could boss me around instead of being bossed around by people who tell her when to eat, when to pee, make her take pills. At home with me, she'd be empowered again. She would be the boss. From her perspective, hell no, she should *not* embrace the situation. She should fight to go home. She should try her best to convince me. Use any means at her fingertips, all the tricks that she knows—charm, anger, sympathy—whatever she can use, she should use it to the max to get out of this place. And, honestly, who can possibly blame her for fighting? If you thought there was a way to get out, anybody would try to get out. That makes a lot of sense to me.

Facilitator: What about a **turnaround** to the self? *I should embrace myself as I am?*

Client: Definitely. When I was able to be more centered and more open, everything was so much better. Lots of times, I've felt impatient and snuck out of the place. I left her feeling angry because she tried so hard to get me to take her home. I felt so guilty after that. I wasn't doing my mom any good. I wasn't embracing my own learning process, my own shortcomings in the situation. An example could be, if I left my mom sad and mad in the nursing home, I should embrace the fact that I wasn't able to help her, I wasn't able to help myself. I failed and it's part of the learning process.

I should embrace myself when I'm sitting with my mom and she says, "Get me out of here! I've nothing left to live for now!" I should take deep breaths and pour love on myself and feel that love in that moment. Even though I feel alone in facing my mother's apparent torment, I really am not. I'm connected to the universe and everything's okay. In doing so, I'm probably helping my mom, too. I think it's true, in this situation.

I should love and embrace myself in that situation instead of being focused outward if Mom's happy. What about me here? I'm in distress, too. I should try to calm myself and give myself an inner hug. I haven't thought about that before. Usually, I'm the last one on my list to attend to. I should be realizing that it's a hard situation and I'm suffering, and pay attention to what's going on inside me. That's a good one.

Facilitator: Let's look at statement #4.

Client: In order for me to be happy in the situation, I need Mom to be happy in the nursing home.

Facilitator: You're visiting her. She's complaining…

Client: And she is very unhappy, and I'm thinking, "Mom, I want you to be happy so I can be happy, so we can be happy together right now, so we can have a great visit and have fun!" No, not gonna happen.

Facilitator: Slow down. Meditate on that. "I need Mom to be happy"—**is it true**?

Client: No. I can be happy even when she's unhappy.

Facilitator: **What happens** to you during that visit **when you believe the thought**, "I need Mom to be happy"? **How do you react**?

Client: I get tense. I get mad because I think my happiness depends on Mom's happiness and she won't cooperate. I get stressed out. I try to talk her out of being unhappy. I'll say, "But what about this and what about that?" or, "Maybe it'll change in the future." She doesn't buy any of it. I try to talk her out of it or change the subject. I get frustrated. She gets even more frustrated because she knows I'm trying to change her mind. The frustration escalates.

When I have the thought that I need her to be happy for me to be happy, I'm putting a tremendous burden on her. I'm thinking, "I can't be happy unless you're happy. Be happy, dammit! I can't tolerate your unhappiness. I can't be a true friend to you. I can't hear about your sorrow and anger. I can't be a witness to it because then I'm not happy." I smile at her. I'm fake. I put on a phony exterior of myself so I can make her happy and that's not being a friend at all. I'm being unreasonable. No one would be happy in that nursing home. It's crazy on my part.

Is it true that I can't be happy unless my mom's happy? No. I can enjoy learning how to listen to her and be a witness to her unhappiness. I can enjoy that process of being a friend in that way. There's something relieving about that, accepting her emotions as they are, her ideas, her beliefs, her wishes, her dreams, her hopes. Being a witness to that. That makes me happy because it makes her feel better when I do that. I have the capacity to center myself and remain the calm witness.

[Client moving herself into Question 4.] **Who would I be without the thought**? Without the goofy thought, I'd be a different person. I'd be empowered and possibly I could help my mom be more empowered by being the calm witness to her emotions and thoughts.

[Client moving herself to the turnarounds.] **Turn the thought around**, "I need her to be happy for me to be happy." My mom needs me to be happy. Is that a turnaround?

Facilitator: The thought is, "I need Mom to be happy."

Client: I don't need her to be happy. In that moment when she's unhappy, I don't need that because I know how to center myself and find my happy place. I can take deep breaths, go inside myself. I can look at my mother and see her fierceness, her incredible powerful energy. I can be in awe of it instead of being intimidated and frightened by it. I can wonder at the power of my mother's spirit, which is immense, and I can understand perfectly why she's working on me to get her out of there. And I can tell her, "Mom, I understand. I get it. I hear you. I don't blame you one bit. I don't fault you for your feelings and thoughts and your plans." I can be honest with her and tell her, "Mom, I can't take you home today and I don't know if I'll ever be able to take you home." I've never said that to her. That would take a lot of guts on my part. That would scare the hell out of me. That's a whole other Worksheet.

I don't need my mom to be happy when she isn't happy. If she just did everything I wanted her to do, I wouldn't be forced to grow at all. So, it's perfect. I do love her so much.

Facilitator: Let's look at, "*I need myself to be happy.*" **Turn it around to the self**.

Client: Whatever happens is okay. I learn through my suffering. I can get more centered by experiencing these things. They motivate me to become more aware through a variety of methods. It wakes me up from my coma. I don't need to be happy all the time. Even when I'm sitting with my mom, I don't need to be happy in that moment. It's uncomfortable but that's why I'm there.

Facilitator: What about **turning the thought to the other**, "*I need to be happy for Mom to be happy*"?

Client: That's a really good one. On so many visits, I go there and try to cheer her up, change the subject, tell her happy stories about my life and the cats and tell her this nursing home's a great place, the aides are so kind and good, which they are. I try to focus on the positive and I feel like I need to be happy for my mom. I noticed that the few times I've talked to Mom about my problems she actually seemed happy. She wants to be helpful to me, to be a friend to me. So for me to go in there and be like Pollyanna and say, "Oh, look at the birds and the trees outside your window," instead of telling her about my struggles in life, that I'm unhappy, I'm not really doing her or myself any favors. I've been under the delusion that I need to be happy for my mother when I'm visiting her. I'm slowly learning that's not the case. She wants me to be human, to be myself and that's what makes her, paradoxically, feel better and it makes me feel better too that I can share those parts of my life with my mom. I need me to be happy for my mom. That's not true. I don't need to be happy for my mom.

Facilitator: Let's look at statement #5. What do you think of your mom in that situation?

Client: I'm not usually critical of my mom. I'm usually pretty sympathetic with her and I'm critical of myself.

Facilitator: Look at her, the way she is in that moment.

Client: I think she's stubborn, pig-headed, and overwhelming. She won't listen to me. She is close-minded, fearful.

Facilitator: **Turn it to yourself**.

Client: I am stubborn, pig-headed, overwhelming, close-minded, fearful. Yeah. I'm sure she feels that about me, without any shadow of a doubt.

Facilitator: Don't guess what she thinks or feels. Look at yourself and see if it's true in any way and find authentic examples, if you have them. How are you being…

Client: It's true. I'm afraid. *I'm fearful* about taking her home because I got so deeply exhausted and sick taking care of my husband and my mom. I'm fearful of getting in over my head again. As a consequence, *I'm pig-headed* about not taking her home because I'm afraid for myself. *I'm stubborn* about not showing her that I'm not considering bringing her home. I'm stubborn about keeping her there right now. Also, I'm stubborn about wanting her to accept being in the nursing home. I'm stubborn about finding ways to make her happy there. I'm stubborn about trying to keep her alive. So many times when she had an infection, I raced her to the doctor's and she survived. I wasn't 100% sure that was the right thing to do. If I were her, maybe I wouldn't want to go on. I'm very stubborn and pig-headed.

Facilitator: I am close-minded...

Client: I obsess about my mom all the time. I closed off my mind to everything else that's important in life through these years. I'm very single-minded and worried about her all the time with a very narrow focus. I'm not caring much about other people or myself.

Facilitator: I am overwhelming...

Client: Yeah, I'm like my mom and I'm very intense when I want something. Very bull-headed, very single-minded, and not always thinking how it affects other people around me because I'm forceful about getting what I want. This is really enlightening. I'm a lot like my mom.

Facilitator: **Turn it around to the opposite**.

Client: My mother is brave, open-minded, flexible, relaxing to be with. Sometimes she's like that. If I can be centered and witness her for a while and reflect her feelings and emotions back to her, she becomes more flexible, more brave, more open-minded.

Facilitator: What do you see? Does she say or do something?

Client: If I'm calming myself down and being open to her negative emotions, after a while she'll relax and almost forget that she wants to be taken home today. She'll let that go a little bit. She might say, "Let's go to the dining room and have a cup of coffee." She'll perk up and cheer up. She'll be content where she is when I allow the storm to run its course. She'll miraculously become calm and happy. The more I resist her negative emotions, the more they increase. In those moments when she's switched, when the storm passes, she demonstrates amazing flexibility, courage, and relaxation. She's different. That's true.

During some visits, she's been able to let go of her negativity, her obsessions, her overpowering nature. She was able to let go of the need to make me take her home right then and even say, "Goodbye. I'll see you next time."

Facilitator: Let's look at the last statement.

Client: [Client reads the question for statement #6 on the Worksheet] What is it about this person and situation that you don't ever want to experience again?

Facilitator: "I don't ever want…"

Client: I don't want to experience my mother's anger and sadness again.

Facilitator: **Turn it** to "I'm willing…"

Client: I am willing to experience my mother's anger and sadness again. Yes, yes, I am.

Facilitator: And "I look forward…"

Client: I look forward to [laughs] *experiencing my mother's anger and sadness again*, as well as her agitation, her fear, her pain, her apparent suffering, to her trying to convince me to take her home right now, to the incredible force of her nature. I love thunderstorms because of their power. I look forward to my mother's thunderstorm, the power of it, so immense—it's incredible. I'm looking forward to experiencing the wonder of that and learning how to center myself in the midst of her fear and anger and staying open even in the midst of that. I can do it!

This was so good.

Facilitator: We finished the Worksheet.

Client: That was awesome. It's been very helpful. This is a very deep issue for me. It'll take me doing lots and lots of Worksheets, for sure. I thank you. You gave me the courage to put my toe in the water by just being there. It seems so big that I've been very scared to do that. It really helps to go through a whole Worksheet like that. It takes a long time but you see things more and more and more clearly.

Self-judgments: I-statements

Self-judgments are those thoughts that begin with an "I" that are screaming for your attention and cannot be ignored. For example, "I'm bad," "I have failed her," and "I'm not responsible for her." However, it is largely recommended that you judge another person and not yourself, at least until you get some experience in The Work. Why is that? One reason is that you might apply the brakes in self-defense and not allow yourself to go as far or as deep into Inquiry as you would have been able if you were judging another person. Also, when you are judging yourself, you could be in self-attack mode so it would be kinder to yourself to not direct this energy toward yourself—that would be like throwing a boomerang that will hit you in a way you don't expect. (You might be interested to read about Doing The Work with a Motive in the Appendix.)

Another reason is that, usually, before the self-judgment shows up, we have already made a judgment about the other person. For example, if you think, "I'm a bad son for not visiting my mother more often," it could be that what preceded it was a visit with her when you thought, "She's boring me. She keeps telling the same stories." A self-judgement like, "I'm impatient with my mother," might follow a judgement about her such as, "She talks too much about her favorite TV show. She should show more interest in me." It is valuable to identify the thoughts that precede the self-judgments.

The thing is, Inquiry *is* about you. You get to explore your wonderful self through the questions and the turnarounds—they are all about you. As you do The Work, you educate yourself about your thoughts and emotions and how they make you act and react (in Question 3). You explore who you would be without the stressful thoughts about the people in your life (in Question 4). Then, in the turnarounds, as you get to the I-statements, it happens in a much gentler way once you have been through the four questions first. If you started Inquiry with an I-statement, it will be turned to the other person anyway. For example, "I rejected her," will be turned around to, "She rejected me." So, why not follow the simple directions of the Worksheet and judge the other when you fill it out? (It can be an interesting exercise to write down your reasons for that and do Inquiry on those beliefs as well.)

Regarding the topic of Mother, some people might turn to self-judgments because of their hesitation to do The Work on their mother for different reasons. Some people say they fear criticizing their mother because then they would feel like a bad son or daughter. They feel intimidated because, "She raised/trained us not to criticize her." They fear feeling guilt and shame as if they were doing something that is not allowed, forbidden in their family. In such cases, pointing the finger to the self might seem easier, but is it truly so?

If those self-judgments are hollering for your attention, go for it if you choose to. You can stick with your I-statements—there is no right or wrong way to do The Work. It is personal Work. However, if you feel stuck, not getting in as far or as deep as you would like to, or if you feel defensive, consider turning the statements from yourself to your mother and do Inquiry on the Mother thoughts. Here's a list of self-judgments that I have collected from dozens of people along with a little exercise for turning them to Mother, in case you would like to try it and start your Worksheet that way.

Mind game

Turn the I-statements into statements about your mother.

I-statement	**Turned to mother**
I owe her because she gave me life	She owes me because she gave me life
I was an easy child	She was a difficult mother
I don't enjoy being with her	She doesn't enjoy being with me
I parented her	She did not parent me
I am invisible to my mother	She is invisible to me

Try turning I-statements to "She" with the following judgments:

I feel an obligation toward her

I don't want her as my mother

I have to sacrifice my happiness to make her happy

I need to distance myself from her

I am sick because of her, I am stressed because of her

I was a sad child because of her

I feel sorry for her

I don't love her, I hate her

I should do things for her (because I am her daughter/son)

I'm not good enough for her

I ruined her life

I don't ever want to see her again

I wish she would die

Another angle of self-judgments is about you as the parent you turned out to be.

I-statement	Turned to mother
I can't be a good mother because of my mother	She can't be a good mother because of me/her mother
(I hurt my children because) I was a hurt child	(She hurt her children because) she was a hurt child
I try to be the mother I never had for my children	She tried to be the mother she never had for her children
I'm a terrible mother because of my mother	She is a terrible mother because of me/her mother

Try turning I-statements to "She" with the following judgments:

I am afraid to be a mother because of my mother

I don't want to have children because of her

I am appalled by her mothering style

I identify with her mothering style

I turned out to be just like her

Wishful thinking, complaints, and therapy-related thoughts.

I-statements	Turned to mother
I want her to fix our relationship	She wants me to fix our relationship
I want to feel safe around her	She wants to feel safe around me
I can't contain all her meanness toward me	She can't contain all my meanness toward her
I need Mom to be happy	She needs me to be happy
I want her to be normal	She wants me to be normal
I want her to go to therapy	She wants me to go to therapy

Try turning these I-statements to "She" with the following judgments:

I want her to promise she will never do it again

Where was she all my life?

I don't want any connection with her

I suffer trauma because of her

I kept hoping she will change, I stopped hoping she will change

I am addicted to her, I am addicted to getting attention from her

I don't know what the truth is

I was able to free myself from my mother, I needed a few "slaps" to be able to let her go

I need to save my mother

(Un)acceptance and (un)forgiveness.

I-statements	**Turned to mother**
I have forgiven most of the things she has done to me	She has forgiven most of the things I have done to her
I should have a good relationship with my mother	She should have a good relationship with me
I know she is hurting about what she did to us	She knows I am hurting about what I did to her/ us
My behavior (toward her) is not acceptable	Her behavior (toward me) is not acceptable

Try turning these I-statements to "She" with the following statements:

I understand she did her best

I will never forgive her, I don't want to forgive her, I will never be able to 100% forgive her

I'm mad at her

Facilitation #17: I Abandoned My Mother (1)

Client: The situation is from two weeks ago. I was sitting in the living room and I was thinking about giving my mom a call. I thought she'd be upset with me because I abandoned her. That was it.

Facilitator: When was the last time you talked to her or saw her?

Client: Nearly two years ago.

Facilitator: So, you imagine a future situation when you call her and her reaction will be to accuse you of abandoning her?

Client: I felt guilty for abandoning her, that's all. Yeah, I was imagining she's going to be upset.

Facilitator: "You abandoned your mother"—**is it true**?

Client: Yes.

Facilitator: "You abandoned your mother"—**can you absolutely know that it's true**?

Client: [After a pause] No.

Facilitator: **How do you react, what happens, when you believe the thought, "I abandoned my mother"?**

Client: I feel guilty. I feel like I've done the wrong thing. I have a story about how I should behave: that I should contact my mother, I should talk to her, I should be more forgiving and not make all these judgments about her. I feel guilty because I think I hurt her feelings. I left her confused. I imagine she doesn't know why I don't talk to her.

I've got all these stories about things I should do or should have done in the past. I've got this image of myself behaving in the way I did—not talking to her, not contacting her, not having anything to do with her, and I have images of what I should have done: I should have called her, I should have told her. I shouldn't have hung up after accusing her of being a bitch and telling her off. I'm seeing my behavior as unacceptable. I'm being intolerant of myself.

I'm imagining her being upset, confused, and angry, and not understanding what's going on. I imagine talking to her and her wanting some kind of explanation. I see her taking the two years that I took to get myself straight, to do The Work, and get clear on a lot of things, as unacceptable in her eyes. I see myself as having done the wrong thing and I also see myself as having done the right thing. I feel stressed out. I feel worried about having a conversation with her. I'm worried about what I'm going to say. I'm in her business about how she feels, and I feel responsible if she feels hurt. I think it's my job to behave in a certain way that makes her happy. That means being there on her birthday, going to visit her, staying in contact with her, communicating with her about what I'm doing. I feel guilty about not talking to her and cutting her off completely. I carry a lot of self-recrimination about being the cause of her pain and her confusion and thinking it's my responsibility to make her happy, or at least not to make her unhappy.

Facilitator: Do you see images of the past when you have that thought, "I abandoned her"?

Client: An image of the past that comes straight to mind is when I was a teenager and I left home, lived with my father, and I didn't speak to my mother for about three years. It's a hazy memory.

Facilitator: Is there anything else that comes up with this thought?

Client: Not really. It's just a general feeling, thinking that I've done something wrong and I'm responsible for making her feel bad, if she feels bad. But also looking at what I've done over the last two years, which included a lot of The Work on my mother and whatever else and not really seeing that as acceptable. What I'm seeing is a whole different behavior as acceptable, like staying in contact with her, visiting her, and having a normal relationship with her rather than taking the time out and having a relationship with myself and finding some kind of peace and happiness with myself.

Facilitator: How do you treat her when you believe the thought, "I abandoned my mother"?

Client: I avoid talking to her. I imagine her to be upset. I'm not giving her an opportunity to let me know how she feels or what she feels. I'm imposing this story on her about her being upset and how she's going to react—she's going to be angry, she is going to be hurt, etc., and I remove myself from actually experiencing her and seeing what's actually going to happen, what she thinks and feels, and how she reacts. I've cut her out of my life and replaced her with an imaginary story of what I think is going to happen.

How do I treat myself? I'm angry with myself, I'm intolerant of myself, and I cut myself out of having a relationship with her.

Facilitator: What future images do you see with the thought "I abandoned my mother"?

Client: I see images of having a conversation with her in the future, talking to her, and having to explain why I haven't talked to her in nearly two years. I feel guilty and a bit ashamed of myself and it comes from the idea that I've done something to hurt her and make her feel bad. I also see an image of never speaking to her again. She could die tomorrow; she could die any time between now and whenever and I wouldn't like that to happen without ever having contacted her again. Let's move to Question 4.

Facilitator: She'll die without you ever talking to her, "and that means that…" What does it mean?

Client: There's a feeling of regret. I feel like I should have a relationship with my mother. I should be in contact with her. I think that, sometime in the future, I will have a relationship with her again. I think I'd feel regret if that didn't happen because I'd waited too long and she died before it happened, because she's getting old. She's in her eighties now.

Facilitator: So, you're sitting where you are now and you're thinking about calling your mother. **Who would you be without the thought** "I abandoned her"?

Client: I think I'd just call her and talk to her and see what happens. I'd feel more accepting of myself and what I've done in the last two years. I've taken care of myself and that's completely fine. I feel that what I've done is acceptable.

I feel comfortable with what I've done, with taking the time out to look out for myself and needing that separation. I can see that I was in no place to have a relationship with my mother anyway. I wasn't in any kind of mental place to be able to have a relationship. I'm seeing what I've done in the last two years with more acceptance and understanding for myself and I have a lot more contentment and peace with that. I have a feeling about her, just believing that what she feels—if she's upset, angry, or hurt—that's her problem and I can understand that without taking responsibility for it.

Facilitator: When you answered, "No," to the second question, where did the "No" come from?

Client: It comes from the place of expectations other people have, or that I inherited from everyone else in the world, that these are the things that I should do. It's the judgment I place on other people who are confused, thinking somebody needs to do a particular thing to make them happy. It's not my responsibility to make my mother happy or do anything to ensure that she's happy. I'm not responsible for how she feels or her experience in life or her happiness.

Facilitator: Let's look at the **turnarounds**. "I abandoned my mother."

Client: I abandoned myself. I was completely in her business imagining how she'd react and how she'd feel. I was imagining what she's going to think and taking responsibility for her feelings and thinking it was my job to make her happy.

I also abandoned myself in the sense that I'm not really accepting that I took two years to do The Work, taking the timeout and space that I needed from my mother to get some clarity. I'm abandoning myself by not having some kind of understanding or patience that this is what I've done and what I needed to do. I'm thinking I should be talking to her and being in a relationship with her rather than what I actually did, which was to cut myself completely from her and work through all these issues.

I abandoned myself by not being open to having a relationship with her and by going into the story of what will happen if I call my mother in a future scenario. I abandoned myself by avoiding putting myself in a situation where I could feel guilt or shame and not giving myself the opportunity to see what happens, how I'd feel, and what I'd think, and work through all sorts of feelings, whatever they are, if they come up.

Another turnaround is *I didn't abandon her*. Oh, my God, here we go. No, I was just looking after myself. I was doing The Work and I needed the space to work through all the thoughts and feelings I had about her. Also, it's not my job to make her happy or ring her or have any kind of relationship with her at all, unless I decide I'm ready to have a relationship with her.

I haven't abandoned her yet. I've been sitting here in the last two years doing The Work on her [laughs]. I think I've done the right thing, actually, in the sense that if I'd had anything to do with her over the last two years, it probably wouldn't have been a nice, happy relationship anyway. In that sense, I looked after her by staying away from her.

She's never ever said that I abandoned her or indicated to me that I abandoned her. I'm just imagining this whole situation. She does have my phone number, it hasn't changed. *She abandoned me?*

Facilitator: It's a **turnaround**.

Client: Well, she hasn't called me in the last ten years. True. She called me once in the last ten years. She never comes to visit on my birthday, she never stops to visit, she doesn't seem to have the… This turnaround doesn't seem right. She abandoned herself.

Facilitator: That turnaround is in her business.

Client: Yeah, that's fine. Being in other people's business is where we find understanding. She abandoned herself. Look, I don't know. In my imaginary scenario, she abandoned herself by thinking it's my job to make her happy, I guess. Thinking I should call her or have contact with her or visit her on Christmas or ring her on her birthday, or go see her on Mother's Day, etc. She abandoned herself by not reaching out to have a relationship with me and not talking to me and not giving herself the opportunity to do that. She abandoned herself by not giving herself the experience of having a relationship with me.

Facilitator: These sound like examples for the turnaround, "She abandoned me."

Client: No, it's completely different. She abandoned herself. It's her decision supporting what she did, what actions she's taken, what she expects, and all that. It's all completely personal to her and has nothing to do with me. If I go to "She abandoned me," it's not a turnaround. Well, I guess it is.

Facilitator: "I abandoned my mother." **Turn it around**—"My mother abandoned me."

Client: No, she abandoned herself—that's better. When I look at my mother and understand how she's hurt herself, I can see compassion and understanding and have more kindness toward her.

Facilitator: Is there another **turnaround**?

Client: I could do *I abandoned her—Yahoo!* [laughs]. Yay! I got two years of peace and I had so much time without her giving me the pushes that I didn't need. I had a beautiful time to do The Work and look after myself. I wasn't ready to have a conversation with her or to have any kind of relationship with her. I've done her and myself a favor by not having anything to do with her.

I abandoned her—Yahoo! It gave her an opportunity to deal with me not being in her life and reflect on it and learn from it. If that's what she wanted to do, it's her business. It gave her an opportunity to deal with not having her son in her life, to see if she could learn something from it. Do you see any other?

Facilitator: There is the **turnaround** *She abandoned me* and the connection, "I abandoned her because she abandoned me."

Client: Yeah, that's another thought, blaming somebody else.

Facilitator: That's what we do, blaming and judging others.

Client: Did you see anything that stood out, that sounds really true?

Facilitator: I heard some additional thoughts you mentioned and maybe you'd like to take them to further Inquiries: My behavior is unacceptable, I cut her off, I should be in a relationship with my mother, I should be in contact with her, I will feel regret, I waited too long.

Client: It's all self-judgment. I could do The Work on them. There's more kind understanding toward myself, with maybe a tinge of guilt on the side.

Facilitator: Well, we inquired only one thought. You chose an "I" statement, and there are more Worksheets to do—yahoo to that!

More Work to do!

Reading this facilitation, you might have identified additional Inquiry-worthy judgments that can start a new Worksheet. For example, you can start with statement #1, "I am (emotion) at my mother because she abandoned me," or, "I am (emotion) at my mother because she abandoned herself," questioning each thought separately.

Anchor in a specific situation when you had the thought and do The Work on that.

The judgments can be included in a full Worksheet or on a One-Thought-at-a-Time Worksheet:

She doesn't call me, she isn't talking to me

She thinks I should call her, she thinks I should have contact with her, she thinks I should ring her on her birthday

She doesn't come to visit me, she doesn't visit me on my birthday

She thinks I should visit her on Christmas, she thinks I should come to see her on Mother's Day

She thinks it's my job to make her happy

She isn't reaching out to have a relationship with me, she isn't giving herself the experience of having a relationship with me

Facilitation #18: I Abandoned My Mother (2)

Client: I abandoned my mother. I thought that's a worthy thought to do Inquiry on even though it's a self-judgment. It's a recurring thought. It comes up in many moments.

Facilitator: Okay, can you recall one situation when you had the thought?

Client: When I talked to my cousin and she told me she'd visited her mother and I made a comparison. I was comparing myself to my cousin—she's a good daughter and I'm not.

Facilitator: You're sitting with your cousin having a conversation...

Client: Yes, on the phone. She tells me she ran some errands for her mother and she's going to visit her and she says how much she dislikes her mother. When she talks about her mother, there's an automatic comparison happening. I compare her with me, and my aunt with my mother. I abandoned my mother and my cousin didn't, even though she keeps saying how she doesn't like her mother.

Facilitator: Okay. "You abandoned your mother"—**is it true**?

Client: Something in me says yes and there's something else in me that says no. I need to sit with this more. [After a long pause] Can you ask me again?

Facilitator: "You abandoned your mother"—**is it true**?

Client: [After a long pause] No.

Facilitator: **How do you react, what happens, when you believe the thought** that you abandoned your mother?

Client: I feel guilty. I think I've done something wrong. I'm a bad person. There's mostly beating myself up about it and it makes me choke a little. I feel like an immoral person. There's a thought that it shouldn't be this way. I should have been doing all kinds of things for her. There's a long list of should-haves.

I see images of a future where she's getting older, weaker, sick, and lonely, and I feel sad about it. I imagine that she needs me and I'm not there for her. I think I'm selfish, ungrateful, self-centered, cold-hearted, mean, and bad because I'm just thinking about myself and what's good for me. It's all about me. I criticize myself for abandoning her.

I think about my cousin and I make comparisons in my head about us. She calls her mother even though she resents and dislikes and complains about her mother. I'm guessing she does like her mother to some extent because she does things for her. She rants about her mother, but she still goes and visits, and she talks to her on the phone. Then, I contemplate maybe actually it's easier to be in touch and talk to my mother and visit her and then rant about it instead of cutting her off completely, which is also torture. I'm confused. I don't know what's the right thing to do and right for whom—right for me, right for her, right for us? I don't know and I feel restless and stressed about it.

I compare myself to other people as well. Most of the people I know like their mother. Some of them don't like their mother so much, and they still talk and visit her. I don't know a lot of people who are disconnected from their mother and loving it—there's always something off about it. So, I'm in other people's business, watching what they're doing.

[Client asking herself a sub-question.] How do I treat her with the thought I abandoned her? Like she's a victim. I've done something wrong to her. I hurt her. I imagine her suffering. I imagine her thinking about me [laughs]. I imagine her as hopeless, helpless, and miserable without me [laughs]. I feel responsible in some way for her well-being and her happiness. I treat her as if she didn't have a choice, it's something I forced on her, something I inflicted on her, and she's innocent. She's a victim of having such a selfish daughter. I've always perceived her to be miserable and a victim. Like there's always someone doing something mean or bad or insensitive to her and she's just weak and insane. I put myself inside her mind as if I'm looking at the world through her eyes, and then there's the belief that, "There's no justice in the world. The universe is a cruel place, and living is hard and miserable and depressing." So, she's innocent and I'm the bad person who's doing something wrong and I constantly believe this is not the way things are supposed to be between mother and daughter.

When I was sitting with Question 1, I saw an image of two people on a battlefield, and one of them, which is her, lying on the ground, reaching her hand out to me, and I'm just walking away. It's like I deserted her on the battlefield, left her behind—that's the movie behind the thought that I abandoned her. I treat her as this person who's hopeless and helpless, wounded, bitter, angry, depressed, and she needs love and support, and I walk away. I don't give that to her. And there's a thought, "You just don't do things like that." Also, I get in her business. I want her to have love, I want her to have a good life, but I feel like I'm not the person for this job. And when I say that, I think about the past when I thought it was my job and, apparently, I didn't do a good job because I wasn't very successful at making her happy. I wasn't able to make her happy and, at some point, I started resenting her for being the way she is and I mentally started to walk away from her and the distance grew with the years. And then there was physical distance when I moved out of her house and I moved farther and farther physically, mentally, and emotionally. It didn't happen in one day that I abandoned my mother. It was a long process that started when I was a teenager.

I've done many Worksheets, but there's something in me that doesn't want to get closer again. There's just a sense of obligation and I compare myself to other people, like my cousin, and I believe I'm expected to do certain things as a daughter, which I don't want to do. That's it.

Facilitator: What images of the future do you see when you believe the thought you abandoned your mother?

Client: I imagine her getting older, sick, needy. I see her alone in her apartment. There's no one there—no siblings, no husband, or friend. I imagine how lonely and abandoned by everyone, not just by me, she is. Forgotten… I imagine her as forgotten. I recall when I was younger and she'd talk about old people who die alone and are found days later when their bodies are rotting and stinking—it's one of her fears. I'm imagining her fear coming true in the future. [Pause] Sometimes I play with thoughts about what if she dies and we haven't spoken before that. I imagine I won't feel regret. I've already given up on her. I imagine there'll be some sense of relief that this part of our relationship is over and then just whatever relationship is left with a dead person, I can deal with that.

I think I abandoned the fantasy that things can be different between us so there's some loss of interest in the relationship. There's acceptance, this is how it is. I don't love it, I don't hate it, it feels fairly neutral. With the thought, "I abandoned her," I want to leave it behind and move on. So it's mostly that I believe that not maintaining some relationship with my mother and not taking care of her as she gets older is wrong. And behind that, there's a thought that she needs me.

[After a pause] There are still nagging thoughts that a mother should be all kinds of things that she isn't. "Should be, should be, should be"—it's obsessive thinking. It's stressful. If only I could take the word "should" out of my vocabulary... besides what I think she should do or I should do about my mother, everything in life is fine. I don't want to change anything.

Facilitator: **Who would you be without the thought** that you abandoned your mother?

Client: [After a long pause]. What comes to my mind is, I have two options. One is to free myself from the person, the other is to free myself from the judgments about the person. I don't want to be in a relationship with a person I don't like and I constantly judge and criticize. As long as I'm stuck in that spot, I prefer to distance myself from the person, which means not talking to her or seeing her until I'm free from the criticism because I experience it as more hurtful to me and to her. Without the thought, it feels kinder to me and to her to stay away. Well, I'm not sure about her because I don't know what she thinks. But for me, it seems kinder to me to stay away at the moment.

I don't have to know what will happen in the future, and the past doesn't matter so much since it's done. I don't resent her for things that happened in the past.

Without that thought, I see that in the present there are other things I prefer to do and other people I prefer to focus on, and other areas in my life I prefer to put my time, energy, and attention into. I don't need to make excuses or justify why I do what I do. Without the thought, I don't ask why things are like this and why they aren't different. I don't need to understand anything. It's what life is in the moment, without the stories that are background noises that disturb me and cause me to enjoy life less and be unhappy about myself and the way I live my life. Without the thought, all of this chatter and noise fades away, it's gone, and I enjoy my life and I feel complete, present.

Facilitator: It's interesting, isn't it? Without these thoughts, it would be fantastic.

Client: Without torturing thoughts, it's fantastic. Yes, life is good.

Facilitator: You want to do a **turnaround**?

Client: Okay.

Facilitator: "I abandoned my mother."

Client: I did not abandon my mother. I didn't make an active, conscious decision to abandon my mother. So, I didn't abandon her in that sense. Last time she reached out to me and she asked for help, I went to her and helped her. Then things got back to how they were before, and we drifted our separate ways. We somehow went back to how we used to be before—it just phased out, faded away, and again, there was silence between us.

It's not something that I did on purpose, with intention. It felt more like when you touch something and it hurts, and then you touch it again and again, and it happens so many times until one day you ask yourself, "Am I stupid? I'm not going to touch that again." There's something in me that doesn't want to get close to her because it hurt enough times. So what I'm saying is, it doesn't feel like I abandoned my mother. It feels more like I see a future where I'm going to be hurt again if I get close to her because I'm still believing that things should be different.

[After a long pause] *Facilitator:* You want some help?

Client: Yep.

Facilitator: You didn't abandon your mother because you're still sitting here doing The Work on your mother and trying to sort out all the issues you have with her. And you care about your mother being lonely, and her health, and having a relationship with you. You haven't abandoned her at all, at least, not mentally.

Client: Exactly. I think, mentally and emotionally, I haven't abandoned her but I'm focused more on the physical connection, actually talking with her, seeing her, having some sort of communication, like my cousin.

Facilitator: It's all the should-haves and shouldn't-haves.

Client: Yes, it's a thought around, "She needs me." Well, the last time she needed me, I didn't abandon her. I got in my car and drove over and did everything I could.

Facilitator: You still talk to her when she needs you. You still help her when she needs you. Okay, what's the next **turnaround**?

Client: What hurts is the thought that *I abandoned myself*. It's actually more painful than thinking that I abandoned her. I'm thinking about the years when I hated my life and I wanted to die and I blamed her for it. I've done hurtful things to myself, like abuse alcohol. I was beating myself up, criticizing and judging myself for years and I believed it was because of the way she is and the way she treated me. I hated her. [Long pause] I had relationships with other people where I could find proof again that no one cared about me, I wasn't good enough, not pretty enough, not funny enough, and all that stuff. That was bad and mean to myself.

The last time that I saw her, when I went to help her, I was standing by her bed at the hospital and again reliving the thoughts, "She doesn't care about me," "She only cares about herself," "She only needs me to fulfill her needs," "I'm not important to her other than for my services to her," and, "She's using me like she uses other people." Every time I'm with her, I abandon myself because I think she only needs me to do something for her, like listen to her, cook for her, shop for her, or run errands for her. I abandon myself when I believe she only cares that I serve her in some way and I don't have any value to her beyond that. Whether it's true or not, it's a story I tell myself and it makes me feel invisible and insignificant to my mother.

She abandoned me. This turnaround is going to bring up a lot of Worksheets. She abandoned me when she got divorced from my father and she didn't want to be a divorced woman with a baby, so I lived with him and his parents in my early childhood. It feels like she abandoned me.

I felt like she abandoned me when I became a mother and expected her to come to help me and mother me. My understanding was that she was expecting to be a guest when she said she didn't want to be a burden. As I've known her all my life, I expected I'd have to cook for her, care for her needs, and it was challenging enough with a newborn, so I asked her not to come. I felt abandoned, motherless. I decided it was better that she didn't come at all because I was worried about having to take care of a baby and her. I found proof in the past when I had to take care of her plenty of times and abandon myself and my wants and needs and focus on her needs.

She abandoned me a few times when we had a conversation over the phone and she hung up on me. She does that to people when she doesn't want to hear what they have to say. I was young and gathering the courage to be honest and truthful and say my opinion about something that she apparently didn't want to hear, so she hung up on me! This happened a few times, followed by weeks of silence. I felt so abandoned by her. I was young and I needed her. [Pause] She abandoned me when she stopped calling me on my birthday. I remember the first time—years ago—I was surprised. So, one more proof that she doesn't care about me.

I have a memory coming up from when I went to therapy for the first time in my life. She came to visit me one time and I started talking to her about our relationship. I wanted to discuss some stuff and she walked out the door and left and I ran after her and tried to persuade her to come back and stay and talk. I understood from that situation that I can never really talk to her about what's bothering me about our relationship. So she abandoned me in the sense that I can't talk to her openly and honestly. She's not interested in hearing me or she can't handle it or whatever, and I'm left alone with it. I want to be heard and she doesn't want to hear it. That makes me abandon myself again because I have to be considerate to her emotions and difficulties and put my emotions and difficulties aside for her sake. I'm not willing to do that anymore. I don't want to abandon myself.

Facilitator: I've got one more for you. You want to hear it?

Client: Yes.

Facilitator: In this situation, what's happening is that you're distancing yourself from your mother and then you feel like you shouldn't be doing this and you should be helping, and it should be different. You know you need to also look after your own mental and emotional health until you work through all this stuff, and you can have a relationship with your mother, perhaps, and feel safe and comfortable and peaceful about however she is and yourself. But for now, it's not where you are.

Client: Yes. Thank you.

Facilitator: Thank you.

More Work to do!

As you sit in Inquiry, additional stressful thoughts and situations will come up. Identify them and take notes, as you might want to work on them later and go deeper. In this facilitation, from the turnaround, "She abandoned me," a new Worksheet can begin using the examples that were found. For example,

Additional stressful thoughts:

She doesn't care about me, she only cares about herself

She needs me to fulfill her needs, she is using me

She needs me to listen to her

She wants me to cook for her, she wants me to run errands for her

Go back to those moments when you did something for your mother or when you had to take care of her and had a judgment about it. Question these thoughts.

Additional stressful situations:

Memories and images that come up as examples can serve as ground for further Inquiry, like, "She didn't call me on my birthday." You can have a separate Worksheet for each year when she didn't call you on your birthday. You can work on situations when you became a mother or father, and your mother wasn't there to support you when and where you needed or wanted her to—at the hospital, at home, when you wanted her to cook for you, help with your baby, listen to your problems, give you a hug, show you she loves you, and she wasn't available physically or mentally to do that for you.

Investigate the situations you still feel stressed about.

I Need My Mother to Love Me

"It's not your job to love me."
Byron Katie

"I need my mother to love me," is a universal thought that shows up in different variations on the Worksheet when we identify our beliefs. For example, "She should love me for who I am, as I am," "She doesn't like me," "I want her to love me," "I need her approval," "She should accept me," "She should care about me," "She doesn't care about me," and, "She hates me."

This need for a mother's love is connected to core beliefs such as, "Mothers should love their children," "Mother's love is a natural thing," "Mothers should put their children's needs first," "Mothers should love unconditionally," and, "Women have a maternal instinct to love their children." We worship the idea of a mother's natural, unconditional love for her children from the moment a baby is born, or even conceived. We are very much attached to the idea that this is the right order in the universe—this is how things should be, must be, naturally. Deep down inside us, there is something that cannot let go of this thought, this need, even when we are adults and our mother is an elderly woman and even when, in reality, this is not our experience.

Cause-and-effect thinking about Mother's love

People believe thoughts like, "If my mother loved me, I would have been more successful in school," "I can't be a good mother/father because I had a bad mother," and, "If she is not a great person, how can I be a great person"? This is a cause-and-effect way of thinking that places a connection between being showered with mother's love or being deprived of it, and how we turned out to be and how our life has unfolded. It places an "if" that comes before the thought, "I need my mother to love me," or a "because" that comes after. There is a belief that a desired outcome could have happened (in the past): "If she loved me more, that turn of events would have been better for us." We're imagining that something good can still happen, hoping that things will change for the better (in the future) as a result of receiving love from her.

There are people who believe that, because their mother did not love them (enough), they allow their spouse/partner to hurt them, or they tolerate their spouse/partner cheating on them. They believe that because of that lack of Mother's love, they lack confidence, are incapable of having a romantic relationship, cheat on their partner, and are looking for love outside the relationship/marriage. Some people believe that, because of their mother not loving them (enough), they were unpopular at school, have no friends, are the victims of exploitation, abuse drugs or alcohol, are depressed and even suicidal, and they have not succeeded—or have even failed—in their education and career.

Your cause-and-effect thinking may tell you that, because your mother did not (or does not) love you (enough), you are unlovable, worthless, damaged, lonely, depressed, and incomplete. You might make a connection between "(because) my mother didn't love me"—the cause—and "I don't love myself," "No one loves me," "My spouse/partner doesn't love me," and, "My children don't love me"—the effect. Your thinking may tell you that if you had been raised by a (more) loving mother, none of the bad things that happened to you would have happened, and you would have been a (more) joyful, positive, optimistic, successful person. Your thinking might tell you that, because she did not or does not love you, there is something wrong with you. Would you like to know if this is true? Take this stressful cause-and-effect way of thinking to Inquiry and find out.

Conditional thinking about love

People dream about having unconditional love in their life. What stands in the way of experiencing unconditional love is conditional thinking about love as if it were a transaction, an exchange between people. When it comes to our mother, it could be that we are placing ourselves on the receiving end more than on the giving end. From the moment we are born, we need and want something from our mother. This way of thinking might be rolling innocently in your mind like this: She is the mother, I am the child, so she (naturally) must give this love to me. That is a story that many people believe in—does it make it true for everyone?

Conditionally thinking about love manifests itself transactionally with beliefs such as: if you do loving things for me, I'll do loving things for you. When you don't listen to me, I stop listening to you. If you hurt me, I'll hurt you. If you won't express regret for what you did, I won't forgive you. This is a transactional way of thinking about love that puts conditions on giving and receiving love from someone else. It's easier to love her when she gives me what I want, when she answers my needs. It could be more challenging and I love her less (or I hate her) when she's disappointing me, refusing my requests, not living up to my expectations. As a result of this way of thinking, we might find that we believe our mother loves us conditionally, we love her conditionally, we love ourselves conditionally, and unconditional love remains a fantasy.

We make our perception of self-worth dependent on the "birth mother" or "the mother (I think) I have" giving us what we want or need from her as proof of her love for us. This is how we turn conditional love back on ourselves—we become conditionally loving ourselves! Even as adults, we can get confused and believe that our mother is responsible for our sense of value, lovability, and happiness. This way of thinking is a hopeless, stressful way of living as there is not much we can do to control how someone else feels about us. It is pointless to try and dictate to our mother (or anyone) her awareness or behavior. Sure, it feels nice and fuzzy inside when (we think) she is giving us this magical, unconditional love. "I need Mom to love me," is a belief that takes our focus away from ourselves. If you need her to love you, love yourself first. Can you give yourself this love regardless of what you think your mother (or anyone) feels about you or how they treat you?

Taking the thought to Inquiry

While sitting in Inquiry with clients, I noticed the thought, "I need my mother to love me," often popping up in different forms. I also noticed that this belief has the power to build or break the believer.

How do you treat your mother and yourself in those moments when you believe she does not love you? How does believing this thought affect you? What are you unable to see when you believe this thought? How do you live in the world when you believe your mother does not love you (enough)?

Here is a sample of clients' answers when this thought (or its variation) was questioned in Inquiry.

Question 3: How do you react, what happens, when you believe the thought, "I need my mother to love me"?

My focus is on her and how I can get that love. I feel unloved, vulnerable, helpless, hopeless, unhappy. I feel sorry for myself. I feel rejected. I feel lonely, abandoned, desperate, weak, needy. I have resentment toward her. I don't want to live, I don't want her to live. I don't want to be with her, I want another mother, I don't want to be her son/daughter. I compare her to other mothers who seem to be better to their children. I believe mine is the worst mother on Earth. I want so much to be important to her, to be the center of her universe.

There's a heaviness in my body. My shoulders and my chest, my arms feel heavy. My heart hurts, my throat hurts.

I feel like I need to do better, to do more, I'm not good enough as I am, I'm bad. My sense of worthiness depends on her judgments of me. I'm looking to her for approval. I lose myself. I get busy trying to figure out how to get her love. My happiness and self-worth depend on my interpretation of her reaction toward me.

Question 4: Who would you be without the thought, "I need my mother to love me"?

I can see her as a person, a woman. I can see that what she did to me is not personally against me or about me. I won't feel like a victim, I'd feel less sorry for myself. I'd be grounded, present, not desperate. I'd notice I'm okay, I'm safe. I'd be less imprisoned in the story of the child who's deprived of his mother's love and all the drama around it.

I can see she's in distress. I'd see a woman who's frustrated and angry, who wants peace and quiet. I can have some compassion for her. I can see she's not the perfect mother. I can see that she has her own issues. I can see she's unhappy in her work, she's unhappy with my father, with herself, and that doesn't have anything to do with me. I'd be able to see it's not personal. I can be kinder. I'd be able to cope better in the situation.

My body's more alive. My body's straighter and there's no heaviness. I can breathe more deeply.

I'd be free from her, not depending on her, not emotionally attached. I can grow up. I could choose if and how I want to be in a relationship with her. I won't be so focused on her. I can find love in other places.

I wouldn't try to change or to be a certain way to make her love me. I'd be completely free to be myself, I could be whoever I want to be. I'd be enjoying myself, my life, and my own self-expression. I'd be peaceful, calm, lighter, more connected with myself, more focused, more relaxed, more open, more confident, more carefree.

Let's look at the **turnarounds**. How can the turnarounds be as true or truer?

The **turnarounds** to, "I need my mother to love me":

1. *I need (me) to love myself*
2. *I need (me) to love my mother*
3. *I don't need my mother to love me*, or *I need my mother to hate me*

I need (me) to love myself.

How can you love yourself? Here are a few examples from clients' insights:

I need my own love and approval, I'm the one who should be complete with myself, with my life choices, accept my way of living. I need to care about my opinions. I need to be at peace with myself. I need to be explaining to myself what's going on with my mother and sticking up for myself.

I need to not compare my situation with other children's families that I don't know much about. I need to not feel ashamed of my mother, I need to not overreact and overstate how bad she is, especially when comparing myself with other kids. I need to see I have a fantasy of how other children's lives are better and their mothers are better than mine and how that makes me feel bad. I need to ask myself, can I absolutely know it's true that those mothers and those families are better and happier? I need to love myself especially for believing that I'm in a much worse situation than I actually am.

I need me to love me because she's not available, able, or capable of that so I'm the only one available for that. I need to recognize that I can get love from other relatives, like my grandmother or my aunt.

I need to not get sucked into the violence, I need to protect myself. I need to be present and without the story of how a mother should be and what a child should be, what our roles should be, and all the drama around that. My stories create more pain than the physical pain of the beating. Without this story, I'd suffer less, it would hurt me less.

I need me to think of something I can do for myself at that moment, what I'd enjoy doing, like go and read a book, play, or go for a walk. I need me to approve of the qualities that are in me.

I need (me) to love my mother.

I need to love her for the good things she provided, to be grateful. She fed me, made sure I was clean, got me clothes, sent me to school, guided me in my education and toward a good job. There are plenty of things that I'm grateful for and I love her for.

I need to understand that she got upset about what I've done. I need to care about her frustration or impatience with the situation. I need to respect that she wants peace and quiet. She looks happy doing what she's doing in that moment when I was disturbing her. I need to care that she doesn't want to be disturbed. I need to care about what's important to her.

I need me to love her so I can be happy. Feeling resentment or anger toward her is painful to me. If I want her to be happy, I need to love her. I need to give my mom my approval that she's a good mother. I need to accept her as a human being. I need to be happy for her when she's doing something she loves and enjoys, even if it means she isn't giving me the attention I seek at that moment.

I need to understand that she's depressed and messed up. I need to love her because I see that she's struggling. I see she's attached to her own beliefs about how things should and shouldn't be in life. I can have more patience and understanding for her.

I need to love her for the challenges she gave me because it helped me grow, made me dive deeper into myself and I'm grateful for that and that's thanks to her. Without those challenges, I wouldn't have any need to search for psychology, spirituality, and everything else—that's a big thing for me.

I need to not call her names like a monster, evil, and bitch. I need me to not create a story that I have the most evil mother in the world and I'm the victim in this story with no other place to go to. I had a lot of criticism and poison aimed at her and I'm sure she felt it. I had no compassion for her. I do love her, I need to bring this love into the relationship with her. I need to respond from my heart and not from my ego. I need to apologize to her. I need to not kick her out of my life.

I don't need my mother to love me. I need her not to love me.

When I need her love, I become dependent and attached to her. Without this need, I become much more independent and self-sufficient and I love that about myself. It leaves me free to be myself. I'm not waiting for her attention or approval and it gives me the freedom to go and do whatever I want.

Not needing her love leaves me out of her business, focusing on myself and I can see the situation is not about me. I can see that she's focused on other people or other things at the moment.

In that situation, I don't need her to love me. I get other things that I need at that moment, I get a challenge, a lesson in life about values, education, responsibility—she's teaching me something.

It's clear that I needed her not to love me, at least not in the gentle way that I preferred. It leaves me free to leave that home and not come back. It feels clear to me that her role was not to love me but to give me challenges that I've benefited from, that made me who I am. Whether she loves me or not, I see that I'm okay.

I need my mother to hate me.

This is the complete opposite turnaround to "I need her to love me." How could that be true for you (even only for a moment)? Could there be any part of you that wants or needs your mother to hate you? Any part that believes you deserve it for any reason?

I haven't met anyone yet who tried out this turnaround. Personally, I can't recall a time I ever thought, "I need my mother to hate me," either. I do remember there were plenty of moments when I thought, "I hate her." Did you ever experience a moment when you felt you hated your mother, or even told her you hated her? Have you been violent toward her, in your actions or your thinking? Have you wished that she would die? Have you done something related to her you feel ashamed or guilty about?

"I need my mother to hate me." How could this be true?

The things we'll do for love

What's the motive behind our wanting and needing the magical, unconditional motherly love? As we have seen above, we believe that kind of love from her has the power to build, destroy, and repair us. It can create and eliminate our self-esteem and confidence. It makes us feel good about ourselves, and it gives us a sense of safety and security in this world. Underneath the thought, "I need my mother to love me," there is a horrifying belief that, "If my own mother doesn't love me, no one will love me." If no one loves me, that means something frightening; it means that no one will take care of me. Therefore, we need to make her love us, we must squeeze that love out of her, and we need proof.

To gain mother's love, approval, and appreciation, we are willing to do many things, some of them against our true nature. To please her, we are willing to pretend, play nice, put on a façade, and be inauthentic. The focus of our attention is directed at her. To figure her out, we try to read her mind. We make assumptions and stories about what and who she is, "the mother (I think) I have." We try different strategies to teach her, even punish and hurt her into showing us proof of her love. We get involved in her business, leaving our own business unattended, and that in itself can create a sense of loneliness, abandonment, and alienation from ourselves.

Needing Mom's love makes people go into competition and rivalry with others. It could be with your father, her boyfriend, your brother or sister, her friends, her plants, her hobby, even a pet—pretty much anyone she gives her attention to and anything that you might think she loves more than she loves you could be a target for some sort of hostility from you.

In reality, whether your mother loves you or not is her business and you have no control over that. You can be the most adorable or most awful child in the universe and it's her business whether she loves you or not, how much she loves you, how she loves you, and the ways she shows it. In the meantime, attaching to this thought, "I need my mother to love me," while experiencing that you are not getting it might cause you misery, depression, desperation, even self-hatred. It can bring you to express violence toward yourself and her, even if only in your mind, in your thoughts, and imagination.

Not depending on your mother's or anyone's love, approval, or appreciation as a condition for your well-being and happiness leaves you free to do and to be whoever and whatever you want, and to live authentically. Can you give love unconditionally to yourself and to others? Can you receive love unconditionally? In my experience, the path to change that conditional way of thinking is by offering the mind the question, **Is it true?** followed by **Can you absolutely know that it's true?** followed by Questions 3 and 4 and then the turnarounds. One belief at a time, Worksheet after Worksheet, false beliefs dissolve, the truth—your truth—comes out and self-love enters.

Violent, Abusive, and Neglectful Mothers

"You cannot experience rage unless you are in a movie."
Byron Katie

With all this talk about love and unconditional love, in reality, there are children and adults who experience their mother as violent, abusive, and neglectful. We believe and defend this belief that mothers (and fathers) should care for their children at least until they are of a certain age when they can take care of themselves. We believe that children have the right to at least basic care from their mother (and father), like food, shelter, education, and clothes, and we make laws to ensure this happens. Reality, however, tells a different story.

Reality shows us that a mother can be neglectful, abusive, or otherwise uncaring or unable to provide basic physical and emotional care for her child. There are plenty of examples of mothers doing all kinds of things that are not what we believe they should be doing. When we believe something shouldn't be happening and it does, we argue with reality and suffer twice—opposing reality also hurts. You can insist, "I want my mother to hug me and show me affection," "A mother should keep her child safe," "She should not be the one who attacks me," and, "She is the one who is supposed to protect me." Do these beliefs help you when in reality, she doesn't do it?

Doing The Work on violent, abusive, neglectful situations does not mean we do not condemn them. Asking **Is it true?** and **Can you absolutely know that it's true?** does not mean we are denying what happened. We are not using The Work to manipulate ourselves or others into tolerating a situation that we find intolerable. We are not using The Work to lie to and deceive ourselves. On the contrary, The Work brings us closer to our inner truth. The important question is: can you end the violence, abuse, and neglect that exists in you, targeted at yourself or others? Can you end the war within yourself?

With Inquiry, you can stop the war for at least one person: you. Question the thoughts and beliefs that weaken and deflate you like, "She should be normal," "My mother is the worst," "I am scared of my mother," or "She is dangerous"—all could be correct observations. Investigate the social conventions that claim, "Mothers should protect their children," "Home should be a safe place for children," and "Children should not be scared of their mother," which might not be what is happening for you in reality. Question what you were taught to believe (and blindly or obediently follow) when it's not true for you. It might be more accurate and truthful to you in the way you experience your mother, that you should be scared of your mother and not expect her to hug you or care about you.

Underneath the suffering, there is a story that if only she, "the mother (you think) you have," was different, normal, and more like the other mothers, you would have been happier, healthier, stronger, more educated, or successful, and your childhood dreams would have come true. If only she was normal like the other moms—and in your experience she is not—you could have had a beautiful relationship with her and, therefore, a better life.

Living by stressful, unquestioned beliefs is how we become imprisoned by our story. The Work is an invitation to test everything for yourself and see which thoughts are true for you and bring you peace and freedom instead of stress, war, and prison. Instead of going to war with another person or with yourself, put your mind on paper. We are not doing The Work on people. We are doing The Work on our thoughts about people. Take a Worksheet and a pen and write your thoughts down, get still, and meditate on them. Question your beliefs and turn them around, then turn your life around.

Mind game

You might have had an experience with your mother when she violently beat you, she was drunk and out of control, or when she threatened to kill you or herself. Inquiry is an opportunity to investigate your state of mind about these situations.

Identify and test the beliefs that cause you suffering to free yourself from arguing, fighting, and opposing reality, leaving you weak, hopeless, and helpless.

1. There is an exercise in The Work called, "What's the worst that can happen?" Imagine yourself in the stressful situation and identify, what were you thinking and believing in the moment? For instance,

   My mother can kill me, she can mutilate me, she is going to kill my brothers, she can hurt me, she will hurt my face and my eyes, she will handicap me.

   She can kill herself, I will be alone, there will be no one to take care of me.

   I'm not the daughter/son that she wants, she doesn't love me, she hates me.

   She will never stop …

   _____

   _____

   _____

   Take your thoughts to a Worksheet and do Inquiry on them.

2. If you are open to it, try and question "How the worst that can happen is the best that can happen?"

   _____

   _____

   _____

Mind game

What is it costing you?

A possible outcome of experiencing violent situations with our mother (or father) can be the stories we create about what it means about ourselves, her, other people, and the world that is costing us our right to be free and happy.

Identify what it means to you about yourself, your mother, your family, the universe, God, humanity, reality? Write your beliefs and take them to Inquiry.

For example, "She beat me," and that means...

That means that I..._____

That means that she is..._____

That means that people are..._____

That means that the world is..._____

Mind game

I complain to God: Have you ever prayed in a moment of violence, suffering, and despair that God will save you or replace your mother with a better mother, or that God will somehow make your mother disappear from your life?

Fill out a Worksheet with your judgments about God (or call it what you want—universe, reality) and do The Work. For example,

#1 I am <u>angry and frustrated</u> with <u>God</u> because <u>God didn't give me a loving mother, God gave me a crazy mother.</u>

#2 I want <u>God</u> to <u>make her stop being violent toward me, to change my mother, to make her gentle and kind to me.</u>

#3 <u>God</u> should <u>fix my mother, do his/her magic and make her normal.</u>

#4 I need <u>God</u> to <u>send another mother into my life, to use his/her power to make my mother a better person, take my mother out of my life, to save me.</u>

#5 God is <u>asleep, unfair, cruel, doesn't care about me, forgot about me.</u>

#6 I don't ever want <u>God to allow my mother to be violent toward me again, to experience violence from my mother again.</u>

Facilitation #19: I Shouldn't Suffer Because of My Mother

Client: I've done so many Worksheets about my mother and I still suffer from things related to her. When will my Work be done? When will it end? I'm still suffering because of her, no matter what I do. She's constantly on my mind. I want to be free from suffering. I should be able to stop suffering because of my mother.

Facilitator: You should be someone who is not suffering because of your mother anymore—**is it true**?

Client: Yes, I have a strong desire for that.

Facilitator: Yeah, right, and that's what you're trying to use The Work to fix. **Can you absolutely know it's true** that you should be someone who is not suffering because of her mother anymore?

Client: No.

Facilitator: Notice how that brings you closer to yourself. Even that little, "I can't know for sure," allows some space for you. **How do you react, what happens, when you believe the thought,** "I should be someone who is not suffering because of my mother anymore"?

Client: I've dedicated my life to it, to being free from her. I'm willing to do everything within my power to achieve that. [After a pause] When I was younger, I dreamed of the day I'd be able to leave home and never come back. I wanted to disconnect from her. [Pause] I studied psychology. I went to therapy a few times in my life. I studied and tried many therapeutic and healing methods to make the suffering stop. I do The Work. I'm on a lifelong journey trying to discover the thing that will stop the suffering.

[Pause.] I can't breathe. It's like a chain around my neck. I want to be able to breathe. I want to be free. I don't want to let anyone constrain me, and she's the most powerful one constraining my freedom. I blame her for many negative experiences in my life—it's because of the kind of mother she is.

Facilitator: So you see images of yourself as being free from this, liberated from your beliefs about your mother, peaceful, and happy. Then you compare them to how you perceive yourself now and you become dissatisfied with who you are now, not liberated from this suffering.

Client: Yes, and I try to learn from other people. I observe their relationship with their mother and I try to find answers there; maybe they know something I don't know that might work. Some people disconnect from their mother, some stay in touch with her and complain all the time. I try to figure it out. I contemplate what I should do to suffer less.

Facilitator: Yes… all these strategies so you can suffer less. It's a mess, trying to be someone you're not. Look at how you treat your own present suffering with that belief, the one in you that hurts from this, the one you want to get away from, the real you who's suffering from beliefs about your mother. How do you treat her with this desire to get away from it, the part in you that you won't accept?

Client: There's the self-image that I want to see myself as a good person, a good daughter. I should be someone who has found the way to be in a peaceful relationship with her, complaint-free, leaving the past behind. I hold myself to high standards and I'm stressed with my thinking, "I shouldn't be doing what I'm doing to her."

Facilitator: And how does it feel to hold yourself, to expect from yourself something you can't do?

Client: Not good.

Facilitator: No, it's a constant attempt to correct yourself, constantly making yourself wrong for being just what you are. Not good enough, it's not right, it's wrong, I should be different—"I should be better than this." And with that comes the despair of not being able to actually do it… not being able to make yourself free.

Client: And then I criticize myself for being spoiled, self-indulgent, selfish, and thinking only about myself and what's good for me.

Facilitator: Yeah, "I should be someone who is not suffering from my beliefs about my mother anymore." I should be different from what I am. What I am is not good enough.

Client: And I should find the way. I should figure it out.

Facilitator: So stressful, and then you start using The Work as a tool to become that person, right?

Client: I did, and I'm wondering if I still do. I know I was, until I realized there's something stronger in me that resists that.

Facilitator: We're only talking about when you believe this thought. We're not talking about "you." We don't even know what that is. When you believe, "I should be someone who's past the suffering with my mother," then you'll use anything, including The Work, as a tool to fix yourself. You'll use The Work against yourself instead of as a kind way of holding yourself to uncover, "Sweetheart, what's going on with you?"

Client: Yes, and that was confusing, too. I stopped criticizing and judging or expecting something from her, but not from myself.

Facilitator: Yeah, and that's not only confusing but also painful.

Client: Yes. I didn't understand what was going on, and I did Worksheet after Worksheet after Worksheet… and it's still not done.

Facilitator: Exactly, because the proof of when it's done is when you become someone who isn't suffering anymore, because you think, "I should be someone who is not suffering from my beliefs about my mother anymore." **Who would you be without this thought**?

Client: I'd be humble, ordinary. Accept life as it is, just like anyone else who's struggling. Doing Worksheets as they come. It feels like my body's getting looser and softer. I don't need to fight for anything, I don't need to try harder. It feels like the journey is over, I'm there. The searching is over. I'm at the end of the journey.

Facilitator: Could it actually be true that *you shouldn't be someone who is not suffering over this*? It's the first **turnaround**.

Client: It feels very peaceful. I'd be like everybody else. I'd accept that, like everyone else, I complain about my mother, whatever the complaint is—it can be small or big—it's just how it is. I was hoping to get over it, to be free of complaints and judgments but maybe it's not going to happen in this lifetime.

Facilitator: What I'm hearing from you is that what you're trying to achieve is a sense of peace with yourself—you'll be good enough to relax. But there's a quicker way, which is to accept who you are now and then you can also relax. That could be a reason why you shouldn't be different than you are. You can achieve what you're going for without having to change yourself, which seems to be a difficult task—to make yourself what you're not.

So, could it be true that you should not be someone other than who you are on this? That you should simply be someone who suffers when you suffer?

Client: What comes to my mind is that it seems only fair that I should suffer like everybody else.

Facilitator: Yes, you're human, like the rest of us. Why would you be different? Everyone suffers from time to time.

Client: Especially about their mother [laughs].

Facilitator: Certainly. They suffer over having a mother, they suffer over not having a mother… it seems to be part of our lives, like gravity. You can think all you want that gravity shouldn't be here, but it's here. You can think all you want, "I shouldn't be experiencing suffering," but you do. It's part of the condition here on planet Earth.

Client: Yeah, I think there's no way out of suffering. Maybe a few individuals have been able to do it.

Facilitator: Where this reconciles, at least for me at this point, is not by trying to get away from the suffering, but by embracing the suffering—then it begins to change into something that feels less like suffering, and more like being alive. Our belief that we have to move away from the suffering in order to not suffer, is how we might use The Work in the beginning. Then, at some point, there's a shift to use The Work to move into and hold the suffering. When all emotions are allowed, when you let it in, they seem to shift. Have you had that experience?

Client: Yes, in Question 3 and Question 4.

Facilitator: When you really let yourself feel the anger or the sadness, it doesn't stay forever, it evolves into something else and then it disappears. By embracing or being with the suffering, which we're working on right now—"I should be human, like everybody else," seems to be part of the program. It's by owning that, that something happens to the suffering. The suffering doesn't go away in the sense that I'm suffering-free, but it shifts into something tolerable and even sweet, letting it break your heart open. It's through the grief that there's an opening to sensitivity and kindness to ourselves, not through perfecting ourselves. It goes through accepting and allowing that, "Okay, pain is here." And that goes for this as well: "You should be someone who suffers from your beliefs about your mother." It's truer than "you should not" for all these reasons.

Client: Since a young age, I tried to push through and make it stop…

Facilitator: Such hard work. It's impossible. It's an uphill battle and there's always one more peak to climb. The peace isn't quite there yet. I need to improve one more thing and then I'll be at peace.

Client: Yes, exactly. There's always one more peak to climb and one more thing to do or improve. *I should suffer because of my mother* actually feels more peaceful to me. It feels like I can relax my shoulders and lean back in my chair. It feels less of a struggle this way.

I want to turn it around to *I am willing to suffer because of my mother* and, *I look forward to suffering because of my mother* and see how it feels. Yes, I'm looking forward to being like everyone else, not better, not worse, and feeling normal about it. I'm looking forward to talking with her on the phone and rolling my eyes, I'm looking forward to losing patience when I'm listening to her ongoing complaints. I'm looking forward to complaining about my mother and then writing a Worksheet about it and inquiring it. I'm looking forward to experiencing her irritating behaviors and then finding them within myself and doing The Work about it. I'm looking forward to the wisdom that follows. She gave me some pushes in my life, that's for sure, but my life turned out okay.

I'm looking forward to the possible additional freedom from false thoughts about her, myself, and the world, to embracing pain and not trying to avoid feeling it. I'm looking forward to experiencing the disappointment that she's far from being the mother I dream of, far from being perfect. I'm not perfect either. I'm looking forward to feeling humble, unspiritual, and ordinary. I'm looking forward to it. Yes, this feels really good, more peaceful, and true. Thank you.

Mother Yourself

"Nothing outside you can ever give you what you're looking for."
Byron Katie

Some people have an overall healthy, happy relationship with their mother, dotted with random moments of irritations every now and then. In their experience, when they are dealing with their (birth) mother, the difference between the images of "the mother (they think) they want" and "the mother (they think) they have" is small. Other people might experience a huge rift between those two mother images in the case of an abusive, violent, neglectful, abandoning mother. Deprived and continuously longing for that motherly love, it might seem like a fantasy that will never come true in a life filled with heartbreak, physical and mental pain, and even fear.

Whatever your personal story is, reality shows us that there are moments in childhood and adulthood when we find ourselves without a mother, whether she is dead or alive. Whether the reason is justified or not, in such situations when our mother is not available to us physically, emotionally, or mentally, we have to fend for ourselves and be our own mother. How do you react, what happens, when you argue with reality and believe, "She should mother me," "It's her job," and, "She should take care of me," when she does not, or cannot? Who would you be without the story that your mother should mother you?

There were times in my life when I could not see beyond the story of what my mother (and father) should be and do for me. Just as addictive as the thought, "I need my mother to love me," was the thought, "I need her," when she was not available. I experienced myself as motherless from time to time. It did not feel good. Then I heard this idea of "mother yourself" from Byron Katie and I was curious to explore it. It sounded like a good solution and I played with it in my mind. Then, one day, as I made myself lunch and looked at the food on my plate, I realized that no mother on Earth could have done it better for me than myself, exactly the way I like it, with the right amount of food on the plate and served at perfect timing.

A thought came to my mind: "I am Mothering myself," and it flooded me with emotions of self-love and I felt butterflies in my stomach. It felt so right, so true. It was quiet and peaceful. It was truer than the thought, "I want my mother to mother me," or, "I want my mother to cook for me." In that moment, I was the mother that I want for myself.

I believe we all have that internal mother (and father) inside of us, taking care of us, parenting us, guiding us, and protecting us. In other words, it can be named "self-love" and we experience this love when we are present, grounded, awake, and not confused. Unlike the internal mother that is in us, any external mother is bound to disappoint us every now and then (or more frequently for some of us), and it's pointless to expect it not to happen. An external mother can never live up to your expectations and make you 100% satisfied and happy. An external mother cannot read you like an open book, know you better than anyone else, read your mind, and answer your wishes, wants, and needs. (Turning it around the role, I am willfully surrendering to the idea that, as a parent, I am not able to answer all my children's expectations, wants, and needs, so I disappoint them at times.)

Even good intentions and kind gestures can go wrong, be misunderstood, and be rejected. A hug, a kiss, a kind word, even a cookie that your mother offers you might not be to your liking. (Again, in the role of a parent, my children have rejected a hug from me, a kiss, or a cookie, and that is okay.) No one other than you can know exactly what you need or want, how or when you want it, or when you no longer want it. Mother (and other humans around us) can try to guess and do their best but, really, no one knows better than you what is best for you. (Do *you* always know what's best for you?) Why wait for another person to make your dreams come true when you can do it just the way you like it, by yourself—especially when reality shows you that they can't or they won't do it?

I can tell myself the story of, "I'm sick, I need help. If only mother/husband/children would go to the store to buy groceries and make me chicken soup…." And I can check with myself, "It looks like no one's available. Can I do it? Yes, I can." I'm not saying that it's not nice when someone else pampers and takes care of me. It is nice. But when no one is around (for whatever reason) it does not do me any good to tell myself such a story. It is so freeing to stop waiting for my mother (or any other person) to do things for me or change and become who she is not. It is way easier and more peaceful to mother myself. I love the mother that I am to myself; she is so good to me (and she makes a delicious chicken soup!). It is the end of confusion. The end of waiting. The end of dreaming about what is not, and opposing what is.

If you wait for your mother to mother you and your experience is that she does not, you might be attempting to hand over this job to other people in your life. You might expect your romantic partner/spouse, boss, teacher, or friend to mother you. You might expect your children to mother you! It can turn into a never-ending childhood when at the age of twenty, thirty, forty, fifty, sixty, or seventy you are still waiting for your mommy to mother you.

Searching outside for external substitutes, or substances, to mother you, will not fulfill this need. No one can nourish you mentally, emotionally, and physically as perfectly as you can nourish yourself when you are present and awake to reality. No one can understand your needs better than you do. When we look for a mother outside ourselves, we have to settle for that "good enough mother" (a term coined by Donald Winnicott). However, when you experience your mother not being good enough (or not good at all), this means you just have to suck it up with your "good enough mother." How frustrating is that?

Mothering yourself, on the other hand, brings you back home to yourself. The mother that I am to myself is meant for me only; it's an internal experience. She is the ideal mother to me, she understands me, she gets me. However, I am not confused into believing that she is the ideal mother to my children! As it turns out, my children don't want or need the sort of mother that I am to myself. In the past, I used to believe they would love and adore her—she is so perfect, so how can they not? As it turned out, each child of mine has his/her own personal story of the mother they think they want and she is different from my story of her. That was (and sometimes still is) a cause of confusion and conflict between me and my children every now and then. When this happens, I take my judgments to a Worksheet. This war that goes on in my mind happens between me and myself and it belongs on paper; it's not a war I want to have between me and my kids. I do my Work, I sort it out in Inquiry, and peace returns.

As long as you are waiting for someone else to love and mother you in the way you crave to be loved and mothered, it is an invitation for disappointments and relationships that go downhill. Be the mother of your dreams, the mother you think you want to yourself—no one else can do it for you. In The Work, I turned around, "I want my mother to mother me," to myself, "I want me to mother myself," and that was where I found my perfect-for-me mother. After a while, there was no need for that, either, as I was just a "woman looking at a plate with food on it at lunchtime" without a story that I needed a mother.

Forgiveness

"None of us would ever hurt another human being if we weren't confused—that's my experience. Confusion is the only suffering on this planet."
Byron Katie

Dwelling in the past, fearing the future, and attaching to your story might leave you lingering in the "victim" identity. Forgiveness is challenging when you feel like the victim. Forgiveness might even be out of the question when you experience your relationship with another person as being troubled or abusive in any way. Katie explains that, "Forgiveness is about seeing that what I believe happened didn't necessarily happen."

Forgiveness was not on my mind when I started my way with The Work. It snuck up on me as I plowed my way through a tall mountain of Worksheets about my mother and the rest of the universe. (That mountain got taller and taller until, one day, it was mostly over). Each thought, moment, situation that was met with, **Is it true?** opened a crack, an opportunity to check again, a possibility to see things I was blind to before meditating on the question. Nothing changed in reality about the situation, the past, or my mother, only my unquestioned mind sitting in Inquiry. That gave forgiveness a chance. Then, one day, there was peace, and I realized there was nothing and no one to forgive.

How does The Work enable forgiveness?

As I reflected and tried to retrace the stepping stones that allowed forgiveness to happen, I found a few possibilities for how this might have come about.

1. What I believe happened, didn't happen.

Yes, there were Inquiries where I found that what I believed happened didn't happen the way I perceived and understood it at the time, and my interpretation of it was inaccurate or partial. I also found my part in contributing to some stressful situations where I wasn't as passive a player or as much a victim as I had thought. From Worksheet to Worksheet, I acknowledged that my version of the story is not the ultimate, one and only objective truth, and that other stories and versions are as true as mine. I found I can't know for sure—I can't absolutely know that it's true—and I grew to love that I-don't-know mind.

You might believe thoughts such as, "Mom loves my sister more than she loves me," "My mother gave me a bad childhood," or, "She kicked me out of the house." In Inquiry, you might discover that it wasn't the case. For example, if you question, "My mother gave me a bad childhood," go back to a time when you had that thought. Watch it again like a movie in slow motion. In meditation, can you see how confused, fearful, or too emotional you were to notice all kinds of details? Were you really paying attention to what your mother was saying as you were caught up in your own story? In Inquiry, you can look and listen again to what she did and said and how you understood it when you believed your story (Question 3). You might understand things she said or did in a different way when you look at it again without your story (Question 4). Can you see your part, your confusion, your innocence, and hers? Try the turnarounds; can they be true as well, or even truer? For example, "I gave myself a bad childhood," "I gave my mother a bad childhood," "She did not give me a bad childhood," "She gave me a good childhood." Meditate on each turnaround to find authentic examples. You might discover that what you believe happened, didn't happen (or, at least, not exactly as your version of the story goes). These insights and realizations enable a letting-go, a detachment from your story and hence, from the identity formed around the story.

2. What I believe happened, did happen.

Sometimes, what happened was a physical act or fact, like, "She hit me." It cannot be denied. By asking, **Is it true?** we are not trying to deny it. When we work on a factual statement there are two options: 1) work on the fact, the physical act, "She hit me," and 2) work on the story, the meaning of it. For example, "She hit me," and that means, "She is violent," and, "She doesn't love me."

2.1 Working on a fact

When you do The Work on a fact like, "She hit me," you can answer "Yes" or "No" to Questions 1 and 2. There is no right or wrong answer. Answer "Yes" if this is your truth. This is not a trick question trying to manipulate you into denying that what happened actually happened. Don't force a "No" if it's not an authentic answer for you. Move on to the next questions and trust the process, as Inquiry is about getting to know yourself. Discover in Question 3, how do you react, what happens, when you think this thought? In Question 4, look into who you would be without the thought, "She hit me." (Again, that does not mean denying that she did, in fact, hit you. It's just looking at the situation without the thought.) Then, proceed to the turnarounds. Can you find examples for, "I hit her," and "I hit myself"? It can be metaphorically speaking, or a hit that happened in your mind, in your imagination. Were you hitting her or yourself in that situation or in other events, either physically, or in your thinking? Can you find examples of when she didn't hit you in other moments? Can you find an example where, even when her hand touched your cheek and she slapped you, she did not hit *you*? For instance, was it "you" that she hit? Was it about you at all?

It takes an open mind to sit in the questions; it's a meditation. And, again, it does not mean lying to yourself. We're only looking and exploring possibilities. Don't force yourself to believe what is not true for you. The Work is personal work and you will have to find your own answers. In my experience, forgiveness happened as I did The Work with a commitment to know the truth. In meditation, as I recreate the situation in my mind's eye, I notice additional details to which I did not pay attention in real time, being caught up in my story. When I cling to a story that is not true for me, I am imprisoned by the story and it feels like that. A story about facts is still a story.

Inquiry gives an opportunity to investigate what happened. From Worksheet to Worksheet, I became more aware, more educated about myself. I could consider: What can I do that would be kind to me and the other person? What is true for me? I set myself free when I focus on myself instead of the other person, not waiting for them to change (or trying to force them to change)—that just steals my time, energy, and power. I can change my self-experience by taking responsibility for my beliefs and judgments. I have the power to change my thinking. I stop arguing with the reality that things should not be a certain way when reality shows me this is how they are. The past is over. My story of what happened stopped defining me. I was no longer living the story that I am a victim. When I was no longer a victim, there was nothing and no one to forgive.

2.2 Working on the story

When the situation is over and the physical pain is gone, what's left is the story, and what hurts is its meaning. I can do an Inquiry on what it means to me that, "She hit me." For instance, it means, "She is violent," and, "She doesn't love me." I'd work on those statements as described in section 1.

After sitting in the four questions, strangely enough, I can find in the turnarounds examples of how I am violent toward myself and her, and how I do not love myself or her. I connect with the violence in me, my violent thinking or behavior aimed to hurt myself and/or my mother, or other people. I would ask, how am I violent? How do I scare and hurt myself, her, and other people sometimes? How do I not love (or even hate) myself? How do I not love her? I find that all of it exists in me, so how can I judge another person for being just like me? I cannot criticize another person or expect another person not to do what I am (capable of) doing. There's humility and a letting-go, a peaceful surrender with this realization. There is a quietness in the mind and heart that follows this sense of connection about humanity, there is no "me" and "her" or "them"—we are all the same—and that is peaceful.

3. The turnaround to the role of the mother

As I was doing Worksheets on my judgments about my mother, my children, and myself as a daughter and a mother, I gained new perspectives, insights, and realizations. It became unreasonable not to forgive my mother for some past situations.

When I judged my mother and could not see how a turnaround was possible, I tried the turnaround to the role of the parent. As a parent myself, I experience the daily effort of juggling work, family, home, health… or, in one word, life. As a human, I sometimes need to take care of my own needs first (when I'm tired, hungry, or upset) before I can attend to my child's needs. As I attempt to be the best mom I can be and find a balance with all of this, I become more understanding of the challenges of being a parent. It helps me to give my mother a break for being too busy to play, too tired to cook, absent from my school events, physically and emotionally unavailable at times, choosing to do something for herself and putting her needs first, and even for yelling or acting in ways I perceived to be violent.

I can see how I behaved as a child and teenager—not listening, not helping enough, uninterested, indifferent, deceitful, sneaky. I can see my part and contribution to some stressful moments. I can see how the ways I behaved toward my mother could have upset her. From the point of view of myself as a mother interacting with my children, I can understand her possible upset and frustrations with me. I see how the turnarounds can be true. I can also see my innocence as the child in some situations and how what might have upset her was not personal against her or about her at all.

In the turnaround to the role of the parent, I can see about myself, as a mother, that when I get upset with my children, most of the time it is not about them at all. It is about what I am thinking and believing that argues with reality, causing my confusion; it is something else that causes my distress. In those moments when I was about to explode (or did explode) with frustration at my child or snapped at my teenager when I believed he or she should have behaved differently, I experience how being captivated by my beliefs of right and wrong affects me. I see it all exists in me. I find compassion for myself as a person, a parent, the child or teenager that I was, and I can find compassion for my mother (and father) and my own children. How can I expect anyone to behave or act differently—better—when I cannot do it? I find it impossible not to forgive.

I used to believe that "I am the way I am because of her," then I considered: **Is it true?** She did not change but my thinking changed. I questioned what I believed, ending more thoughts with a question mark and was left with fewer words, fewer stories, less noise, less war, more understanding, acceptance, and staying in my business. I realized that forgiveness is for my own sake, my own benefit. I do not owe anyone forgiveness—it is not meant for them, it is meant for me to stop my suffering. It means living my life without an identity and a story of, "I am a victim" with all the ways it spreads and affects other relationships and takes over other areas in my life. I have not made a decision or a choice to forgive. At the bottom of the big pile of Worksheets, I found there is nothing left to forgive. My thinking changed and forgiveness happened.

You might not be ready yet to understand, accept, or forgive your mother for things she has done to you, and that's okay. Keep in mind that, as long as you are not at peace about something, you will find it in other people in your life. When I suffered over, "My mother doesn't care about me," not surprisingly, I found it also in, "My husband doesn't care about me," "My children don't care about me," "My friend doesn't care about me," and so on. It was just as interesting to look at, "I am not interested in my mother," "I am not interested in my husband," "I am not interested in my children," and, "I am not interested in my friend," and see when and how that's true.

Forgiveness to yourself

You can't have war within yourself and live a happy life.

After blaming your mother for this and that (for years, possibly), you might feel like a fool when you start doing The Work and realize *your* part in causing trouble in the relationship (or at least in some situations). For example, it can happen when you see that "It's her fault," or, "I am suffering because of her," turned around to "It's my fault," and, "She is suffering because of me," is just as true or truer than your original statements.

When you find that what you believe happened didn't happen the way you remembered or told it, it might throw you off balance. If things were dramatic between you two, there might be fear of unpleasant self-judgments kicking in like, "I'm a horrible person," "I was wrong," or, "I wasted my life blaming, hurting, hating another person." You might feel guilt, shame, anxiety about what you discovered—the truth—and that it's backfiring on you. It might move you to do The Work with a motive like self-defense or avoid it altogether. However, The Work is not about finding out who is guilty, who is at fault, and who should be punished. It's about knowing the truth, and that is different.

The Worksheet is your friend, and the questions and turnarounds are there to enlighten you, to show you how to make things right. They are there to help you understand yourself better, to see your innocence. They are an invitation to be gentle with yourself, to make amends to yourself. It's the end of the war with yourself, with your thinking, and so it is the end of the war with other people. As you continue to do Worksheets, you find the innocence in yourself and everyone, meaning you recognize the innocence in reacting and acting out of what you (and others) were thinking and believing, out of your unquestioned mind. It's what happens when The Work becomes a part of you.

As with any practice, it gets easier. You might even be excited and looking forward to a realization such as, "Oh, I was such an idiot!" (I remember the first time I did—it was thrilling). Your I-know mind becomes a don't-know mind. It brings an openness and a willingness to not know anything besides knowing when you're making up a story.

As I kept doing The Work, one thought at a time, one situation at a time, I discovered again and again that I could not have reacted or acted in any different way in a given situation. When I was confused, caught up in my story, believing my thoughts, I was operating out of them. But later, in Inquiry, I get a chance to go back and figure things out, discover the cause of the confusion, find what is true for me, connect with myself, and stop the futile arguing (even fighting) with reality. When I find it was my fault, I own my part. I make amends when I can, how I can, when I'm sincere about it. Inquiry is where I can find kindness and forgiveness for others and it makes it possible to find kindness and forgiveness for myself.

It was easier for me to forgive others (although I did not go into Inquiry with that intention in mind—it just happened on its own). However, it was more challenging to find forgiveness for myself. I asked myself for quite some time, how come I can forgive others but I can't forgive myself? And then one day, forgiveness for myself happened, too. Whatever your starting point is, it works both ways: when you find forgiveness for others, you can find forgiveness for yourself. And the turnaround is true as well: when you can forgive yourself, you can forgive others.

A World Created with a Word

"The world is nothing until it is named. And it's still nothing until you believe that name."
Byron Katie

When "Woman" gives birth, she is named "Mother." Then, there is "Child," separated and not separated from her at the same time. After naming things, stories are being born of how things should and should not be, of what is right and what is wrong. Once we give it a name, "Mother" and "Child" are no longer free to be whatever they can be or want to be.

The story of "She is my mother" comes with a big, fat manual of laws, rules, regulations, instructions, and expectations about how she should be, how we want her to be, and what we need her to be so that we will survive, thrive, and be happy. From the moment we come out into the world, we begin wanting and needing something from our mother until the day she dies (and even after). The only problem is reality. Reality doesn't always follow the guidelines in the Mother-Child manual of what should and should not be.

Mother is a name. You can read this book all over again and every place you see the word "Mother" replace it with any other person—father, brother, sister, husband, wife, son, daughter, I, boyfriend, girlfriend, friend, teacher, boss, God, stranger, neighbor, and so on. Try it.

I found that when I replace "Mother" with a different name like Woman, Aunt, Friend, or Neighbor, my expectations change and some of my judgments about her shift or fade away. For example, when I name her Friend, it changes my experience and I listen to her the same way I listen to my friend. When I name her Aunt, I experience the conversation with my mother the same way I do with my aunt. Naturally enough, I notice similar judgments I have about my friend and my aunt showing up in the conversation. If I name her "friend," or even "fiend," I will treat her so. And, when I go with Person, I find there is no problem at all—I am free, and so is she.

Mind game

Try giving your mother different names and see if, and how, your story about her shifts. Play with woman, human, person, friend, teacher, guru, stranger, boss, tree, God, object, it, or any other word you would like to try.

Notice, does it open new possibilities for you? Do you have the same judgments about your mother when you name her something else?

A world is created with a word. With a word, an identity is born—"I." Then, "I" becomes, "I am a daughter," "I am a son," "I am a mother," "I am a person who…." As we add more words, the story develops, the plot thickens, and we get attached to it. We believe there's a certain way for how things should be and we start collecting evidence, proof, and facts to support it and back it up. However, reality shows us that it can be very different from what we want it to be, need it to be, dream it to be, or strongly believe that it is the way it should be. We have two choices—argue (even fight) with reality and suffer, or inquire and discover the truth, our inner truth, and experience the freedom and the end of war and suffering that comes with that.

Mind game

It takes an open mind to sit and meditate on **Is it true?** When The Work is alive in you, everything ends with a question mark—it's the questioning mind.

The whole world says, "She is your mother." It happens when you believe it (and you don't have to believe it). Have you ever questioned:

"She is my mother"—**is it true?**

"I am her son/daughter"—**is it true?**

This book is an invitation to do The Work on these beliefs and discover for yourself, who would you be without these stories?

In the end, you might find you have no story to tell other than, "I don't know."

Personal Words to Conclude

It's morning. My body wakes up, then my mind wakes up. A few thoughts pop in my head, "Get out of bed. Go get your first School of The Work binder. There are valuable notes in it." I kick the blanket aside, I sit, I stand, my feet touch the floor and drag me to my home office. Still sleepy, I'm too lazy to move the chair that blocks access to the glass door of the bookcase. It opens just a crack and I reach my hand in as far as I can and pull out one of the brown binders, hoping it's the right one. Back in bed, I look and see it's the binder from the last School—The School for The Work, November 2019. I flip through the pages and come across a Worksheet I filled out at that School. It's about my mother. I read it and my tired eyes fly wide open—I can't believe what I see. *"I'm impatient with my mother because she doesn't let me finish a sentence. She's not interested in what I have to say," "I want her to hear me out," "She should listen to me," "I need her to not interrupt me," "She is a bad listener, talks too much, self-centered,"* and *"I don't ever want to be ignored in a conversation."* I'm stunned that I still hold the same judgments from a year ago! After all the mountains of Worksheets and (what feels like) a gazillion of Inquiries I've done… still the same judgments!

A self-judgment comes up, "My thoughts are not only recycled but also *re-cycled*!" That is, "recycled" as in not original, being thought by millions of people worldwide—and that's okay. And "re-cycled" as in they are pesky, and they reappear out of nowhere again and again. Re-cycled, it feels like I'm going in circles, back to square one, and not only about my mother but also about friends and relatives, neighbors, and all kinds of people I know. That should not be happening!

I notice the reactions and emotions that flood me: a sense of deflation, defeat, despair, embarrassment, and failure. I am disappointed in myself. I experience an inner tantrum. I identify the thought that is causing all of this. I'm believing, "Nothing has changed." Plenty of Worksheets and facilitations have been done, mine and others, in the past year, and I believed I'd moved far away from my starting point. And now…. this Worksheet throws me back. It makes me want to burry this manuscript, to keep it locked in my laptop forever, and never let it see the light of day. What's the point in publishing this book if my thoughts are re-cycled? "I have failed."

I carry with me these thoughts and emotions all day long, playing with, "Nothing has changed," in my mind. I know that The Work is an ongoing practice and not a quick solution. I know it's reasonable for there to be multiple Worksheets on the same situation, same person, and even the same thought and moment. But all this knowing is unhelpful. This is the I-know-mind, it's logical thinking and does not dissolve my inner emotional tantrum. I do know what to do in this case. "Nothing has changed…" I offer my mind the finest question—**Is it true?** and I dive into Inquiry to meditate on it.

Appendix: About The Work

If you are new to The Work and you have read your way up to here, you have a pretty good idea of what The Work is and how it is done. To expand and deepen your knowledge and understanding of The Work, I suggest you read Byron Katie's books (especially *Loving What Is*), visit her website www.thework.com, and watch her videos on YouTube. You might want to consider signing up for a workshop to get some hands-on practice because the best way to understand The Work is to *do* The Work.

Katie says that practicing The Work is like learning how to ride a bike. At first, you might wobble and lose your balance, but keep doing it until it gets easier. In this appendix, I give only a brief overview of The Work. There are plenty of resources where you can learn about The Work and practice Inquiry—books, videos, podcasts, courses, and workshops are available worldwide by many good and experienced facilitators.

What is The Work?

The Work is,

- A deep, ongoing process of self-realization.

- A meditative practice.

- An experience (to understand it, you have to do it yourself).

- More than a technique, it is a way of thinking and living.

The Work is a way to…

- End the arguing and fighting with reality.

- Notice when your thoughts oppose reality and cause you stress and suffering in life.

- Inquire and meet your thoughts with understanding.

- Become aware when you are telling yourself a story that is not true to you.
- Stay in your business and not get involved with other people's or God's business (things beyond your control).
- Stop wanting or needing the world to change so you can be happy.

What's to love about The Work?

- Its simplicity—only four questions that are easy to remember, and a few turnarounds.
- It's available to everyone anytime, anywhere, worldwide.
- It is an efficient way to make stressful, recurring thoughts, emotions, and situations dissolve and fade away as a result of Inquiry.
- It's free and you can do it on your own or with a partner. (Experienced facilitators are also available worldwide.)

A quick guide to Inquiry

1. The Work is magical but don't expect it to give you a quick fix—it is not called The Work for nothing. Roll up your sleeves and be ready to put in some... Work!

2. Choose a specific situation and person that is stressing you. Don't do Inquiry on your whole relationship with the person. Observe the situation closely, see all the details, listen to everything that was said, and watch yourself and the other/s.

3. Get still and allow the situation to come to life and recreate itself as if you're watching a movie. Get in touch with a specific moment in the situation when your feelings were most intense. Feel it in your body, experience again the emotions you had at the time.

4. Write your thoughts on the Judge-Your-Neighbor Worksheet following the simple directions given on it, answering each question

with short and simple sentences. (The Worksheet is available free on www.thework.com.)

5. In statement #3 on the Worksheet (In this situation, what advice would you offer him/her?), offer advice that is practical, would solve your problem, and that the person is capable of doing. For example, if the situation happened in a crowded elevator, don't offer advice such as, "He should take yoga classes to calm himself," as that is not possible in the moment. Instead, think of advice that can be fulfilled such as, "He should stop talking," or, "He should take deep breaths."

6. For statement #4 on the Worksheet—"In order for you to be happy in this situation, what do you need him/her to think, say, feel, or do?"—express the needs that are relevant to that specific moment, the ones that will make you happy. Be specific about what you need from that person.

7. Imagine yourself in the situation at the age you were when it happened. For example, if you were five years old at the time of the event, be the five-year-old child as you sit in Inquiry.

8. Get still and quiet. Work slowly, take your time to meditate on the questions. Let the answers meet the questions.

9. Be honest with yourself. Don't try to be the "good guy," spiritual, or sugar-coat what you really think and feel. For example, you could rationalize and write, "She did her best," when what you really believe deep down inside is, "She is crazy," or "She was the worst mother ever." (You can inquire "She did her best" as well—this is your personal work.)

10. Let yourself experience all emotions and sensations as they appear. Cry, smile, frown, laugh, let yourself feel the anger, sadness, frustration… whatever arises, it's all allowed and welcome.

Doing The Work with a motive

The Work is often mentioned as "a way to end your suffering." I have done my Inquiries about my mother determined to find relief, solutions, and some answers for this stubbornly irritating and challenging relationship. I needed to know what to do and I wanted to make some decisions. I wanted to get rid of the judgments, negativity, criticism, and resentment that I targeted at her and myself. I had plenty of motives and, "The Work is the way to end your suffering," sounded good to me.

People use The Work for all kinds of reasons. One of them is as a way of self-development where the underlying belief is, "I'm not good enough" (so I need to improve myself, I should change, be different, better than I am)—I fell for that one, too. Other reasons could be to stop being angry, to find a better way to deal with someone, or just to find peace of mind. All of them are good reasons. However, The Work has no goals to achieve.

Let's separate goals from side effects. "The end of suffering," is not the goal, it's a side effect, a result of doing The Work. I must say, there are plenty of wonderful side effects to practicing The Work. Personally, I gained more clarity about self, others, and life, improved my communication skills, experienced an increased sense of happiness and freedom, reduced levels of stress, and hence an improvement in my health. I love the feeling of living in my integrity and becoming less judgmental and more tolerant of others and their opinions. I feel more open and curious. These changes happened on their own as a result of making The Work an ongoing practice in my life.

The Work works best and does its magic when we enter Inquiry with an open mind and a willingness to discover whatever shows up, without trying to manipulate the questions or navigate the answers. Trust your inner truth (I also refer to it as my inner compass or my inner voice), follow the simple directions of the process—it's fairly easy—meditate on the questions, and let them guide you (instead of you attempting to guide them). So far, that has seemed to work best.

I find the main reason to dive into Inquiry is that I want to know the truth. It's the truth that sets me free, and freedom is addictive. I go into Inquiry not knowing where it's going to lead me, what I'm about to discover, or what's going to unfold—I trust the process. If you're not ready for this yet, that's okay. If you are, you will see that, as side effects of Inquiry, you get to be more connected with yourself, your mind expands, your heart softens, and something new awakens and shines inside of you—a free and authentic you.

Tips for doing The Work without a motive

Ulterior motives might interfere with your Work and make you use The Work to achieve some purpose. Here are some signs that you are stepping away from doing The Work. Notice when you are:

- Defending your story as the correct or only version of what happened, seeking validation, or wanting to prove you are right.

- Attempting to solve a problem, looking for an answer, solution, resolution, wanting to make a decision, or imagining a future when your issue is resolved.

- Wanting to fix or heal yourself or someone else, seeking to be free from pain, sadness, resentment, and all other negative emotions and sensations.

- Afraid of experiencing shame, blame, guilt when you anticipate you are about to discover your part in the situation's escalation, fear of consequences, or wanting to be the "good guy" in the story.

- Defending a self-image, fearing change about losing or shifting in your identity, not knowing "Who am I?" after Inquiry.

- Trying to make yourself a good, spiritual person.

- Not ready or willing to know the truth yet, or see yourself without your story.

Notice if you're letting your answers meet the questions, or if you're manipulating them in any way and by doing so, you're stepping away from doing The Work. When you go to Inquiry with a motive, you might catch yourself:

- Defending, justifying, explaining, apologizing.
- Playing nice, sugar-coating, positively thinking about the person or thing you are judging.
- Going into a story, starting a conversation.
- Changing your statements, answering too quickly.
- Caring about the facilitator's opinion about you, asking the facilitator for his/her opinion, advice, or guidance.

You are not only the star in the movie of your life but also the storyteller, the director, and the producer. In Inquiry, the spotlight is on you. Enjoy the show. Enjoy your Work.

Books about The Work

Loving What Is / Byron Katie with Stephen Mitchell

A Mind at Home with Itself / Byron Katie and Stephen Mitchell

A Thousand Names for Joy / Byron Katie with Stephen Mitchell

I Need Your Love—Is That True? / Byron Katie with Michael Katz

Who Would You Be Without Your Story? / Byron Katie

How to End the Stories that Screw Up Your Life / Ernest Holm Svendsen

Acknowledgments

I would like to express my gratitude to the wonderful and generous participants (clients) who shared their Work, their mother, and their wisdom with me. You have educated and enlightened me—I learned so much from you.

I am thankful for the friends The Work has brought into my life: Kieran Gardner, Daniel Vukomanovic, Trine Thomsen, Dafna Chen, James Stewart, Karen Budd, and Shir Mordechay Schleyen. Thank you for your support in conversations, discussions, reading parts of the manuscript, and giving meaningful feedback. Thank you for facilitating me on stressful thoughts like, "This book writing is never going to end," "I'm not on schedule," and "It's one more book about mothers," etc.

Thank you to Tom Compton and Ernest Holm Svendsen for opening my mind to new depths and ways to do The Work and having fun with it.

Thank you to the editor, Julie Phelps, for being flexible and willing to bend some rules of proper English here and there.

To my husband, for your friendship, love, and support, and for reading each and every word of this book.

To my children for giving me plenty of free time to write, and for showing me the turnaround to the role in action.

My heart is exploding, thank you all.

Made in the USA
Monee, IL
02 July 2021